Twentieth-Century Latin American Revolutions

Twentieth-Century Latin American Revolutions

Marc Becker

ROWMAN & LITTLEFIELD
Lanham • Boulder • New York • London

Published by Rowman & Littlefield
A wholly owned subsidary of The Rowman & Littlefield Publishing Group, Inc.
4501 Forbes Boulevard, Suite 200, Lanham, Maryland 20706
www.rowman.com

Unit A, Whitacre Mews, 26-34 Stannary Street, London SE11 4AB, United Kingdom

British Library Cataloguing in Publication Information Available

Library of Congress Cataloging-in-Publication Data

Names: Becker, Marc (Professor of history), author.
Title: Twentieth-century Latin American revolutions / Marc Becker.
Description: Lanham, MD : Rowman & Littlefield, [2017] | Includes index.
Identifiers: LCCN 2017011418 (print) | LCCN 2017020205 (ebook) | ISBN
    9781442265882 (electronic) | ISBN 9781442265868 (cloth : alk. paper) | ISBN
    9781442265875 (pbk. : alk. paper)
Subjects: LCSH: Revolutions—Latin America—History—20th century. | Revolutions—
    Latin America—Case studies. | Revolutionaries—Latin America—Biography. | Latin
    America—Politics and government—20th century.
Classification: LCC F1414 (ebook) | LCC F1414 .B43 2017 (print) | DDC 980.04—dc23

Printed in the United States of America

Contents

v

Preface

This book presents a synthetic overview of revolutionary movements in twentieth-century Latin America at a level appropriate for an undergraduate classroom or a general audience. Scholars will quibble over the selection of case studies, claiming that some were not sufficiently violent, transformative, or permanent to warrant that moniker. Events that appeared revolutionary at the time may not appear so in retrospect, and sometimes, looking back, it may surprise us how forward-looking our predecessors were. In short, no canon of Latin American revolutions exists, and the selections in this book are based on my years of study and analysis of transformative movements.

The book begins with a theoretical introduction that explores theories and assumptions that inform the concept of "revolution." This chapter provides a brief overview of the global **left** (bolded terms are defined in the glossary at the end of the book) in order to situate events in Latin America, analyzes persistent and ongoing issues facing the Latin American left, and examines factors necessary for a revolution. Each subsequent chapter presents an interpretive narrative of a single case study in chronological order, except for chapter 8, which explores the most significant **guerrilla** movements that failed to capture state power. The final chapter scrutinizes contemporary leftist governments in Latin America with an eye toward what they can teach us about past revolutionary movements.

Each chapter begins with a list of key dates and concludes with discussion questions designed to encourage deeper exploration of the key issues that each revolution raises. Each case study also includes a biography of a significant revolutionary leader. Given the gendered nature of revolutionary movements, these inevitably focus on a man, and often one from a privileged background. The intent is not to reinforce a traditional historiographical approach but rather to critique the theme of vanguard leadership that runs throughout the book. Similarly, each chapter includes a primary source document that reflects the movement's ideology. Each chapter closes with a short list of English-language books that provide an entry point for further study, as well as a list of films that offer visual representation of each revolution.

A brief note on capitalization: The *Chicago Manual of Style*, 16th Edition (section 8.37), indicates that names of ethnic and national groups are to be capitalized, including adjectives associated with these names. Because "**Indigenous**" and Black refer to such groups of people, these terms are capitalized in this book. That convention is based on, and followed in respect for, the preference that the board of directors of the South and Meso American Indian Rights Center (SAIIC) specified as an affirmation of their ethnic identities.

This book was drafted while teaching "Latin American Revolutions" at Truman State University. I thank my students in that class for their suggestions and insights into conceptualizing this project and writing the text. Kevin Young, Patti Harms, Cheryl Musch, and others read the manuscript and provided suggestions for improvement. Once again, it has been a pleasure to work with my editor Susan McEachern and her staff at Rowman & Littlefield.

Twentieth-Century Latin American Revolutions

Latin America

1

Theories of Revolution

KEY DATES

1640	English Revolution
1789	French Revolution
1791	Haitian slave revolt
1848	Karl Marx and Friedrich Engels publish *The Communist Manifesto*
1910	Mexican Revolution
1917	Bolshevik Revolution
1944	Guatemalan Spring
1949	Chinese Revolution
1952	Bolivian Nationalist Revolution
1959	Cuban Revolution
1970	Chilean Road to Socialism
1979	Nicaragua's Sandinista Revolution
1999	Venezuela's Bolivarian Revolution

LATIN AMERICA IN THE EYE OF THE HURRICANE

Historian E. Bradford Burns once aptly described Latin America as a place where "poor people inhabit rich lands." Many people assume that Latin America is poor because of a lack of natural resources, but that is not the case. Today Bolivia is the poorest country in South America, but five hundred years ago its Potosí silver mine made it the most valuable colony in the world. Sugar production on the Caribbean island of Hispaniola in the late eighteenth century similarly made it the richest colony in the world, but today Haiti is the poorest country in the Americas. In comparison

1

to the incredible wealth of Potosí and Hispaniola, North America had relatively few resources, but today the United States is the wealthiest country in the world.

Scholars refer to a "resource curse" that has impoverished Latin America to explain this dramatic change in economic standing, but such blanket statements gloss over intentional political and economic decisions that have underdeveloped the region. The Uruguayan journalist Eduardo Galeano condemned the imperialist powers that pillaged the continent in his book *Open Veins of Latin America*. Galeano observed that some areas of the world win and others lose, and that Latin America specialized in losing. "Our defeat was always implicit in the victory of others," he wrote. "Our wealth has always generated our poverty by nourishing the prosperity of others." Advanced industrialized countries in Europe and North America extracted wealth from Latin America in the form of labor and natural resources. Even more damaging to the region, those industrialized countries turned the cheap raw resources into expensive finished products that they imported back to Latin America, with most of the value of that production remaining in the industrialized countries. It was in their economic interests to maintain Latin America in a politically subservient situation. As Burns, Galeano, and others came to realize, Latin America was not poor through any fault of its own but because of its location in a global capitalist system.

Poverty was not the only problem that Latin America faced. Extreme economic inequality further underdeveloped the region. In 1912, the Italian statistician Corrado Gini developed what has come to be known as the Gini coefficient as a measure of the distribution of assets, and now scholars commonly use it to measure inequality. A Gini coefficient of zero represents perfect equality in which everyone shares equal access to the same amount of resources, whereas a Gini coefficient of one represents maximum inequality where one person owns everything and leaves everyone else with nothing (see figure 1.1). A Lorenz curve (named after economist Max O. Lorenz) graphically represents the unequal distribution of income or wealth in a society. By this measure, Latin America is the most unequal part of the world. While many people in Latin America suffer from deep poverty, the region is also home to immense wealth. The Mexican business magnate Carlos Slim, for example, is one of the richest people in the world, even as almost half of the country's population lives in poverty.

The twin problems of poverty and inequality create a wide range of difficulties, including high crime rates, political instability, short life expectancies because of a lack of access to healthcare, and low productivity because of a lack of education. In this situation, the promises of a socialist revolution that would end poverty, eliminate inequality, and solve many of Latin America's associated economic, social, and political problems are very appealing. Revolutionaries identified their twin opponents as the U.S. imperial extraction of their resources and local capitalists who benefited from this extractive system to the detriment of the rest of society. Their goal became to free themselves from the control of the United States and to remove the wealthy ruling class from power, by any means necessary.

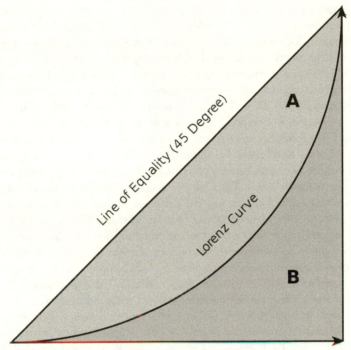

Figure 1.1. Gini Coefficient

Writing in a nineteenth-century European context, Karl Marx (1818–1883) contended that an urban **proletariat** with a developed awareness of their role in society would lead revolutionary changes. He considered Latin America, with its lack of an advanced industrial economy, not yet ready for a revolution. In the twentieth century, however, Latin America experienced more revolutions than any other part of the world. Furthermore, rural **peasants** rather than industrial workers led many of them. Revolutionaries debated how quickly profound political and economic changes could be implemented and whether violence was necessary to achieve these changes. Did their movements need charismatic leaders to inspire people to action, or could everyone collaborate equally in the construction of a new society? Revolutionaries debated these and other compelling issues and in the process created a dynamic environment in which to study struggles for a more equal and just society.

* * *

This book includes seven case studies of revolutionary movements in twentieth-century Latin America, plus one chapter on guerrilla movements that failed to take state power and a concluding chapter on contemporary leftist governments at the dawn of the twenty-first century. The case studies begin with the 1910 Mexican Revolution that introduced a century of revolutionary activism and laid the groundwork for other revolutions that followed. The Mexican Revolution is often seen as a standard-bearer through which other subsequent Latin American revolutions are interpreted. A series of leftist movements followed with varying degrees of success. The Guatemalan Spring (1944–1954) appeared to create an opening for a deep transformation of society, but both internal and external opposition collapsed the experiment. A short insurrection on April 9–11, 1952, brought the Revolutionary Nationalist Movement (MNR) to power in Bolivia and led to some of the most militant labor and peasant unions in Latin America before reversing course and collapsing in a military **coup**. The 1959 Cuban Revolution was the longest lasting, furthest reaching, and most successful of the twentieth-century revolutions. It fundamentally influenced subsequent leftist paths to power. The Cuban Revolution inspired a decade of guerrilla uprisings across Latin America, but the defeat of Ernesto Che Guevara in Bolivia in 1967 and the 1970 election of the Marxist Salvador Allende to the presidency in Chile swayed leftist sentiments toward searching for constitutional and institutional means to fundamental revolutionary changes in society. **Nationalization** of U.S.-owned copper mines contributed to U.S. support for Augusto Pinochet's brutal September 11, 1973, military coup that ended that experiment. The 1979 triumph of the Nicaraguan **Sandinistas** provides a second example of a successful armed struggle in Latin America. Unlike Cuba, however, their willingness to implement **neoliberal** reforms eroded their domestic support and led to their electoral defeat in 1990. Similar attempts in Colombia, El Salvador, and Peru failed to take power through armed means, although their struggles led to highly politically aware societies. The election of Hugo Chávez in 1998 brought his uniquely styled Bolivarian Revolution (named after independence leader Simón Bolívar) to Venezuela and introduced a new wave of revolutionary movements in the twenty-first century. Chávez embodied many of the debates that swirled around revolutionary movements throughout the twentieth century. An examination of his administration and those of others that followed closes this book and provides an opportunity to reflect on lessons learned from twentieth-century revolutions.

Global events influenced political and ideological changes in Latin America, and these were reflected in shifts with alternations between a preference for armed struggle or institutional paths toward capturing power (see figure 1.2). The 1917 Bolshevik Revolution in Russia introduced a Marxist ideology of class struggle and a historical materialist interpretation of Latin American realities that had a notable influence on leftist insurgencies after the 1910 Mexican Revolution. Although the left came to power in both Guatemala and Bolivia through breaks in the established order, revolutionaries in both countries quickly established electoral systems that provided a mechanism to consolidate their reformist policies. In contrast, guerrilla leaders in Cuba rejected electoral paths in favor of armed struggle to transform their country's political and economic structures. After a string of guerrilla defeats in the 1960s, the electoral victory of Allende in 1970 briefly

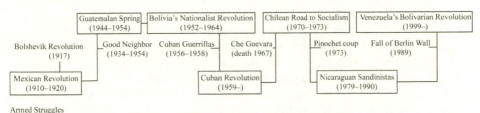

Figure 1.2. Timeline: Armed Struggle and Electoral Paths to Power

shifted popular sentiments back toward an emphasis on electoral paths to power. The 1973 Chilean coup strengthened the hand of those who argued that the Latin American left could only take power through armed struggle, and the 1979 Sandinista victory in Nicaragua bolstered that position. The Sandinista electoral defeat in 1990, as well as the fall of the Berlin Wall and the collapse of the Soviet Union, reinforced **capitalism**'s hold over the entire world. The possibilities of the left gaining victory, whether in Latin America or elsewhere, through whatever means, appeared remote. Chávez's presidential win in Venezuela less than a decade later, however, firmly placed the left back on Latin America's political landscape and established the region in the vanguard of progressive changes around the globe. Chávez's victory also boosted the idea that elections were the preferred—if not the only—means for a socialist transformation of society.

Scholars debate which events can properly be characterized as revolutionary. Developments that at the time seemed to be truly transformative can in retrospect appear quite moderate or reformist. In contrast, previous policy proposals may now strike analysts as surprisingly progressive when compared to contemporary administrations. This is part of the terrain that this book enters. What was the intent of each movement? Did it seek to transform society in favor of previously dispossessed sectors of society, or simply reform or modernize society to the benefit of those who already held power? Interpretive explanations of each case study create a historical context for the appearance of each revolutionary movement and offer an understanding of its main goals and achievements, its shortcomings, and its legacy. Biographies of each movement's principal leader provide an opportunity to explore the importance of charismatic and vanguard leadership. Primary source documents illustrate the goals and tenets of each movement and connect to a broader theme of the importance of ideology in mobilizing support for a mass uprising.

WHAT DOES "REVOLUTION" MEAN?

Revolutions are a relatively rare although often studied but only vaguely understood historical phenomena. The word "revolution" comes from the physical world and refers to the rotation of an object. For example, the speed of a car's engine is measured in revolutions per minute, or RPM. In the political realm, a revolution happens when those in power are replaced with a previously dispossessed class of people. Much like a crankshaft in a car's engine, society has rotated so that those who were previously on the top are pushed to the bottom or out of power, and those previously on the bottom move to the top and gain control over decision-making processes.

The term "revolution" is sometimes used so loosely as to refer to any palace coup or change of government that it loses all meaning. Alternatively, some historians will restrict usage to highly exceptional events such as the 1640 English Revolution, the 1789 French Revolution, and the 1917 Bolshevik Revolution. Some scholars contend that even the structural changes accompanying these events were not profound or permanent enough to warrant use of the term. Others argue that the social changes that accompanied the industrial revolution were more significant than those in the political realm where the term is commonly applied. A true revolution in which society is completely flipped upside down is an exceedingly rare occurrence. Perhaps it has never happened, and if it did it would be so disruptive of society that it might be an undesirable development.

A previous generation of scholars commonly applied the term "revolution" to early-nineteenth-century anticolonial revolts against Spain and Portugal that resulted in Latin American independence. Many scholars now view those as upper-class movements that while leading to a political separation from European powers also entrenched preexisting and very unequal social, political, and economic structures. Much as in the United States, a powerful land- and slaveholding class of men replaced the previous European overlords. Independence did not lead to African slaves gaining their freedom or an advance in rights for women. In Latin America, under the newly independent governments and without the paternalistic protection of distant European monarchs, many Indigenous communities lost access to their lands and were reduced to the status of serfs working on the estates of wealthy landowners. Those "revolutions" were not necessarily beneficial for the most dispossessed members of society.

Some argue that revolutions follow a natural cycle with a complete rotation from the collapse of an old regime to the radicalization of popular aspirations for a new society and finally to a **conservative** reaction against the excesses of the revolutionaries, which leads back to where everything started—a complete 360-degree cycle. It is not uncommon to use this model to read the unfolding of the French Revolution onto other events. In France, workers stormed the Bastille fortress on July 14, 1789, which led to the collapse of the monarchy and the execution of Louis XVI. The Jacobins (so named because of the Dominican convent where they met) arose to power in that political vacuum as the most radical wing of the revolution, and their ruthlessness led to a 1793–1794 Reign of Terror. A conservative coup d'état in the month of Thermidor led to a restoration of the old order. Some scholars build a career out of looking for the inevitable moment of a conservative "Thermidor" reaction against radical revolutions. Such mechanical models, however, ignore the unpredictability of revolutionary developments and how they emerge at their own pace and with their own rhythms.

Scholars have not reached consensus on which events to characterize as revolutionary. For some, a revolution is an inherently violent event that removes a previous government from power through force. Typically the change must be rapid and profound. Participants in a revolution sometimes unify around a limited goal of overthrowing an entrenched and repressive **dictatorship** and once that goal is achieved will not necessarily support a more thorough transformation of society. For others, a political project needs to embrace an explicitly socialist ideology to be categorized as a revolution. The case studies in this book vary significantly in terms of the strategies and ideologies that advocates employed to come to power. None of them began as an explicitly socialist project, and often they did not entail significant violence. All of them, however, sought a rapid shift in wealth and power from the upper class to an impoverished and dispossessed working class. From this perspective, a successful revolution requires an eventual adherence to an anticapitalist ideology that informs a coherent program that seeks to fundamentally alter economic and political structures in favor of marginalized people. An ultimate goal is a more equal and just society that erases profound class divisions.

ANTICOLONIAL REVOLTS

Twentieth-century revolutionaries drew inspiration from previous generations of insurrections. Scholars debate the intent of these earlier movements, including whether they envisioned progressive political changes or sought to hold on to a quickly disappearing past. In either case, these prior mobilizations offer models for action as well as cautionary tales of what could go wrong when idealists seek to turn the world upside down.

Tupac Amaru

The 1780 Tupac Amaru revolt was one of the largest and most significant mass uprisings ever witnessed in the Americas. The movement is named after its leader, an Indigenous rights advocate named José Gabriel Condorcanqui, who traced his lineage to the last Inka emperor, Tupac Amaru. In 1572, the Spanish viceroy Francisco de Toledo executed the emperor after a failed revolt against the European invaders. Inka rule came to an end, but the memory of a society without colonial oppressors remained imprinted in the minds of their descendants. Similar to his ancestor, Condorcanqui witnessed Spanish abuses of native communities that contributed to growing discontent with colonial rule. He initially sought relief through legal means but realized little success in gaining the attention of colonial authorities. With institutional paths to change closed off, on November 4, 1780, Condorcanqui captured and executed a Spanish official. He took the name of Tupac Amaru (sometimes called the second to distinguish him from his predecessor) and called for the expulsion of the Spanish and for the establishment of an independent Inka Empire. As news of the uprising spread, supporters flooded to join the insurgent forces and its ranks quickly grew to sixty thousand troops. They attacked Spanish estates, freed Indigenous prisoners, and removed colonial authorities from power.

Most studies focus on Tupac Amaru's leadership and minimize the interests and motivations of a mass movement that wanted change and was prepared to fight, kill, and die for it. After suffering under centuries of Spanish colonial abuse, Indigenous peoples in the South American Andes were attracted to a vision of a society without economic exploitation and racial discrimination. Their hopes to regain control over their destinies spread like wildfire and rocked society. Without that pressure from below, the revolt never would have reached the dimensions it did. It is difficult to judge whether Tupac Amaru inspired others to follow him in the uprising, or if the population wanted to take action and only needed the opportunity that he had created. Inevitably, both a strong, charismatic vanguard leadership and a disgruntled mass of people ready to act created the necessary conditions for the spread of the revolt.

Traditional treatments of revolts emphasize male leadership and ignore the important contributions that women made. Tupac Amaru's wife, Micaela Bastidas, played a key role in the movement. She served as the movement's chief propagandist and pushed Tupac Amaru to take more militant actions against colonial rule than he had initially proposed. When he was absent, she took command, but more importantly she was a skilled strategist and ideologue in her own right. Her name has become a powerful feminist symbol of a capable woman playing a role equal to that of men in a movement for human liberation. On April 6, 1781, the Spanish captured the leadership of the revolt and on May 18 executed Tupac Amaru and his family members in the old Inka capital of Cuzco. In a patriarchal legal system that defined women (as well as Indigenous peoples and African slaves) as incapable of rational thought and thereby denied political rights, the Spanish took the unusual action of executing Bastidas for her active participation in the revolt.

After the uprising, the Spanish engaged in a campaign of severe repression designed to destroy cultural elements of neo-Inka nationalism that the movement had inspired. Historians have subsequently debated whether the uprising was a messianic movement for ethnic rights, a class-based struggle against economic exploitation, or a failed anticolonial revolt that was a precursor to independence forty years later. Did it have an ideological underpinning, and did it articulate a vision for a new and better future? Or was it a mindless reaction against changes people did not understand or could hope to influence? The answers to these questions are not simple or obvious. In any case, the name Tupac Amaru remains a potent symbol of resistance. Guerrilla movements in Uruguay in the 1970s and Peru in the 1980s took their names from the revolutionary leader, and the Black Panther activist Afeni Shakur gave the name to her son, the legendary rap superstar. More than two centuries later, Tupac Amaru still inspires people to action.

Haitian Slave Revolt

A 1791 slave revolt that led to Haitian independence in 1804 provides an example of what is perhaps the most thorough social revolution, in the sense that it completely inverted an established social order. Although not traditionally included in the pantheon of classic revolutionary movements, it is an example of one of the deepest and most profound revolutionary changes in the modern world. After ten years of sustained warfare, plantation slaves in this French colony overthrew the planter class, destroyed the sugar-based export economic system, and created a new government under the leadership of former slaves. Unlike other anticolonial movements, the Haitian slave revolt is the closest the world has come to a true revolution with extensive social, economic, and political changes.

For more than a century, Haiti was a French colony known as Saint-Domingue. In the eighteenth century, it was the richest colony in the Caribbean and supplied half of the world's sugar and coffee. It also had the densest African slave population in the Americas. The overworked and underfed slaves led to soaring profits for a small French planter class. On August 22, 1791, the slaves revolted against their treatment. The revolt was long, bloody, and devastating, but unlike the Tupac Amaru uprising, it was ultimately successful in evicting the colonial power. A former slave named Toussaint Louverture rose to a position of leadership in the movement. In 1802, the French ruler Napoléon Bonaparte captured Louverture and held him prisoner in France, where he died the following year. Louverture's lieutenant, Jean-Jacques Dessalines, continued the insurrection in his absence. Dessalines finally defeated the French forces and, on January 1, 1804, declared independence for the colony. In a symbolic break from European control, the Black revolutionaries named the country Haiti, the original Taíno word for the island. Former slaves were now in control, while the French planters were either dead or in exile.

Although the Haitian Revolution provides a successful example of exploited Blacks transforming social structures, the victory came at great cost. The war destroyed the island's infrastructure, and the new leaders lacked the technical or administrative skills necessary to run the government. The government faced difficulties in growing the economy without laborers for the export-oriented plantation system. More significantly, both France and the United States were determined to undermine Haiti's model of independent development designed to benefit the working class. The United States refused to recognize the government, both because of their alliance with France and because they did not want the example of a successful slave revolt to spread in its own slave-owning borders. More important, France forced Haitians to pay reparations in exchange for international recognition. Haiti never recovered from that financial bankruptcy and today remains the poorest country in the Americas. The country's macroeconomic statistics would seem to indicate that the island was better off as a slave colony, but that conclusion ignores the role imperial powers played in deliberately undermining an independent Black republic.

Some have taken the Haitian Revolution's levels of brutal violence and the independent country's resulting impoverished condition as a caution against attempting revolutionary changes. Before venturing out on such an endeavor, protagonists must count the costs and weigh those against potential benefits. Others argue that such profound changes in social and economic structures cannot occur successfully in a single location but must happen simultaneously on a global level to be sustainable. As long as wealthy capitalists remain in power anywhere in the world, they will continue to do battle against examples of local endogenous development that seek to enhance the fortunes of marginalized populations.

Religious Movements

In Mexico at the dawn of the nineteenth century, Father Miguel Hidalgo rallied his rural parishioners in support of independence. Early on the morning of September 16, 1810, Hidalgo rang the church bells in his parish of Dolores. He appealed to the Virgin of Guadalupe and called for death to the Spanish and their bad government policies. He marched on Guanajuato, picking up tens of thousands of unarmed but enthusiastic recruits along the way. He appeared to be heading a social revolution with promises of social programs, including land reform and a redistribution of goods. A conservative reaction, however, feared that Hidalgo was releasing a race war on behalf of Indigenous and African-descent peoples against European landholders. In an attempt to put an end to the revolt, the Spanish captured and executed Hidalgo. A decade later, Mexico gained its independence but under the control and direction of wealthy landowners. Hidalgo's uprising represented an inspired but ultimately futile effort to transform society.

During the nineteenth century, many millenarian movements emerged from marginalized societies. One of the most famous of these surfaced in the desperately poor zone of Canudos in the semiarid backlands of Brazil. A local leader, Antônio Vicente Mendes Maciel, became known as Antônio Conselheiro (the Counselor) because of the legal advice he dispensed to poor people. He worked as an itinerant mystic preacher, and his promises of a better world attracted thousands of followers. In 1893, he organized a religious commune at Canudos that quickly grew by leaps and bounds. The community functioned along communistic lines without money and with a common ownership of property. The community alarmed the government, which in 1897 sent in troops and killed almost all of the thirty thousand residents. Conselheiro is alternatively remembered as a religious fanatic, saint, or messiah. Only recently in 1888 had Brazil ended slavery, and a republic was declared the following year. Opponents denounced Conselheiro as a monarchist who opposed the progress that the country was making and desired the return of the recently disposed Pedro II. Others claim that Canudos was a utopian community that expressed the aspirations of marginalized peoples who had lost their land and that the ferociousness of the government's attack was fueled by racism and scorn for lower-class people.

Scholars debate whether these social aspirations were progressive or reactionary, whether protagonists imagined a new and better future or sought to hold on to a quickly disappearing past. Anticapitalist discourses can easily take both aspects, but their underlying ideology and ultimate objectives are diametrically opposed. Some call these early movements prepolitical and contend that they lacked an ideology and clear demands for systemic and transformative change. Key questions to consider are whether the movements engaged the consciousness of a dispossessed class of people and addressed the structural issues that maintained them in an impoverished situation, rather than simply improving the lot of an individual leader or a small group of people. Some movements seek to return to an imagined and nonexistent past rather than moving society forward to a better future. As these early anticolonial revolts reveal, mass uprisings can have reactionary as well as progressive characteristics. Violence and the disruption of an established society alone do not make for a revolutionary situation.

BIOGRAPHY: JOSÉ CARLOS MARIÁTEGUI, 1894–1930

José Carlos Mariátegui was a Peruvian thinker who is commonly revered as the founder of Latin American Marxist theory. His most famous book, *Seven Interpretive Essays on Peruvian Reality*, is a foundational work on Latin American Marxism and commonly cited as the one book to read to understand Latin American realities. Mariátegui presents a brilliant analysis of Peruvian, and by extension Latin American, problems from a Marxist point of view.

In October 1919, the Peruvian dictator Augusto B. Leguía exiled Mariátegui to Europe. Mariátegui studied in France and Italy, where he interacted with many European socialists. His time in Europe strongly influenced the development and maturation of his thought, and solidified his socialist tendencies. Upon returning to Peru in 1923, Mariátegui declared that he was "a convinced and declared Marxist."

José Carlos Mariátegui
Source: Casa Museo José Carlos Mariátegui

Mariátegui interacted dynamically with European thought in order to develop new methods to analyze Latin American problems. He favored a nonsectarian "open" Marxism in which Marxist thought should be revisable, not dogmatic, and adaptable to new situations. Rather than a rigid reliance on objective economic factors to foment a revolutionary situation, Mariátegui also examined subjective elements such as the need for the political education and organization of the proletariat, a strategy that he believed could move a society to revolutionary action.

In 1926, Mariátegui founded *Amauta*, a journal that he intended to be a van-guard voice for an intellectual and spiritual movement to create a new Peru. In 1928, he launched a biweekly periodical called *Labor* to inform, educate, and politicize the working class. Mariátegui published two books, *La escena contem-poránea* (The contemporary scene) in 1925 and *7 ensayos de interpretación de la realidad peruana* (*Seven Interpretive Essays on Peruvian Reality*) in 1928, in addi-tion to many articles in various Peruvian periodicals.

Unlike orthodox Marxists who denied the revolutionary potential of the peas-antry, Mariátegui looked to the rural Indigenous masses in addition to an indus-trialized urban working class to lead a social revolution that he believed would sweep across Latin America. Mariátegui argued that once Indigenous peoples had seized onto **socialism**, they would cling to it fervently, since it coincided with their traditional communal forms of social organization. To be successful, modern socialism would fuse the legacy of "Inka communism" with modern Western technology.

Mariátegui's revolutionary activities did not remain only on a theoretical level. He was influential in the organization of communist cells all over Peru and served as the first secretary-general of the Partido Socialista Peruano (PSP, Peruvian Socialist Party) that he founded in 1928. In 1929, the PSP launched the Con-federación General de Trabajadores del Perú (CGTP, General Confederation of Peruvian Workers), a Marxist-oriented trade union federation. Both the CGTP and the PSP were involved in an active internationalism, including participating in **Communist International**–sponsored meetings. Twice the Leguía dictatorship arrested and imprisoned Mariátegui for his political activities, although he was never convicted of any crime.

Although the political party and labor confederation that Mariátegui had helped launch flourished, his health foundered. In 1924 he lost his right leg and was confined to a wheelchair for the rest of his life. In spite of his failing health, Mariátegui increased the intensity of his efforts to organize a social revolution in Peru. Mariátegui was at the height of his intellectual and political contributions when he died on April 16, 1930, two months short of his thirty-sixth birthday.

DOCUMENT: JOSÉ CARLOS MARIÁTEGUI, "ON THE INDIGENOUS PROBLEM," 1928

Mariátegui reinterpreted Marxist thought for Latin American realities. In this es-say that he wrote in 1928 at the request of the Tass News Agency in New York, Mariátegui focuses attention on the need to address the economic exploitation that Indigenous peoples faced. It complements and extends his discussion in his 1928 book Seven Interpretive Essays on Peruvian Reality.

According to conservative estimates, the population of the Inka Empire was at least ten million. Some place it at twelve to fifteen million. The conquest was, more than anything, a terrible carnage. The Spanish conquerors, with their small numbers, could not impose their domination but only managed to terrorize the Indigenous popula-tion. The people regarded the invaders' guns and horses as supernatural beings, which created a superstitious impression. The political and economic organization of the colony, which came after the conquest, continued the extermination of the Indigenous race. The viceroyalty established a system of brutal exploitation. Spanish greed for precious metals led to economic activities directed toward mining. The Inkas had worked those mines on a very small scale because the Indians, who were largely an agricultural people, did not use iron and only used gold and silver as ornaments. The Spanish established a system of forced labor to work the mines and textile sweatshops that decimated the population. They created not only a system of servitude, as might have been the case had the Spanish limited the exploitation to the use of land and retained the agricultural character of the country, but also a system of slavery. Humanitarian and civilizing voices called for the king of Spain to defend the Indians. More than anyone, Father Bartolomé de Las Casas stood out in their defense. The Laws of the Indies were intended to protect the Indians. It recognized their traditional community organization. But in reality the Indians were at the mercy of a ruthless feudalism that destroyed the Inka economy and society without replacing it with something that could increase production. The tendency of the Spanish to settle on the coast drove away so many aboriginals from the region that it resulted in a lack of workers. The viceroyalty wanted to solve this problem through the importation of African slaves. These people were appropriate to the climate and challenges of the hot valleys and plains of the coast, but were inappropriate for work in the mines in the cold sierra highlands. African slaves reinforced the system of Spanish domination. In spite of Indigenous depopulation, the Indians still outnumbered the Spanish. Even though subjugated, the Indians remained a hostile enemy. Blacks were devoted to domestic service and other jobs. Whites easily mixed with Blacks, producing a mixture of a type characteristic of the coastal population that has greater adherence to the Spanish and resists Indigenous influences.

The independence revolution was not, as is known, an Indigenous movement. It was a movement of and for the benefit of creoles and even the Spanish living in the colonies. But it took advantage of the support of the Indigenous masses. Furthermore, as illustrated by the Pumacahua, some Indians played an important role in its development. The independence movement's liberal program logically included the redemption of the Indian as an automatic consequence of the implementation of its egalitarian principles. And so, among the republic's first acts, were several laws and decrees in favor of the Indians. They ordered the distribution of land, the abolition of forced labor, and so on. But independence in Peru did not bring in a new ruling class, and all of these provisions remained on paper without a government capable of carrying them out. The colony's landholding aristocracy, the owner of power, retained their feudal rights over the land and, therefore, over the Indians. All provisions designed to protect them have not been able to do anything against feudalism, and that is still true today.

The viceroyalty seems less to blame than the republic. The full responsibility for the misery and depression of the Indians originally belongs to the viceroyalty. But in those inquisitorial days, a great Christian voice, that of the Friar Bartolomé de Las Casas, vigorously defended the Indians against the colonizers' brutal methods. There has never been as stubborn and effective an advocate of the aboriginal race during the republic.

While the viceroyalty was a medieval and foreign regime, the republic is formally a Peruvian and liberal regime. The republic, therefore, had a duty the viceroyalty did not have. The republic has the responsibility to raise the status of the Indian. And contrary to this duty, the republic has impoverished the Indians. It has compounded their depression and exasperated their misery. The republic has meant for the Indians the ascent of a new ruling class that has systematically taken their lands. In a race based on customs and an agricultural soul, as with the Indigenous race, this dispossession has constituted a cause for their material and moral dissolution. Land has always been the joy of the Indians. Indians are wed to the land. They feel that "life comes from the earth" and returns to the earth. For this reason, Indians can be indifferent to everything except the possession of the land, which by their hands and through their encouragement is religiously fruitful. Creole feudalism has behaved, in this respect, worse than Spanish feudalism. In general, the Spanish *encomendero* (grant holder) often had some of the noble habits of feudal lords. The creole encomendero has all the defects of a commoner and none of the virtues of a gentleman. The servitude of the Indian, in short, has not decreased under the republic. All uprisings, all of the Indian unrest, have been drowned in blood. Indian demands have always been met with a military response. The silence of the cold, desolate highland *puna* region afterward guards the tragic secret of these responses. In the end, the republic restored, under the title of the road labor draft, the system of *mitas* (labor system).

In addition, the republic is also responsible for the lethargic and weak energies of the race. The cause of the redemption of the Indians became under the republic a demagogic speculation of some strongmen. Creole parties have signed up for their program. And thus the Indians lost their will to fight for their demands.

In the highlands, the region mostly inhabited by the Indians, the most barbaric and omnipotent feudalism remains largely unchanged. The domination of the earth in the hands of the *gamonales* (landowners), the fate of the Indigenous race, falls to an extreme level of depression and ignorance. In addition to farming, which is carried out on a very primitive level, the Peruvian highlands also have another economic activity: mining, almost entirely in the hands of two large U.S. companies. Wages are regulated in the mines, but the pay is negligible, there is almost no defense for the lives of the workers, and labor laws governing accidents are ignored. The system of *enganche* (debt peonage), which through false promises enslaves workers, puts the Indians at the mercy of these capitalist companies. The misery of agrarian feudalism is so great that Indians prefer the lot offered by the mines.

The spread of socialist ideas in Peru has resulted in a strong movement reflecting Indigenous demands. The new Peruvian generation knows that Peru's progress will be fictitious, or at least will not be Peruvian, if it does not benefit the Peruvian masses, four-fifths of whom are Indigenous and peasant. This same trend is evident in art and in national literature in which there is a growing appreciation of Indigenous forms and affairs, which the dominance of a Spanish colonial spirit and mentality had previously depreciated. **Indigenista** literature seems to fulfill the same role of *Mujika* literature in pre-revolutionary Russia. Indians themselves are beginning to show signs of a new consciousness. Relationships between various Indigenous settlements that previously had been out of contact because of great distances grow day by day. The regular meeting of government-sponsored Indigenous congresses initiated these linkages, but as the nature of their demands became revolutionary they were denatured as advanced elements were excluded and representation was made apocryphal. Indigenista currents press for official action. For the first time the government has been forced to accept and proclaim indigenista views, and has decreed some measures that do not touch gamonal interests and are ineffective because of this. For the first time the Indigenous problem, which disappears in the face of ruling-class rhetoric, is posed in its social and economic terms and is identified more than anything as a land problem. Every day more evidence underscores the conviction that this problem cannot find its solution in a humanitarian formula. It cannot be the result of a philanthropic movement. The patronage of Indigenous chieftains and phony lawyers are a mockery. Leagues of the type of the former Pro-Indigenous Association provide a voice clamoring in the wilderness. The Pro-Indigenous Association did not arrive on time to become a movement. Their action was gradually reduced to the generous, selfless, noble, personal actions of Pedro S. Zulen and Dora Mayer. As an experiment, the Pro-Indigenous Association served to contrast, to measure, the moral callousness of a generation and an era.

The solution to the problem of the Indian must be a social solution. The Indians themselves must work it out. This understanding leads to seeing the meeting of Indigenous congresses as a historical fact. The Indigenous congresses, misled in recent years by bureaucratic tendencies, have not yet formed a program, but their first meetings indicated a route for Indians in different regions. The Indians lack a national organization. Their protests have always been regional. This has contributed in large part to their defeat. Four million people, conscious of their numbers, do not despair of their future. These same four million people, though they are nothing more than an inorganic mass, a dispersed crowd, are unable to decide its historical course.

Source: José Carlos Mariátegui, "Sobre el problema indígena," *Labor: Quincenario de información e ideas* 1, no. 1 (November 10, 1928): 6 (translation by author).

COMMUNIST INTERNATIONAL

Even as international currents influenced leftist ideologies in Latin America, revolutionaries debated what relationship they should have with those international trends, or whether they should project their movement as rooted primarily or even exclusively in domestic events. The most significant external influence was the October 1917 Bolshevik Revolution that set Russia on the path of a rapid transition to socialism. Inspired by the Bolshevik drive to move a rural society toward a modern, industrialized one, many socialist and anarchist activists in Latin America formed communist parties in the 1920s. Under the leadership of Vladimir Ilyich Ulyanov (alias Lenin) (1870–1924), the Bolsheviks organized the Communist International in 1919 to lead this international movement to world **communism**.

Previous attempts to organize an international socialist organization had failed. The International Workingmen's Association (1864–1877), often called the First International, was founded in London to revive the European labor movement after their defeats in the 1848 socialist uprisings. Karl Marx led and dominated the First International, but sectarian divisions collapsed it. The Second International (1889–1914) was founded in Paris and was less torn by internal disputes, but its passivity in the face of the First World War led to its collapse. The Second International later regrouped as the Socialist International that gathered together mainstream social democratic parties.

The First and Second Internationals were federations of different national groups and political parties, whereas the Communist International, also known as the Comintern or Third International, was designed as a single, centrally organized party, radiating out from its base in Moscow with the aim of world revolution. The Peruvian Marxist José Carlos Mariátegui observed that whereas the Second International was an organizational machine, the Third International was a combat machine designed to transform society. Its goal was to lead a global revolution.

Initially, the Comintern focused its efforts on what it thought would be an imminent revolution in Europe. No Latin Americans attended the Comintern's first congress in Moscow, and few participated in the next several congresses. It was not until the sixth congress, in 1928, that the Communist International "discovered" Latin America and began to play an active role in the region. At the same time, the Comintern entered its "third period," during which it adopted an aggressive and militant strategy of engaging in a class-against-class struggle. Communist leaders optimistically believed that capitalism was entering a period of final collapse and turned against moderate left-wing parties in an attempt to hasten the revolution.

The Comintern recognized the revolutionary potential of anticolonial struggles and defended the rights of self-determination for national minorities, including the right to secede from oppressive state structures. The policy led to advocating for the establishment of "independent native republics" for Blacks in South Africa and the United States, and a proposal to carve an Indigenous Republic for the Quechua and Aymara peoples in South America. Mariátegui adamantly maintained that an independent republic would only replicate the existing class contradictions in society. He argued that communists should focus instead on a class struggle that would force changes in a land tenure system that impoverished rural dwellers. Elsewhere, including in neighboring Ecuador, communists picked up the slogan of the rights of Indigenous nationalities and used it as a rhetorical device to advance their struggles. As a result, communism became associated with the liberation struggles of African-descent and Indigenous peoples.

One of the largest international communist campaigns in the 1920s was in defense of Nicaraguan patriot Augusto César Sandino, who was fighting against the U.S. Marines who had occupied his country since 1911. Sandino had previously worked in the oil fields of Tampico, Mexico, where he was caught up in the revolutionary fervor of the Mexican Revolution. The anarchist Industrial Workers of the World (IWW) organized the oil workers and strongly influenced Sandino's ideology. He drew on liberal, socialist, and spiritual ideologies to shape his struggle. The Mexican muralist Diego Rivera and other notable communists, including Mariátegui, organized an international campaign called "Hands Off Nicaragua" in defense of Sandino's anti-imperialist struggle. By 1933, Sandino had fought the marines to a standstill and the United States agreed to withdraw its military forces. In their place, the United States trained and installed a **national guard** that ambushed and killed Sandino in February 1934.

Scholars have long debated the nature of Sandino's ideology and whether his struggle extended beyond a nationalistic struggle to free his country from U.S. occupation. His ideology revealed a mix of liberal, anarchist, and socialist influences, including anticlerical, antiauthoritarian, and anticapitalist positions. Sandino embraced policies that emphasized social legislation, **agrarian reform**, and a downward redistribution of wealth to benefit marginalized people. Sandino's private secretary

Agustín Farabundo Martí attempted to convince him to accept a more explicitly communist position, but Sandino wanted to emphasize the nationalist aspects of his struggle in order to gain a wide base of support. He believed it was necessary to avoid anarchist and communist labels in order to launch a successful, broad-based revolution. The benefits and liabilities of linking local and global struggles were a constant theme of debate among these militant activists.

Martí became frustrated with Sandino's reticence at joining a global movement and returned to his native El Salvador, where he organized the first communist-inspired armed insurrection in Latin America. Martí set up local political councils, denominated "soviets" after the Russian term the Bolsheviks had used. He developed a socialist program that quickly inspired a large peasant mobilization. In January 1932, the Salvadoran military rapidly and brutally suppressed the rural uprising, killing as many as thirty thousand people in the process. The peasant insurgents simply did not have sufficient arms, training, or popular support to defend themselves. Scholars continue to debate what role (if any) the Comintern had in organizing the uprising, or whether the attempted revolution emerged primarily in response to local peasant demands. The army **massacre** targeted Indigenous peoples and led to an abandonment of native dress and language because of their association with the communist insurgency. While some condemn Martí for leading a rural population into a massacre, others celebrate him as a leftist hero for launching a struggle against grinding poverty and extreme socioeconomic inequality in the face of overwhelming odds.

The Comintern held its seventh and final congress in 1935. With the rise of the Nazis in Germany, the congress reversed its policy of class struggle adopted seven years earlier and embraced a **popular front** strategy. Communist parties were now instructed to collaborate with other democratic forces that opposed **fascism**, rather than basing themselves only in the working class. Chile was the only place in Latin America where a popular front strategy successfully brought the left to power through electoral means. In 1938, communists entered into a center-left coalition with socialists to help elect Pedro Aguirre Cerda of the Radical Party as president. That alliance did not result in the implementation of much of the socialist agenda, which highlighted the limitations of the popular front strategy of collaborating with others who were not committed to a radical transformation of society.

In 1943, in the midst of a battle for the very survival of the Soviet Union during the Second World War, Joseph Stalin dissolved the Comintern as a way to calm the fears of his British and U.S. allies that communists were attempting to foment a world revolution under the guise of fighting a common fascist enemy. Following Moscow's lead, during the 1940s and 1950s most Latin American communists opted to work for progressive social changes through existing institutional channels. They pursued peaceful and electoral paths to revolutionary transformation. As would later emerge in Cuba with Fidel Castro, the most violent and radical options materialized outside of the communist orbit. Even so, conservatives denigrated revolutionary movements as emanating out of Moscow rather than responding to local conditions.

The issue of whether to collaborate in one unified global communist revolution or to build a local movement of national liberation continued to divide the left.

IDEOLOGIES

The twentieth-century revolutionary left emerged out of three distinct ideological currents: utopian socialism, anarchism, and Marxism. Advocates of each tendency shared a common vision of a society without oppression and exploitation in which authoritarian structures including governments had disappeared. The goal was socialism in which private ownership of the means of production no longer existed and everyone had equal access to sufficient resources to enjoy life to its fullest. The three ideologies differed greatly in their approaches to the realization of such a dream. Over the past two centuries, each ideology in turn held dominance over the left, and elements of each survive to the present. The boundaries between the different currents were not always entirely clearly established. Aspects of each can be found in the other branches, as they influenced each other's ideas of how best to transform society.

Utopian Socialism

Utopian socialism was the first current of anticapitalist thought to emerge in the nineteenth century. Adherents contended that they could move people in the direction of a more ideal society with intellectual arguments. Individuals would voluntarily adopt their program and establish alternative communities that would set an example for others to follow. This transformation would occur without the destruction of a violent class struggle. Those who advocated these ideas did not identify themselves as utopian socialists. Rather, other socialists subsequently dismissed their ideas as unrealistic and pejoratively labeled their current as a "utopian" or fanciful and unrealizable way to change society.

The English philosopher Thomas More (1478–1535) introduced the concept of utopia through the publication in 1516 of his book *Utopia* (meaning "nowhere"), in which he describes an imaginary socialist society. Three centuries later, the French political theorist Henri de Saint-Simon (1760–1825) formulated ideas that provided the basis of utopian socialism. Saint-Simon was born into an aristocratic society but with his writings sought to guide society away from feudalism and toward social improvements. From his perspective, enlightened leaders would provide technological solutions that would improve society. These developments would occur without class conflict or a violent revolution in which the working class would overthrow the ruling class in order to capture control over the political and economic system. Rather, with the proper ideas and guidance, society would naturally evolve to a higher and more perfect state of being.

The author Edward Bellamy (1850–1898) did much to popularize the ideas of utopian socialism in his 1888 novel *Looking Backward*. The book provides a Rip Van Winkle–like tale in which the protagonist falls into a deep sleep and wakes up in the year 2000 in a socialist utopia. Bellamy describes a society in which property was held in common, money had ceased to exist, technological advances drastically reduced working hours, and everyone enjoyed a life of plenty. Bellamy's vision inspired the creation of clubs and utopian communities to propagate his ideas. Critics complained that his book failed to explain how such a perfect society could be achieved without class conflict or violent struggle. Would wealthy individuals willingly give up their class privileges in the interests of the entire society?

While utopian communities still exist (for example, the Hutterites, an Anabaptist religious sect that practices a communal way of life), utopian socialism largely lost force by the end of the nineteenth century and only echoes of this ideology survived into the twenty-first century. In Latin America, utopian socialism never achieved a strong presence. Mostly, this tendency attracted members of the aristocracy who became aware of the inequalities and oppression in society, and sought to improve the lives of the most marginalized people without sacrificing their own advantages. Other leftists criticized this approach as advocating romantic ideals that could not be realized without addressing underlying class contradictions. Many of the utopian goals of a better society, however, did not disappear and survived under the umbrella of anarchism.

Anarchism

Anarchism is popularly thought of as a lack of order that leads to chaos, and as a result the term acquires negative connotations. Politically, it refers to an anti-authoritarian ideology that opposes hierarchies as unnecessary and fundamentally harmful to the realization of a more just and equal society. The word "anarchism" comes from the Greek word *anarchos* that means "without rulers." Rather than seeking to reform government policies, anarchists fought to destroy existing institutions, eliminate governments and capitalism, and create a new society. Far from advocating for chaos, anarchism at its core is a philosophy of freedom, both in the sense of gaining freedom from imposed authority as well as being free to celebrate the full human potential.

The category of anarchism incorporates a wide range of ideas, stretching from extreme individualism to complete collectivism. The two main traditions can be broadly grouped under individualist anarchism and social anarchism. Individualist anarchism emphasizes personal will over external determinants such as groups, society, traditions, and ideological systems. In contrast to this perspective, which opposes state or social control over individuals, social anarchism emphasizes liberty to realize a person's potential. Social anarchists reject private property because it creates inequality and instead call for the public ownership of the means of production and democratic control over organizations, without any government authority or coercion.

The French philosopher Pierre-Joseph Proudhon (1809–1865) was the first person to describe himself as an anarchist and is commonly considered to be the founder of anarchist thought. Proudhon asserted in his 1840 book *What Is Property?* that "property is theft," which subsequently became a common slogan for anticapitalist movements. Instead of private property, masters, and hierarchies, Proudhon advocated for worker self-management through mutualistic societies that would allow for individuals to realize their full potential.

The Russian revolutionary Mikhail Alexandrovich Bakunin (1814–1876) was one of the most famous and influential anarchists. He advocated for a collectivist anarchism that favored the abolition of state structures as well as the private ownership of the means of production. Instead, workers would collectively own and manage production. Bakunin opposed Marx's strategy of the working class taking control of political power in order to rule from above to implement policies that would benefit the rest of society. Rather than the enlightened rulers of utopian socialism guiding society, Bakunin advocated for the immediate abolishment of government structures because they would inevitably lead to oppression. Socialism remained a common shared end goal, but intense debates raged over how to arrive at that point.

Emma Goldman (1869–1940) played a pivotal role in the development of anarchist thought at the beginning of the twentieth century. Goldman was born in Lithuania and immigrated to the United States in 1885. She was a renowned writer and lecturer on anarchist philosophy, women's rights, and social issues, and was repeatedly imprisoned for her political activism. Goldman was deported to the Soviet Union during the 1919 Red Scare when Attorney General A. Mitchell Palmer suppressed radical organizations. She soon left the Soviet Union out of disillusionment with the authoritarian nature of the new communist government. Goldman is best known through a quote that is actually a paraphrase of her ideas: "If I can't dance, I don't want to be in your revolution." That statement embodies an anarchist rejection of vanguard leadership in favor of democratic participation in movement decisions.

Anarchists opposed joining political parties or voting in elections because these systems inevitably reproduced the oppressive and hierarchical elements of the society against which they rebelled, and their participation would legitimize an authoritarian system. Instead, anarchists favored direct **democracy** in which people would have control over decision-making processes. Many anarchists also advocated for the development of an autonomous working-class culture. They sought to foster new social institutions through staging theater productions, holding lectures, publishing books and newspapers, and engaging in alternative lifestyles. All were designed to develop new forms of community.

Adherents agreed on the need to transform society, but they disagreed over what was the best way to achieve that goal. Some favored violent tactics, which led to a largely inaccurate stereotype of bomb-throwing anarchists. In the twentieth century, anarchists became one of the most peaceful camps on the left. Even while some did engage in violence, most mobilized workers in labor actions. These actions could take the form of strikes, industrial sabotage, or boycotts. In particular, anarchists are associated with a general strike that aims to disrupt the smooth functioning of a capitalist society. Strikes could either take the form of an armed confrontation against business owners, or more commonly of workers peacefully walking away from their jobs in order to force a change in policies.

Anarchism was particularly influential in the labor movement from about 1880 to 1920. The ideology gained broad exposure through the 1886 Haymarket Affair. On May 1, workers in Chicago engaged in a general strike for an eight-hour workday. On May 4, anarchists staged a peaceful rally at Haymarket Square. At the rally, an unidentified person threw a bomb that killed a police officer. Many suspect the action was by a police provocateur who sought to justify a repressive response to the labor movement, while others contend that the anarchists believed in the necessity of a violent revolution to achieve their goals. In either case, the police opened fire, killing seven police officers and four workers. Authorities arrested eight anarchists and charged them with murder. The anarchists quickly became international political celebrities. Four (Albert Parsons, August Spies, Adolph Fischer, and George Engel) were executed, another committed suicide while in detention, and the rest were sentenced to lengthy prison terms. The Haymarket Affair is celebrated around the world on May 1 as International Workers' Day, but notably not in the United States.

Some anarchists criticized trade unions as inherently reformist and opposed what they saw as their innately vanguardist, hierarchical characteristics. In 1905, militant workers who favored a revolutionary industrial unionism met in Chicago to found the Industrial Workers of the World (IWW, or the Wobblies). It was an anarcho-syndicalist group with considerable influence during the early 1900s. The IWW focused on organizing the working class as a key task and engaged in "direct action" through general strikes, sabotage, and boycotts. Among its most important founders was William D. "Big Bill" Haywood of the Western Federation of Miners, who had led a series of strikes in western mines. IWW organizer Joe Hill became a martyr and folk hero when he was executed in 1915 on a questionable murder charge. He famously proclaimed to his fellow workers, "Don't mourn, organize!"

Anarchism entered Latin America through the influence of southern European immigrants, particularly in Argentina, Brazil, and Uruguay. At the beginning of the twentieth century, anarchists engaged in repeated strikes to defend workers' rights and to agitate for higher pay. The military frequently repressed the strikes, leading to the massacre of thousands of workers. While the repression temporarily halted labor activism, extreme abuses soon led to a resurgence of organizing activity and inevitably a new round of strikes and massacres. In Chile, for example, nitrate miners organized 638 strikes between 1901 and 1924. In Ecuador, a massacre of striking workers at the port of Guayaquil in 1922 gave birth to the modern left through a baptism of blood. In Colombia, Gabriel García Márquez memorialized a 1928 massacre of striking banana workers at Santa Marta in his award-winning novel *One Hundred Years of Solitude*. Through his journalism, Ricardo Flores Magón introduced anarchist ideas that fundamentally influenced the direction of the 1910 Mexican Revolution. In 1926, Sandino returned to his native Nicaragua from exile in Mexico under the influence of these anarchist ideas and launched his own revolution. While utopian socialism expressed aspirations for a better society, anarchism provided an ideology to achieve those goals.

Marxism

Anarchism was the most significant anticapitalist ideology during the first two decades of the twentieth century. The triumph of the Bolshevik Revolution in 1917, however, changed popular perceptions of its relative importance. For the first time, a successful armed insurrection overthrew an established capitalist system and began to construct a new society based on Marxist principles. In the 1920s, many anarchists deserted ranks and joined communist parties in an attempt to replicate the success they observed in the Soviet Union. Whereas utopian socialism expressed aspirations and anarchism provided an ideology, Marxism laid out a concrete path to implement those goals.

While utopian socialism is commonly labeled with its derogatory moniker and schools of anarchism are identified by their core organizational principle such as anarcho-syndicalism, Marxism and its variations (**Leninism**, **Trotskyism**, **Maoism**, etc.) are inevitably known for their founders. Karl Marx was a German philosopher who, with the assistance of his collaborator Friedrich Engels (1820–1895), wrote such notable works as *The Communist Manifesto* (1848) and *Das Kapital* (1867–1894) in which he critiqued capitalism and developed a vision for societal change. He looked to the industrialized working class as the agent of social change, as a class that had both the power and interest to overthrow capitalism. To achieve this goal, the working class needed a revolutionary organization that must struggle to create an alternative form of state power, to reorganize society, and to repress the inevitable reaction that the ruling class would mount against a socialist revolution.

Marx was the first to articulate a conception of history that has come to be known as historical materialism. It is a methodological approach that seeks scientific explanations in the concrete, material world for the causes of developments and changes in human society rather than relying on idealistic notions or the spiritual realm. Furthermore, Marx believed that every society would be defined by its dominant mode of production, or the way productive forces and the relations of production are combined. Productive forces include the means of production such as labor, tools, equipment, and land. The relations of production describe property and power relations that govern society and control the way in which humans relate to the forces of production. The mode of production defines the manner in which productive forces are harnessed to meet material needs, how the labor process is organized, and how the products of that labor are distributed to society. Writing in the context of a nineteenth-century positivist framework, Marx described a linear progression of modes of production through time, from primitive communalism to feudalism, capitalism, and socialism, and finally to its full realization in communism where the scientific management of society through democratic means would establish the maximum good for all without the need for governments or other forms of coercion.

According to Marx, society is divided into antagonistic groups called classes that are locked into conflict with each other. People's relationship to the means of production, specifically whether they are a capitalist who owns the factories or workers who deliver their labor to the owner, determines their location in the class structure. Marx wrote in *The Communist Manifesto*, "The history of all hitherto existing society is the history of class struggles." The antagonism between the classes is a result of marked differences in wealth, power, and prestige, as different groups compete for access to those resources. That antagonism is called class struggle and according to Marx provides the engine for historical change.

People are born into a class structure, whether they realize it or not, and that class position shapes, determines, and constrains their role in society. Marx wrote, "Human beings make history, but under circumstances that they do not control." When people become aware of their location in a class structure they gain **class consciousness**. In that situation, they begin to seek to guide and determine a historical outcome to the benefit of their class. Marx believed that once workers acquired a class consciousness they would engage in revolutionary activity that would destroy capitalism and usher in a process of radical change that would socialize the means of production and eventually lead to a communist society. That process would end exploitation and injustice, including the elimination of restrictive social classes and authoritarian governing structures.

Related to the issue of class consciousness is an interplay between objective and subjective factors in determining when a revolution would take place. Some interpreters of Marx's philosophy argue that a society has to meet certain objective economic conditions before a socialist revolution could take place. Specifically, it was necessary for a capitalist mode of production to develop the economy to a sufficient level to meet people's needs before socialism could succeed. At the same time, a highly developed capitalist economy would alienate the working class, who would then act to destroy capitalism and push society to the next higher stage of socialism. Only an industrialized working class through its experience with capitalist production could develop the consciousness necessary to allow them to see the inherent contradictions in capitalism and the necessity for a socialist state. A competing interpretation is that subjective factors such as political education and organization of the masses were more important than objective economic conditions to move a society to revolutionary action. Those who emphasized objective factors acquired a deterministic view of Marxism that maintained that once capitalist development reached a certain stage a revolution would happen automatically, and it was a serious mistake to push for a revolution before those basic economic conditions existed. On the other hand, a voluntarist interpretation of Marxism stressed subjective factors that contended that humans could create a socialist revolution even if the basic economic conditions had not been met. In this case, a danger was to move toward socialism before society could withstand such a transformation. Others believed that both objective and subjective factors were necessary for a revolution to take place.

The sociologist C. Wright Mills defined four different kinds of Marxists. First are the "dead" Marxists, who treat Marx's texts as a sacred authority with answers to all of life's questions. Second are "vulgar" Marxists, who read for specific ideological interpretations and extrapolate from those to represent Marx's ideology as a whole. "Sophisticated" Marxists look to Marxism as a model for how to structure society and mold Marx's nineteenth-century ideas to fit new situations. Even so, they find Marxist answers for everything, and their rigidity can hinder their analysis, which leads to a substitution of dogmatism for serious reflection. Finally, Mills defined "plain" Marxists as those who work openly and flexibly with Marx's ideas. They reject forcing real and lived realities into an ideological straitjacket in order to conform to hard-and-fast rules. While Marx is foundational for an understanding of revolution, advocates have used his thought in many different ways.

Other Tendencies

In addition to these three trends (utopian socialism, anarchism, and Marxism), in Latin America left-wing liberals on occasion also joined forces with socialists to press for radical reforms. Fundamental ideological divisions normally separated liberals from leftists. Liberals generally emphasized individual rights, such as those expressed in the 1789 Declaration of the Rights of Man and of the Citizen from the French Revolution or codified in the Bill of Rights in the U.S. constitution (freedoms of speech, the press, religion, assembly, etc.). Leftists, on the other hand, believed that social rights that benefited an entire community were more important than individual liberties. These rights include access to healthcare, education, housing, and an assured adequate standard of living. A radical wing of **liberalism**, however, recognized the importance of these social concerns. In Latin America, their agenda included a condemnation of U.S. **imperialism**, a call for agrarian reform, protection of worker rights, and nationalization of the means of production. Liberals embraced a representative government as a positive force to implement a social agenda from above, whereas leftists aspired to participatory governance from below and at the point of production that would empower workers to formulate policies that would be in their own interests.

In parts of Latin America, a fifth leftist influence was the Indigenous (and sometimes Black) movements that fought against racial discrimination and economic exploitation. This tendency sometimes predated other leftist movements. In areas of Mesoamerica and the Andes with sizable native populations, rural Indigenous communities had long engaged in struggles for land, ethnic rights, and their very survival. While some observers disregarded their actions as prepolitical, their lived experiences of discrimination and oppression contributed to a heightened awareness of the class structure of society. Their actions challenged Marx's European assumptions that peasants were inherently reactionary and that only the urban working class would form the motor to move society forward. In Latin America, militant Indigenous and peasant movements emerged in the context of growing labor unions and leftist political parties. Indeed, the rise of these rural movements was often closely related to, and reliant on, labor and leftist movements, even while also influencing the character and demands of urban militants. During a period in which many members of the dominant society manifested deeply held racist sentiments toward Indigenous and African-descent peoples, some communist party members comprised a rare group willing to defend their interests. These Marxists did not remain in urban areas removed from local struggles, nor did they manipulate events at a distance. Rather, they worked hand in hand with rural communities and workers on large estates to develop organizational structures in order to fight for their social, economic, and political rights.

NECESSARY CRITERIA FOR A REVOLUTION

Many people assume that revolutions emerge out of oppression, but Russian revolutionary Leon Trotsky (1879–1940) famously observed that if exploitation alone caused an insurrection the masses would constantly be in revolt. Rather, as historian Crane Brinton (1898–1968) argues in *The Anatomy of Revolution*, revolutions develop when a government is not able or willing to deliver on its promises, which leads to a failure to meet society's rising expectations. Sociologist Theda Skocpol argues that revolutions are not made but come when certain conditions are met. Political scientist Eric Selbin challenges that assertion and instead contends that revolutions do not just happen but are made as a result of leaders' conscious decisions and plans. While social and economic inequalities appear to be prerequisites for a revolution, and perhaps even a given in Latin America, these alone are not enough to move people to action. Human intervention, particularly in the form of leadership and ideology, is also necessary. Furthermore, although socialist revolutions can acquire characteristics of a civil war or a mass revolt, they are rooted in a quite different process. Socialist revolutions require a vision and a plan for moving forward to a better future and are fundamentally different than fearful reactions against change.

Several factors appear to be required for a successful revolution. These include the following:

Ideology. Some scholars present peasant revolts as negative reactions in which a dispossessed population seeks to hold on to the benefits of a quickly disappearing past. Socialist revolutions, on the other hand, are forward looking, with a program and vision for a new and better future. They have a coherent *ideology* and are successful when revolutionaries convince others to join in a struggle to implement those ideas. In Latin America, this ideology assumes a revolutionary discourse that is typically anti-imperialist and anticapitalist, and forwards a vision of a more equal and just society without class divisions. It advocates for changes in the political culture and includes religious influences such as **liberation theology**. An ideology distinguishes revolutions from other violent affairs.

Leadership. Successful revolutions seemingly require charismatic vanguard leaders who set agendas and mobilize and inspire others to support that vision and ideology. As human beings, these leaders often have complicated and contradictory motivations and sometimes can work to advance their own personal interests rather than those of the broader society.

Resources. A successful revolution requires the mobilization of significant organizational and material resources, both to challenge U.S. support for the previous government and to overcome opposition to the new regime. In an armed revolution this includes access to weapons, through either capturing them from the local military or setting up networks to import them from outside the country. In the electoral realm, political campaigns require the mobilization of human capital and the distribution of propaganda. It is impossible to rally the population without access to resources, as well as a hope that proper use of those resources will lead to success.

Discredited previous government. Revolutions only succeed with the collapse of a weakened and discredited ancien régime (previous political system) that has lost popular support. Often revolutions succeed not so much because of external pressure on the government but because the current regime is rotten to the core and collapses in on itself. Personalistic and infrastructurally weak regimes are especially vulnerable. A new revolutionary government can then emerge in that political vacuum, with new and better ideas on how to structure society.

Other avenues for change are closed. Dissidents turn to extraconstitutional means to change a government when it *appears* that all institutional or democratic avenues are closed. It is not necessarily important that other avenues are actually closed, but the revolutionaries must capture the narrative and create in the public mind the idea that a revolution is the best, and perhaps only, path forward.

Revolutions are rare events, and multiple conditions and factors must coalesce to create a suitable environment for the eventual success of such a movement. Revolutions are volatile and unpredictable events, and their emergence, course, and development are not easy to predict.

CENTRAL AND PERENNIAL ISSUES

A series of issues underlie revolutionary efforts across the twentieth century and highlight ongoing fractures within the left into the twenty-first century. These ever-present tensions are not easily resolved, and engagement with these issues characterizes the dynamism that defines revolutionary movements.

Reform versus Revolution

A key debate is how quickly revolutionaries can or should make changes in society. If a revolution moves too quickly it threatens to destabilize society, trigger a reaction, and risk losing the gains it had made. A negative reaction may remove a leftist government from power and eliminate its potential for making any further positive socioeconomic changes. On the other hand, if revolutionaries move too slowly they may lose the support of those who are impatient to enjoy the benefits of a radical transformation of society. A slogan that some reformers have taken up is social evolution, not violent revolution, with the associated goal of realizing a permanent transformation of society without its destabilizing side effects.

Peaceful Roads versus Armed Struggle

The guerrilla leader Ernesto Che Guevara argued that one cannot make an omelet without breaking eggs, that a certain amount of destruction is an inevitable byproduct of making radical changes in society. Chinese revolutionary Mao Tse-tung famously observed that a revolution is not a dinner party, that it required the violent overthrow of one class by another. More radical groups such as the Shining Path in Peru believed that violence would help purify society, similar to John Brown's religious notion on the eve of the civil war in the United States that the evil of slavery could only be purged with the shedding of blood. Others, such as the Marxist president Salvador Allende in Chile, contended that violence was entirely unnecessary to make fundamental changes in society and that socialism could be ushered in through existing institutions. Resorting to violence, from this perspective, provided a shortcut to longer and more complicated political processes and would only contribute to more strife and instability. Others observe that few give up privileges willingly, and force is necessary to create a more equal society.

Institutional versus Extraconstitutional Means

While Allende and later others such as Venezuelan president Hugo Chávez gained power through elections and began to implement socialist changes through existing institutions, others contend that an electoral path only reinforces upper-class rule and strengthens capitalist structures. In a functioning electoral system, a conservative **oligarchy** is largely left intact and can undermine positive social reforms. Rather, revolutionaries should mobilize people on the streets to take power directly and eliminate any possibility of turning back progressive advancements. Marxists have typically been more willing to engage in electoral contests in order to gain control over the reins of government, while anarchists favor a general strike to destroy capitalism at its roots.

Mass Participation versus Vanguard Leadership

Are political changes better made through a mass mobilization, or with a tightly focused and organized cadre that will lead the revolution to victory? A hierarchal and authoritarian structure can be much more efficient in accomplishing desired goals than the messy and chaotic method of attempting to work with the often contradictory ideas of a broad range of individuals or interest groups, but that approach comes with the danger of alienating the very people the revolution intends to benefit. A movement's leadership is inevitably male dominated, which further distorts its perspective and priorities. This division between horizontal and vertical forms of organization lies at the heart of the rift between anarchists and communists.

Role of the State

Related to the issue of vanguard leadership and an issue that also divides anarchists and communists is whether revolutionaries should gain control over government structures or destroy those structures. Communists argue that governments can be used to implement positive programs and that it is necessary to assume authoritarian methods as a transitory phase in the struggle against the entrenched opposition from those who benefited from the previous system. Anarchists, on the other hand, argue that governments are inherently authoritarian and prevent the realization of a more equal society. In interpreting Marx's ideas in a Russian context, Bolshevik leader Vladimir Lenin envisioned a "dictatorship of the proletariat" in which a vanguard briefly takes power and imposes their will over the rest of society but soon state structures would become unnecessary and wither away. In practice, once an individual or group takes power they tend to be reluctant to give up that privilege. Even among Marxists, ferocious debates flourish whether entrenched leaders and political parties rule to the benefit of themselves or in the interests of the broader society.

Urban versus Rural Base

Marx envisioned that a social revolution would first develop among the working class in the highly industrialized economies of Germany or England. Ironically, many of his ideas gained a larger following in countries peripheral to the capitalist mode of production. All twentieth-century revolutions, including those in Russia, China, and Cuba, emerged in countries with underdeveloped, precapitalist, and peasant-based economies. Dogmatic Marxists argue that successful socialist revolutions require the alienation that workers experience under advanced capitalism and that the shortcomings of these revolutions arose because society did not meet the necessary objective economic conditions to move on to socialism. Voluntarist Marxists disagree that revolutions require an urban working class and maintain that in Latin America revolutionary movements should be rooted in rural areas where most of the population lived and engaged in agricultural production. A related debate is whether a primitive communal, feudalistic, or capitalist mode of production existed in Latin America. Some contend that Cuba on the eve of its 1959 revolution, for example, was not a feudal but an advanced capitalist society, albeit with a rural proletariat that experienced alienation and gained a class consciousness through their work on sugar plantations rather than on an urban factory floor. From this perspective, Marx was correct in predicting the necessary objective conditions for a revolution, but in twentieth-century Latin America they occurred in rural environments that he could not have foreseen in his nineteenth-century industrialized European world.

Class Alliances

Was the working class the primary motor for revolutionary change, or do middle-class intellectuals and others also have a role to play in the process? Sometimes Marxists looked to **bourgeois** nationalists to develop a capitalist economy as a necessary precondition for a subsequent move to socialism. Revolutionary leaders are often members of the upper class who gain a social consciousness of the unjust nature of society and bring their privilege to bear in a struggle against their own class interests. Can these leaders be trusted to work on behalf of marginalized people, or will their contributions be inherently paternalistic and self-serving? On a larger level, Marxists have often struggled with the issue of developing a "popular front" to run electoral campaigns in alliance with progressive liberals against common enemies in the conservative oligarchy. The disagreement is whether to maintain an ideological purity or engage in strategic and even opportunistic alliances to advance common (and often short-term) goals.

The Woman Question

Throughout the twentieth century, revolutionary leadership remained overwhelmingly urban, male, and of European descent. Often a good deal of sexism coursed through revolutionary movements, with leaders relegating women to secondary or domestic roles. Women were to participate in underground communications networks, offering shelter to militants, bringing food to political prisoners, and providing secretarial services, but all of these were an extension of traditional domestic roles. Some male revolutionaries subordinated women's interests to broader emancipatory objectives, or assumed that women were inherently conservative. Others criticized **feminism** as a liberal bourgeois value and ignored gender discrimination in favor of focusing on higher priority issues of class struggle. On occasion, revolutionaries emphasized the need to engage gender (as well as racial) discrimination and to embrace women's contributions as equal to those of men. Such activists opposed oppression in any and all forms. These concerns are not just a footnote to revolutionary movements, even as they generally have not been adequately recognized. Women shaped revolutionary ideologies and mobilizations, even as revolutions slowly reshaped societal gender roles.

Catholic Church

The Catholic Church hierarchy, together with military leaders and wealthy land-owners, formed part of a trilogy that dominated Latin America's social, political, and economic order since the advent of European colonization. Since independence, a common nineteenth-century liberal demand was for the separation of church and state. Anticlerical liberal reforms sought to roll back the institutional power of the church that was deeply associated with colonialism and conservatism. Many leftists followed in this liberal tradition. The association of the phrase "religion is the opium of the people" with Marx contributed to an assumption that socialists were atheists. Mariátegui, however, found liberal **anticlericalism** to be a bourgeois distraction from more important underlying issues regarding the class structure of society. Furthermore, Central American revolutionaries in the 1980s turned to religion in the form of liberation theology as an inspiration for action. Debates over whether religion was a positive or negative force in society, including whether it could serve to enhance or retard liberatory struggles, were more complicated than what might initially appear to be the case.

Nationalism versus Internationalism

Should a revolution be led on a local level and in response to local conditions, or should revolutionaries fight against injustice wherever and whenever it occurs? In Latin America, socialist revolutions typically acquired characteristics of a national-ist revolt against outside (usually United States) imperialism. Militants appealed to nationalist images and historic leaders to advance their struggles. Others contend that the overwhelming power of capitalism and imperialism will inevitably defeat a successful revolution if it is attempted in only one country, and for this reason international alliances to build a global revolution are necessary. From the 1920s until its dissolution in 1943, the Communist International served this purpose, and leftists subsequently debated whether they should form a new international. Disagreements over joining an international revolutionary movement or struggling for national liberation in only one country divided the Marxist left into socialist and communist camps, with the former accusing the latter of receiving their instructions from Moscow rather than organizing according to local conditions and needs. On the issue of internationalism, communists tended to be in agreement with anarchists who, as part of their opposition to governments and state structures, believed in the power of an international working-class movement. As Marx and Engels urged in *The Communist Manifesto*, workers of the world should unite because they have nothing to lose but their chains.

All of these complicated issues create challenges for revolutionaries who seek to implement their vision for a transformation of unequal and unjust societal struc-tures. None of them have simple resolutions, but how the left engages them defines possibilities for success.

SUMMARY

This chapter has briefly charted the central social, political, and economic issues that Latin America has confronted and the struggles that the left faces to address these concerns. The Americas have immense natural resources, yet that wealth has not served the interests of the majority of the region's population. Observers commonly highlight factors such as poverty, corruption, and overpopulation to explain Latin America's underdevelopment. Instead, the chief problems that the region faces are persistently high rates of inequality, and these are related to an imperial extraction of wealth to the detriment of internal development.

Revolution is a broad and vague term to refer to movements that have fought to address societal problems. Beginning with the European colonialism of Latin America, conditions of oppression and exploitation led activists to rise up in defense of their rights. In the twentieth century, these movements become ever more powerful. Latin Americans joined international efforts to reshape the world in a way that would benefit common people rather than a small group of wealthy and privileged individuals.

Revolutionaries employed many different ideologies to advance their goals. While a progressive agenda is central to defining a movement as revolutionary, these events also require other aspects to be successful. Revolutions need strong and charismatic leadership, access to material resources, a failed opponent, and the appearance that other avenues for a fundamental transformation of society are closed. Revolutionaries have had to engage a wide range of issues, including how fast and how best to transform society; how much to rely on authoritarian structures to achieve change; and what roles women, peasants, and religion should play in advancing a struggle.

Revolutions are inherently messy and complicated businesses. As the case studies examined in this book will demonstrate, one should not engage in the undertaking of revolutionary actions lightly.

DISCUSSION QUESTIONS

What role does the individual play in a revolution?

What are the relative strengths and weaknesses of basing a revolution in an urban proletariat or a rural peasantry?

Is nationalism a positive or negative factor in a revolution?

Does a movement have to be successful to be considered a revolution? What defines success?

Are social, economic, or political changes most important in a revolution?

FURTHER READING

A very large literature exists on theories of revolution. This selected list includes some of the more important works both on revolutions and on Latin American Marxism.

Brinton, Crane. *The Anatomy of Revolution*. Rev. and expanded ed. New York: Vintage, 1965. A classic comparative study of the English, American, French, and Russian revolutions. Originally published in 1938.

Burns, E. Bradford. *The Poverty of Progress: Latin America in the Nineteenth Century*. Berkeley: University of California Press, 1980. Argues that attempts at modernization in the nineteenth century underdeveloped Latin American economies.

Foran, John, ed. *Theorizing Revolutions*. New York: Routledge, 1997. Edited collection of essays with a range of theoretical approaches to understanding revolutions.

Galeano, Eduardo. *Open Veins of Latin America: Five Centuries of the Pillage of a Continent*. New York: Monthly Review Press, 1973. A classic work that condemns European colonialism for underdeveloping Latin American economies.

Goldstone, Jack A. *Revolutions: A Very Short Introduction*. Oxford: Oxford University Press, 2014. Brief but chronologically and geographically broad sociological study of revolutions.

Laforcade, Geoffroy de, and Kirwin R. Shaffer, eds. *In Defiance of Boundaries: Anarchism in Latin American History*. Gainesville: University Press of Florida, 2015. Outstanding edited volume of new scholarship on Latin American anarchism.

Liss, Sheldon B. *Marxist Thought in Latin America*. Berkeley: University of California Press, 1984. Encyclopedic treatment of Latin American Marxist thinkers.

Löwy, Michael, ed. *Marxism in Latin America from 1909 to the Present: An Anthology*. Atlantic Highlands, NJ: Humanities Press, 1992. An exceptional collection of Latin American Marxist documents, with an excellent introductory overview of Latin America's revolutionary tradition.

Mariátegui, José Carlos. *Seven Interpretive Essays on Peruvian Reality*. Austin: University of Texas Press, 1971. Originally published in 1928, a classic work by a pathbreaking Latin American Marxist.

Marx, Karl, and Friedrich Engels. *The Communist Manifesto*. London: Verso, 1998. A foundational statement on communist aspirations.

Skocpol, Theda. *States and Social Revolutions: A Comparative Analysis of France, Russia, and China*. Cambridge: Cambridge University Press, 1979. A landmark study that has become a theoretical reference point for subsequent studies on revolutions.

Selbin, Eric. *Modern Latin American Revolutions*. 2nd ed. Boulder, CO: Westview, 1999. Applies classic theories on revolution to the Latin American examples of Bolivia, Cuba, Nicaragua, and Grenada.

FILMS

The Baader Meinhof Complex. 2010. Red Army Faction fights a guerrilla war against the rise of fascism in the Federal Republic of Germany in the 1960s and 1970s.

The Battle of Algiers. 1966. Dramatization of the conflict between Algerian nationalists and French colonialists that culminated in Algerian independence in 1962.

Burn! 1969. Depicts a fictional revolution loosely based on the Haitian Revolution under Toussaint Louverture's leadership.

The Internationale. 2000. Chronicles the history of the song that was written in 1871 at the fall of the Paris Commune and later became the anthem of the communist movement.

Katherine (aka *The Radical*). 1975. Loosely based on the story of Diane Oughton, who joined the Weather Underground and was killed when the bomb she was building exploded.

Reds. 1981. Re-creation of the life and work of journalist John Reed, including his eyewitness account of the Russian Revolution and his efforts to found a communist party in the United States.

Rosa Luxemburg. 1986. Biopic of the revolutionary.

The Weather Underground. 2003. Documentary on the Weather Underground that engaged in urban violence in the United States in the 1970s.

Mexico

2

Mexican Revolution, 1910–1920

KEY DATES

1876–1911	General Porfirio Díaz's entrenched dictatorship known as the *Porfiriato*
1910	Francisco Madero's Plan of San Luis Potosí launches Mexican Revolution
1911	Emiliano Zapata issues his Plan of Ayala in support of agrarian reform
1913	Assassination of Madero
1917	Promulgation of a new constitution under Venustiano Carranza's control
1919	Death of Zapata in an ambush
1920	Assassination of Carranza; end of fighting
1922	Ricardo Flores Magón dies in the Leavenworth Penitentiary in Kansas
1923	Assassination of Pancho Villa
1926–1929	Conservative Cristero Rebellion
1928	Assassination of president Alvaro Obregón
1929	President Plutarco Elías Calles forms the National Revolutionary Party, the forerunner of the Institutional Revolutionary Party (PRI) that ruled Mexico for the next seventy years
1934–1940	Lázaro Cárdenas's administration implements progressive reforms
1968	Massacre of protesting students at Tlatelolco in Mexico City
1994	The EZLN launches an uprising in Chiapas
2000	Electoral defeat of the ruling PRI

The anthropologist Eric Wolf included Mexico together with Russia, China, Vietnam, Algeria, and Cuba as the primary examples of rural revolts in his classic book *Peasant Wars of the Twentieth Century*. Many scholars follow his lead in treating the Mexican Revolution, which predates Russia's 1917 Bolshevik Revolution, as the first great social uprising of the twentieth century. The Mexican Revolution is part of an autochthonous revolutionary tradition in Latin America. The revolutionary promises from Mexico provided a model and inspiration for social reformers elsewhere on the continent throughout the twentieth century. Scholars who argue for the domestic roots of Latin American political uprisings often interpret subsequent revolutions through the lens of the Mexican experience. In contrast, opponents point instead to outside influences to explain the appearance of revolutionary movements. During the Cold War, conservatives invariably blamed the Bolshevik example and the Soviet Union for unrest in Latin America.

Historians debate whether the Mexican Revolution was truly a social revolution, a rebellion, a civil war, or a mindless bloodletting. Most agree it began in 1910 with Francisco Madero's (1873–1913) liberal Plan of San Luis Potosí that called for free elections in the face of Porfirio Díaz's (1830–1915) seemingly entrenched thirty-five-year dictatorship. A popular uprising forced Díaz to resign and leave for exile in Europe the following year, but a decade of chaotic warfare continued in his wake. On Madero's left, Emiliano Zapata (1879–1919) and Francisco "Pancho" Villa (1878–1923) demanded deeper social and political changes. Zapata's Plan of Ayala called for agrarian reform and introduced one of the revolution's most noted slogans, "Land and Liberty." These peasant demands, together with a wide-reaching labor code and liberal anticlerical reforms that curtailed the power of the Catholic Church, were institutionalized into a progressive 1917 constitution. Many of these promised reforms were not realized until the 1930s under the Lázaro Cárdenas (1895–1970) administration, which is best known for nationalizing the country's petroleum reserves.

The Mexican Revolution was extremely violent, with one million killed in a country of only fifteen million people. Armed groups roamed the countryside, forcing people to join them as combatants, and the fighting displaced millions of civilians. Previously isolated communities came in contact with one another and for the first time created a truly national sense of Mexican identity. The revolution also transformed Mexico's economic system, as a new government broke up the large landed estates known as **haciendas** where peasants worked in feudalistic conditions, nationalized the foreign-owned oil industry, established public schools, advanced workers' rights, and broke the Catholic Church's hold over the country. Nevertheless, instead of a worker and peasant government taking power, a new ruling class emerged that was dedicated to capitalism cloaked with a nationalist ideology and a **populist** style of governance. Despite its broad historical significance, the promises and potential of the Mexican Revolution were never completely realized.

PORFIRIATO

The Mexican Revolution overthrew General Porfirio Díaz's well-established government, the Porfiriato, which lasted from 1876 to 1911. Díaz rose through the political ranks as a liberal leader in the southern state of Oaxaca, one of the most Indigenous areas in Mexico. He gained national recognition when he stopped the advance of Napoléon III's French army at the battle of Puebla on May 5, 1862, a feat still celebrated as the *cinco de mayo*. The military became Díaz's principal avenue for social advancement. In 1876, he overthrew the previous president, Sebastián Lerdo de Tejada, under charges that he was using fraudulent means to stay in office. Díaz then used the same systems of fraud and patronage to gain reelection seven times and remain in power for thirty-five years. The result was one of longest dictatorships in Latin America.

In contrast to the anticlericalism of most nineteenth-century liberals, Díaz developed close relations with the Catholic Church and relied on conservative politicians and the upper class to guarantee his political survival. Díaz ruled with a positivist ideology that emphasized the scientific administration of the state based on the social Darwinist ideal of "survival of the fittest." This racist ideology argued for the inherent inferiority of Indigenous peoples and mestizos. Although Díaz was part Mixtec, one of the main ethnic groups in Oaxaca, he disparaged Indigenous peoples who comprised the majority of the Mexican population. His government sold rebellious natives into slavery in Cuba or simply killed them. Díaz encouraged European immigration to "whiten" Mexico and powdered his own face to appear lighter in color. He believed only those of European heritage could lead Mexico out of its feudal backwardness and toward a capitalist modernity. The **científicos** who advocated this ideology found natural allies among foreign investors and the Catholic Church.

Díaz emphasized economic development as a mechanism to keep himself in power, while simultaneously creating a large and expensive administrative bureaucracy based on a patronage system. He also used his control over the judiciary to deprive Indigenous communities of their territory. Wealth and land became concentrated in fewer hands, with the majority of the population suffering under impoverished living conditions. The large estates were inefficient and oriented toward the export market, causing domestic food production to decline. Workers labored on the haciendas in situations of permanent indebtedness while those in textile mills and mines toiled long hours for low pay without the protection of labor unions. They were commonly paid in scrip that could only be redeemed in company stores, which further marginalized their economic situation. Diets for workers and peasants were inadequate and living conditions unsanitary, which resulted in high infant mortality rates and short life expectancies.

Díaz revised laws to make the country more attractive to international investors. Foreigners bought many of the country's landed estates and owned much of its industry. Railroad building boomed during the Díaz years, but foreign (largely U.S.) companies laid tracks to extract raw materials rather than to encourage internal development. Foreigners owned the telephone and telegraph companies, mines, factories, department stores, and petroleum operations. U.S. companies had more investments in Mexico than in any other country, and during the Porfiriato those companies came to own more than did the Mexicans themselves. The foreign domination became so pervasive that Mexicans asserted the country was the "mother of foreigners and the stepmother of Mexicans."

Díaz's feared police forces (the *rurales*) viciously suppressed dissent, but equally important, Díaz used the mechanisms of a large (and expensive) government bureaucracy to gain popular backing. Those who supported him received awards of public office, land grants, promotions, and pensions. Dí significantly reduced the size of the military so that it would be less of a threat to his rule, and the generals who remained would be personally loyal to their leader. This dual strategy of *pan o palo*—literally, "bread or the club," or "carrot or a stick," implying a largess for his supporters combined with a vicious repression of his opponents—successfully eliminated any significant opposition. As Díaz acquired more power, elections became farcical. With Díaz loyalists entrenched in political positions from the local to federal level, few possibilities for advancement existed for politically ambitious individuals. Despite the image of modernity that Díaz projected to the outside world, his government was rotten to the core and on the verge of imploding.

MAGONISTAS

The earliest and most significant opposition to the Díaz dictatorship emerged as a critical current within the Partido Liberal Mexicano (PLM, Mexican Liberal Party). The brothers Ricardo, Enrique, and Jesús Flores Magón were social reformers who founded the party to criticize the dictatorship for its lack of democracy. They organized a series of working-class strikes and uprisings against Díaz. Despite the name of their party, they were staunch anarchists who denounced governments as authoritarian, declared private property to be theft, and advocated violent direct action instead of engaging in electoral politics as the best way to achieve change. The Flores Magón brothers organized with the Industrial Workers of the World (IWW) and published a journal called *Regeneración* (Regeneration) in which they advanced their anarchist ideas. Facing persecution, the brothers fled to the United States, where they were promptly imprisoned for their political activities.

Ricardo (1874–1922), the oldest and primary leader of the three brothers, spent the entire revolution in exile in the United States. From that distance, his ideas of worker and peasant power influenced the ideology of other revolutionaries, who came to be known as Magonistas. In 1906, workers in the mining town of Cananea in the northern Mexican state of Sonora struck for higher wages and better working conditions. The U.S.-based owners of the Cananea Consolidated Copper Company sent in armed troops to suppress the strike, resulting in a massacre of twenty-three people, the injury of twenty-two, and the arrest of more than fifty. The workers did not achieve any of their demands, but the strike represented the emergence of vocal and visible opposition to Díaz's government.

From exile in the United States, Ricardo Flores Magón continued his agitation against the Díaz regime. In particular, he wrote an essay on the eve of the revolution entitled "Land and Liberty" that contributed a slogan to Emiliano Zapata's agrarian revolt. Francisco Madero attempted to include the Magonistas in his revolt against Díaz, but Flores Magón refused to join him. The Magonistas viewed Madero as part of a "revolution of the rich" that was far removed from their anarchist ideals. Many supporters, nevertheless, viewed both through the same lens—as opposing Díaz—and eventually followed Madero when he emerged as the stronger leader.

In 1918, Ricardo Flores Magón was sentenced to twenty years at the Leavenworth Penitentiary in Kansas for "obstructing the war effort," a violation of the U.S. Espionage Act of 1917. His health deteriorated in prison, a condition that medical neglect exacerbated. When Flores Magón died in 1922, his supporters were convinced that prison guards had murdered him. Although the Flores Magón brothers were never incorporated into the official pantheon of revolutionary heroes, their anarchist ideology provided an important ideological influence for the radical left wing of the anti-Díaz opposition.

FRANCISCO MADERO

In a 1908 interview with the U.S. journalist James Creelman, Díaz indicated that Mexico was ready for a multiparty democratic system and that he would welcome opposition in the 1910 elections. The statement was only meant to improve his image abroad, but local dissidents jumped at the chance to remove Díaz from power. Francisco Madero, a wealthy landowner from the northern state of Coahuila who had studied in the United States and France, emerged as the leading opposition candidate. Hardly a revolutionary, Madero wanted to reform Díaz's policies in order to prevent a radical revolution that would challenge his privileged position. He favored social control that would allow capitalism to flourish. Madero championed a liberal democratic ideology and pushed for open, fair, and transparent elections. For him, democracy meant upper-class governance, not rule by what he saw as the ignorant masses.

Before the June 1910 elections, Díaz arrested and imprisoned Madero. As he had done in previous elections, Díaz rigged the vote and won nearly unanimously. The blatant fraud convinced Madero that the dictator could only be removed through armed struggle. When released from prison after the elections, Madero fled north to Texas, where he drafted his Plan of San Luis Potosí. The plan made vague references to agrarian and other social reforms but focused primarily on political alterations. Most significantly, Madero declared the 1910 elections null and void, proclaimed himself provisional president, and called for free elections. With this plan in place, Madero returned to Mexico to launch a guerrilla war with the support of agrarian rebels, including Emiliano Zapata. After Madero's forces won decisive victories in May 1911, Díaz resigned the presidency and set sail for Europe. His reported parting words were, "Madero has unleashed the tiger; let's see if he can tame it." In 1915, the former dictator died peacefully in Paris at the age of eighty-five. Ironically, he was the only significant figure in the Mexican Revolution not to meet a violent death. With Díaz gone, in November 1911, the Mexican people formally elected Madero as president.

BIOGRAPHY: EMILIANO ZAPATA, 1879–1919

General Emiliano Zapata in 1911, posing in Cuernavaca with a rifle, a sword, and a ceremonial sash across his chest

Source: Library of Congress, George Grantham Bain Collection, Bain News Service

Emiliano Zapata was the Mexican Revolution's leading advocate of agrarian issues. He was born on August 8, 1879, to a family that had long enjoyed privileged positions of leadership in their community of Anenecuilco in the southern state of Morelos. Under the dictatorship of Porfirio Díaz, they lost their lands and their class status declined. Recognizing Zapata's organizing skills, the community elected him to a leadership position in 1909. When legal negotiations for land titles with landowners collapsed, Zapata impelled community members to occupy their haciendas. He became an armed revolutionary, and his followers were known as Zapatistas.

On November 25, 1911, Zapata issued the famous Plan of Ayala (named after his local municipality). The declaration demanded agrarian reform, including a return of communal lands and **expropriation** of hacienda lands—without payment if the owners refused to accept the plan. The plan highlighted Zapata's most famous slogan, "Tierra y Libertad" (Land and Liberty), which he borrowed from, and which reflected the ideological influence of, the anarchist Ricardo Flores Magón. Over the next decade the plan became the guiding principle for Zapata's forces.

Zapata fought for the rights of rural farmers against overwhelming odds. With his prospects for victory declining and desperately short of weapons, Zapata was lured into an ambush by government troops on April 10, 1919, at the Chinameca hacienda in Morelos. Revealing their fear of Zapata's leadership and symbolism, they riddled his body with bullets and dumped his corpse in Cuautla's town square. Supporters refused to accept Zapata's death, claiming that someone else had taken his place and that he had escaped to the mountains. Nevertheless, with Zapata gone the Liberation Army of the South began to fall apart.

After his martyrdom, Zapata became one of Mexico's most renowned and legendary heroes. The iconic image of Zapata dressed in a broad sombrero with a black mustache and cartridge belts across his chest appeared throughout the country. Contemporaries and subsequent scholars have alternatively interpreted Zapata as a common bandit or a social revolutionary. The distance between rural supporters who viewed Zapata as their champion and urban dwellers who denounced him as the Attila of the South points to persistent social divisions that run through the country.

Over the years, Mexico's subsequent political leaders incorporated Zapata into the pantheon of the country's revolutionary leaders, even though he most certainly would have opposed many of their policies. Although politicians invoked Zapata's name for a variety of causes, his image and fame gained renewed interest in 1994 when the Zapatista Army of National Liberation (EZLN) launched an armed uprising in the southern state of Chiapas. Although Chiapas was isolated from the Mexican Revolution and Zapata never organized in that area, the neo-Zapatistas fought for many of the same issues that their namesake had almost a century earlier. Paralleling the situation in Morelos, Indigenous communities in Chiapas had lost their lands to large landowners and faced a corrupt and repressive regime with a political chokehold on local communities. Zapata's slogan "Land and Liberty" summarized their ongoing struggle and highlighted how few of Zapata's dreams had been realized.

DOCUMENT: EMILIANO ZAPATA, "PLAN OF AYALA," 1911

Mexican revolutionary Emiliano Zapata drafted the Plan of Ayala in November 1911 as a call for agrarian reform in response to Francisco Madero's moderate Plan of San Luis Potosí. The plan denounces Madero for not following through on his promises.

Liberating plan of the children of the state of Morelos, affiliated with the insurgent army that defends the fulfillment of the Plan of San Luis, with the reforms that it has considered convenient to increase the welfare of the Mexican homeland.

The undersigned, constituted into a revolutionary **junta** to support and carry out the promises made by the November 20, 1910, revolution solemnly declare before the civilized world that judges us and the nation to which we belong and love, the propositions that we have formulated to end the tyranny that oppresses us and to redeem to the homeland of the dictatorships that are imposed on us, which are outlined in the following plan:

1. Considering that the Mexican people, led by Francisco I. Madero, shed their blood to reconquer liberties and vindicate their rights that had been violated, and not so that one man could seize power and violate the sacred principles he vowed to defend under the slogan "Effective Suffrage and No Reelection," thereby offending the faith, cause, justice, and liberties of the people; taking into consideration that the man we are referring to is Francisco I. Madero, the same one who initiated the aforementioned revolution, who imposed by governmental rule his will and influence on the provisional government of the former president of the republic, Francisco León de la Barra, causing repeated bloodshed and multitudinous misfortunes to the homeland in an overlapping and ridiculous manner, having no other purpose than satisfying his personal ambitions, his inordinate tyrant instincts, and his deep contempt for the fulfillment of the preexisting laws emanating from the immortal 1867 constitution written with the blood of the Ayutla revolutionaries.

   Bearing in mind that the so-called head of Mexico's liberating revolution, Francisco I. Madero, due to his lack of strength and complete weakness, did not bring to a successful conclusion the revolution that gloriously began with the support of God and the people, since he left most of the governmental powers and corrupt elements of oppression of the dictatorial government of Porfirio Diaz standing, which are not, nor can they be in any way the representation of national sovereignty, and that, being bitter adversaries of ours and of the principles which until today we defend, are provoking the discomfort of the country and opening new wounds to the bosom of the country to make it drink its own blood; bearing in mind that the aforementioned Francisco I. Madero, the current president of the republic, tries to avoid the fulfillment of the promises made to the nation in the Plan of San Luis Potosí, with the aforementioned promises being deferred to the Ciudad Juárez agreement; already nullifying, persecuting, imprisoning or killing the revolutionary elements that helped him to occupy the high position of president of the republic, through false promises and numerous intrigues to the nation.

   Bearing in mind that repeatedly Francisco I. Madero has tried to conceal with the brute force of bayonets and to drown in blood the people who ask him, request or demand the fulfillment of his promises in the revolution, calling them bandits and rebels, condemning them to a war of extermination, without granting any of the guarantees that reason, justice, and the law prescribe; taking into consideration that the president of the republic Francisco I. Madero, has made a bloody mockery of Effective Suffrage for the people, and by imposing against the will of the same people, in the vice presidency of the republic, the lawyer José María Pino Suárez and by designating state governors such as the so-called general Ambrosio Figueroa, executioner and tyrant of the people of Morelos; and entering into scandalous conspiracy with the científico party, feudal landowners, and oppressive *caciques* [local political bosses], enemies of the revolution proclaimed by him, in order to forge new chains and follow the mold of a new dictatorship more opprobrious and more terrible than that of Porfirio Díaz. It has been patently clear that he has undermined state sovereignty, violating laws without any respect for life or interests, as has happened in the state of Morelos and other states, leading to the most horrible anarchy registered in contemporary history. By these considerations we declare the aforementioned Francisco I. Madero, incapable of realizing the promises of the revolution of which he was author, for having betrayed the principles with which he mocked the will of the people in his rise to power. He is unable to govern and because he has no respect for the law and for the justice of the people, and is a traitor to the country, humiliating Mexicans in blood and fire because they want liberties, in order to please the científicos, *hacendados* [landowners], and caciques who enslaved us. Today we continue the revolution he began until we overthrow the existing dictatorial powers.

2. Francisco I. Madero is disavowed as head of the revolution and as president of the republic for the reasons expressed above, procuring the overthrow of this official.

3. We recognize General Pascual Orozco, second of the leader Francisco I. Madero, as head of the liberating revolution, and in case he does not accept this delicate post, we will recognize General Emiliano Zapata as head of the revolution.

4. The Revolutionary Junta of the State of Morelos manifests to the nation, under formal protest, that it endorses the Plan of San Luis Potosí, with the additions that are expressed below for the benefit of the oppressed peoples, and will become defender of the principles that they defend until victory or death.

5. The Revolutionary Junta of the State of Morelos will not accept transactions or agreements until they succeed in overthrowing the dictatorial elements of Porfirio Díaz and Francisco I. Madero, since the nation is tired of false men and traitors who make promises as liberators, and when they arrive to power, forget them and become tyrants.

6. The lands, mountains, and waters that hacendados, científicos, or caciques have usurped in the shadow of venal justice will enter into the possession of the villages or citizens who have titles for those properties, of who have been dispossessed of them by the bad faith of our oppressors, and will keep the aforementioned possessions at all costs with weapons in hand. The usurpers who consider themselves entitled to them will deduct it before the special tribunals that will be established upon the triumph of the revolution.

7. Because the vast majority of Mexican villages and citizens own no more land than that upon which they tread, and are unable to improve their social status or be able to dedicate themselves to industry or agriculture, because the lands, forests, and waters are monopolized in only a few hands, for this reason a third of these monopolies will be expropriated from the powerful owners with previous indemnification so that Mexican villages and citizens can obtain **ejidos**, colonies, legal funds for the villages, or fields for sowing and working, so as to improve the lack of prosperity and benefit the well-being of the Mexicans.

8. Hacendados, científicos, or caciques who oppose this plan directly or indirectly will have their property nationalized, and two thirds will be used for war reparations, and pensions for widows and orphans of the victims who are killed in the struggle to achieve this plan.

9. In order to execute the procedures regarding the aforementioned properties, the laws of confiscation and nationalization will be applied as appropriate. The immortal [Benito] Juárez can be used as a norm and an example for ecclesiastical goods, which have scorned the despots and conservatives who have always tried to impose on us the ignominious yoke of oppression and retreat.

10. The insurgent military chiefs of the republic who rose up in arms to the voice of Francisco I. Madero to defend the Plan of San Luis Potosí and to oppose with force the present Plan will be deemed traitors to the cause that they defended and to the country, since at present many of them for a handful of coins or for bribes please the tyrants and are shedding the blood of their brothers who claim the fulfillment of the promises that Francisco I. Madero made to the nation.

11. War expenses shall be taken in accordance with article XI of the Plan of San Luis Potosí, and all procedures employed in the revolution shall be in accordance with the instructions established in that plan.

12. After the triumph of the revolution becomes a reality, a meeting of the chief revolutionary leaders from the different states will appoint an interim president of the republic, who will call elections for the organization of federal powers.

13. The principal revolutionary leaders of each state, in a meeting, will designate the governor of the state, and this high official will call for elections for the proper organization of the public powers, in order to avoid forced appointments that bring misfortune to the people, as the well-known appointment of Ambrosio Figueroa in the state of Morelos and others, who condemn us to the precipice of bloody conflicts sustained by the dictator Madero and the circle of científicos and hacendados who have suggested this to him.

14. If president Madero and other dictatorial elements of the present and former regime want to avoid the immense misfortunes that afflict the country, and have a true feeling of love toward it, they must immediately renounce the positions they occupy, and by so doing they will staunch the grave wounds that they have opened to the bosom of the homeland. If they do not do so, the blood and anathema of our brothers will fall on their heads.

15. Mexicans: consider that the cunning and bad faith of a man who is shedding blood in a scandalous way, because he is unable to govern. Consider that his system of government is seizing the homeland and trampling on our institutions with the brute force of bayonets. As we raised our weapons to bring him to power, we now turn against him for his lack of commitment to the Mexican people and for having betrayed the revolution he initiated. We are not personalists; we are supporters of principles and not of men!

Mexican people, support this plan with weapons in your hands, and bring prosperity and well-being to the homeland.

* * *

Liberty, Justice, and Law. State of Morelos, November 28, 1911.
General Emiliano Zapata, and other signatures.

Source: Emiliano Zapata, "Plan de Ayala (1911-11-28)," *Wikipedia*, last updated January 26, 2013, https://es.wikisource.org (translation by author).

PEASANTS

Once in power, Madero faced pressure from both the left and the right. He had stirred the passions of agrarian rebels who wanted the return of their communal *ejido* lands. In Morelos, south of Mexico City, Emiliano Zapata confiscated estates and distributed land to poor peasants. Zapata initially joined forces with Madero. When Madero deposed the dictator in 1911, Zapata asked the new president to return communal lands. Madero, however, insisted on following institutional procedures and demanded that Zapata's Liberation Army of the South disarm. Madero, responding to his upper-class interests, opposed radical reforms and encouraged his rural supporters to regain their lands through legal and institutional means. The agrarian guerrillas refused to disarm, arguing that they could achieve their goals only through military force. Zapata's demand for more radical reforms led him to break with Madero.

On November 25, 1911, Zapata issued his Plan of Ayala (included as the primary source with this chapter) that called for agrarian reform and popularized one of the revolution's most noted slogans: "Land and Liberty." Zapata demanded that land stolen from Indigenous communities be returned and threatened that hacienda owners who refused to accept this would have their lands expropriated without compensation. The plan also denounced Madero as a tyrant and dictator worse than Díaz because of his unwillingness to make the necessary deep-seated changes that the revolutionaries demanded. Zapata called for his supporters to arm themselves and continue the revolution by overthrowing Madero.

In the north, Zapata's counterpart Francisco "Pancho" Villa also demanded deep sociopolitical changes. According to legend, Villa became an outlaw when he killed a local wealthy landowner who had raped his sister. The lines between bandit and revolutionary, between criminal and political action, are not always clearly delineated. In contrast to the agrarian economy of southern Mexico, which was based on small peasant landholdings, large cattle ranches dominated northern Mexico. With fewer peasants and less demand for land redistribution, Villa advocated expropriating ranches and using the revenue to finance his revolutionary struggle. Although he was mostly illiterate, he supported schools in order to raise the standard of living and provide for more opportunities for his followers. Villa's actions in favor of the local population earned him a great deal of popular support.

SOLDADERAS

During the Porfiriato, women formed organizations that shaped subsequent developments. Working-class women founded associations that advocated revolution as the best way to realize social change and improve conditions for women. Middle-class women, often primary school teachers, forwarded a reformist agenda that advocated for the expansion of educational opportunities to improve economic opportunities. Feminist organizations published journals that opposed Díaz's government and promoted women's rights.

Women participated in a variety of roles in the revolution, most notably as *soldaderas* who accompanied their husbands into battle. Although warfare is historically thought of as a male affair, women have long partaken in war. Military conflicts fundamentally altered their roles in society. Before the advent of modern military operations, women offered support services to male fighters that the military did not provide. Their roles included cooking meals, washing laundry, handling ammunition and other supplies, caring for the injured, burying the dead, and scavenging battlefields for usable items. The word "soldadera" dates at least to the Spanish conquest of the Americas and refers to soldiers using their pay (the "soldada") to employ women servants ("soldaderas").

All sides in premodern conflicts used women in support roles, and their role in the Mexican Revolution was not unique. Elsewhere in the Americas, women who provided cooking, cleaning, medical, sexual, and other services to a premodern army were called *cholas*, *juanas*, or *rabonas*. Soldaderas have become most commonly recognized for their participation with the insurgents in the Mexican Revolution. At this time, the meaning of "soldadera" shifted from "soldier's pay" to "woman of the soldier," and they were stereotypically seen as women of compromised moral standards. Soldaderas usually came from the lower class, and their employment was at best informal. For many, it was their first experience with wage labor. For men, joining the military provided an avenue for social advancement. Earning a wage and marrying an upwardly mobile soldier could also benefit women. Their pay and working conditions could vary with supply and demand.

While some women were forced into servitude, others willingly accompanied the men into battle for the economic opportunities it offered, out of an ideological commitment to the struggle, or because of a lack of better alternatives. Association with a male soldier provided women with a means of economic survival and protection from rape and other abuse. Premodern warfare led to massive folk migrations as men were pressed into roving armed bands, leaving their families no other option but to accompany them. In a strict patriarchal society, it was difficult for a single mother to feed and care for her family without a male guardian. It could be more dangerous for a woman to remain alone at home during an armed conflict than to accompany her male partner into battle. If another armed band raided her village for supplies, she could be forced to provide domestic and sexual services to other men. Accompanying her partner into war would be the surest defense against being raped by strangers.

Death rates during the Mexican Revolution were high. If a woman's partner, known in common parlance as her "Juan," was killed, she would inevitably be obligated to pair up with another soldier. In such a patriarchal society, it could be difficult to remain an unattached soldadera, but that reality hides other motivations that women might have had for joining revolutionary bands. Undoubtedly, as with their male counterparts, women might participate out of ideological motivation, a desire for economic gain, a search for adventure, or an escape from the constraints of a traditional village life. Although less common, some women became experienced combatants and, on rare occasions, even rose to positions of military leadership. Their multiple roles made the revolution possible.

During the Mexican Revolution, Pancho Villa came to see the women and children accompanying his fighters as a hindrance rather than a benefit for his cause. Sometimes more than a quarter of a military force could be comprised of women and children, and they interfered with rapid troop movements. Villa attempted to modernize his military forces, including providing for all of the soldiers' necessities in order to sidestep reliance on soldaderas. In one of Villa's more famous acts of brutality, one of the soldaderas was implicated in an attack on his life. When none of them would admit culpability or identify the culprit, he executed an entire group of ninety soldaderas. Villa was also a famous womanizer and rapist who left a large number of children behind in the wake of his "conquests." Reflecting his misogynistic attitudes, he told the journalist John Reed that he did not think women should have the right to vote. Zapata had a reputation for treating women better, and some generals would allow women to accompany their troops because it discouraged male soldiers from deserting.

After the Mexican Revolution, soldaderas were remembered in a variety of ways, ranging from heroic participants to parasitic camp followers or even as traitors. Whereas a "Juan" was a common soldier, a famous *corrido*, or folk song, venerated an "Adelita" as a brave and beautiful sweetheart who accompanied her male partner to war. In contrast, "Juana Gallo" referred to a fierce fighter, and "La Cucaracha" was a derogatory term for a base camp follower. This final stereotype led the military to see women as the chief cause of vice, disease, crime, and disorder in their camps, and sought to circumscribe their role.

REACTION

Madero's legalization of labor unions and his inability to prevent peasant revolts alienated conservatives. U.S. ambassador Henry Lane Wilson favored political stability and economic development over democracy and henceforth threatened to invade Mexico to protect U.S. property. With Wilson's tacit approval and the support of Mexican conservatives, General Victoriano Huerta launched a coup against Madero in February 1913. A ten-day battle (called the Decena Trágica) heavily damaged Mexico City and resulted in high civilian casualties, culminating in Madero's overthrow and assassination. Huerta's time in office ushered in a period of chaos and extreme political violence, with the conflict assuming aspects of a civil war rather than an ideologically driven revolutionary struggle. New weapons, including machine guns, brought an unprecedented level of carnage to the battlefield. Various armies moved across the country, drafting people and stealing food along the way. These great migrations broke through Mexico's provincial isolation, creating for the first time a national identity.

Wealthy landowner and former Madero supporter Venustiano Carranza merged the forces of Zapata, Villa, and Alvaro Obregón into the Constitutionalist Army to fight the new dictator. Together, they defeated Huerta and forced him to flee the country. With their common enemy gone, the revolutionaries turned their guns on each other. Carranza wanted to construct a new and modern capitalist state. His rival, Villa, proposed much more radical social policies, including land reform, labor rights, and education. For the next five years, the moderate and radical wings of the revolution fought each other for control of the country's future.

In October 1914, delegates representing Villa and Zapata met at a convention at Aguascalientes to unify their forces and drive Carranza from power. Together, Zapata and Villa occupied Mexico City. Zapata, however, was more interested in solving issues in his home state of Morelos than in governing the entire country. His alliance with Villa fell apart, and Carranza recaptured the capital. Under the impression that the United States was supporting Carranza, Villa raided the border town of Columbus, New Mexico. In response, U.S. president Woodrow Wilson sent General John J. "Black Jack" Pershing into Mexico to capture Villa. Pershing's pursuit was a fiasco, and Villa's popularity increased. Under Obregón's military leadership, however, Carranza gained the upper hand.

In addition to lower-class participation as soldaderas, wealthier women also actively contributed to the Mexican Revolution. Like the English social reformer Florence Nightingale, who is remembered for nursing injured soldiers in the Crimean War, upper-class Mexican women sometimes worked with the Red Cross. Professional women contributed intellectually to the revolution. Dolores Jiménez y Muro (1848–1925) was a schoolteacher, a poet, and a political radical. She admired Zapata, and her socialist convictions influenced his political thinking. The feminist Hermila Galindo (1886–1954) was a public advocate of Carranza. During the war, she edited and wrote articles for the feminist journal *Mujer Moderna* (Modern Woman). Galindo openly attacked the Catholic Church, supported sex education in schools, and demanded equal rights for women, including women's **suffrage**. She employed tactics that later feminists would use and ran unsuccessfully for a seat in the Chamber of Deputies. Some critics complained that Carranza kept Galindo as an ally only to gain women's support for his political positions and aspirations.

1917 MEXICAN CONSTITUTION

Once in power, Carranza convened a constitutional convention that elected him president. The assembly debated many key issues of the revolution, including the roles of the church and state, property rights, agrarian reforms, labor policies, education, foreign investments, subsoil rights, and the political participation of Indigenous peoples and women. Carranza wanted a conservative document, but delegates drafted a more radical constitution embodying the aspirations of revolutionaries who attacked large landholders, the church, and foreign capitalists. Even though many of its provisions were only slowly, if ever, implemented, it was a surprisingly progressive document that influenced subsequent social reforms in other Latin American countries.

The constitution codified much of the revolution's nationalist ideology. In a reversal of policies from the Díaz regime, the constitution tightly restricted foreign and church ownership of property and returned communal ejido lands to rural communities. Even though Carranza did not invite Zapata to the assembly, the latter's Plan of Ayala influenced article 27, which codified an agrarian reform program and claimed mineral rights for the state. The constitution's defense of communal land holdings appears to be a third way between communists who favored state ownership of property and capitalists who argued that land should continue to be held in private hands.

With article 123, the constitution created a detailed and progressive labor code that created a lasting model for other Latin American countries. The Mexican labor code instituted an eight-hour workday, set a minimum wage, abolished company stores and debt peonage, established the right to organize and strike, outlawed child labor, and provided for generous maternity leaves. This lengthy article also expanded government powers over foreign capitalists that laid the groundwork for the nationalization of natural resources.

Article 130 declared that congress could not dictate laws establishing or prohibiting any religion, thereby implementing freedom of religion and a separation of church and state. During the colonial period, the Spanish only permitted the practice of Catholicism in their territory, which left much of Latin America—Mexico included—with a strong religious tradition. The new constitution significantly curtailed the power of the Catholic Church over society. Marriage would now be a civil rather than a religious affair. Only Mexicans could be religious ministers, and they were prohibited from engaging in political acts, wearing their clerical garb in public, or conducting religious processions or outdoor masses. Other articles extended the constitution's liberal anticlericalism, including provisions in article 3 that outlawed religious control over education and article 27 that restricted the church's landholdings.

The 1917 constitution was very progressive in terms of its attack on large landholders, the Catholic Church, and foreign ownership of the economy, even though the ideals written into the law were not always implemented. The constitution assumed a pro-capitalist perspective that protected the rights of private property even as it placed important limits on those rights and sought to control, rather than eliminate, foreign ownership. In that sense, it was a liberal document that attempted to move Mexico from a feudalistic to a capitalist economy, rather than a communist manifesto that envisioned socializing the means of production. Nevertheless, it was a forward-looking document that influenced the ideology of future revolutions in Latin America. Significantly, the constitution was drafted before the Soviets came to power in Russia, which highlights the importance of internal rather than external factors in Latin America's revolutionary tradition.

While progressive in many aspects, the constitution subjugated women's rights to the expansion of land and labor rights. Feminists met in a congress in the frontier state of Yucatán a year before the constitutional convention met. Three positions emerged in the meeting that characterized ideological divisions throughout the first half of the twentieth century. Conservative Catholic women wanted to maintain their traditional roles as wives and mothers. Moderate liberal women believed that expanding educational opportunities was the best way to gain political and civic rights. Leftist radicals advocated that women should be treated equally in all aspects of life, including access to the franchise. Although the constitution expanded women's legal and social rights, it limited citizenship rights, including suffrage and holding office, to men. Conservative delegates in the all-male constitutional assembly had favored giving women the right to vote out of an assumption that they would support their interests, while leftist radicals opposed that provision out of fear that doing so would strengthen the church's influence in society.

AFTERMATHS

In May 1917, Carranza assumed power under the new constitution as the first constitutionally elected president since Madero. Two years later, he rid himself of one of his primary enemies by killing Zapata. Carranza had moved significantly to the right by then and attempted to manipulate the electoral apparatus to remain in power. In response, Obregón, who had become more liberal, overthrew Carranza, who was then killed in an ambush. With Carranza gone, Obregón won the 1920 elections and made concessions that largely brought the ten years of fighting to an end.

With the war over, Villa retired to a comfortable estate in the northern state of Chihuahua. As a result of the revolution, he had transitioned from a landless peon to a powerful landowner. In 1923, Villa was assassinated in an attack that seemed to trace back to old feuds between revolutionary leaders. The identity of his assassins and their motivation were never clearly established.

In the first peaceful transfer of power since the revolution began, Plutarco Elías Calles became president in 1924. His time in office witnessed increased conflict between the government and the church hierarchy, leading to the 1926–1929 Cristero Rebellion. In reaction to the constitution's vast anticlerical provisions, priests went on strike and refused to celebrate masses, perform baptisms, or provide last rites for the dying. Conservative guerrilla bands organized under the slogan ¡Viva Cristo Rey! (Long Live Christ the King!). In opposition to the new public socialist education system, they burned government schools and killed teachers. In retaliation, the government killed one priest for every dead teacher. The military looted churches and converted them into stables. Similar to the previous decade's soldaderas, women's brigades played a crucial role in sustaining the Catholic army. The conflict culminated with a Cristero partisan assassinating Obregón, who had been reelected president in 1928, before he could take office.

Facing endless violence that seemed to be claiming the lives of all the revolutionary leaders, politicians devised a system that would ensure their continued hold on power. In 1929, Calles formed the National Revolutionary Party, the forerunner of the Partido Revolucionario Institucional (PRI, Institutional Revolutionary Party), that ruled Mexico for the next seventy years. The consolidation of a new political party allowed revolutionary general Lázaro Cárdenas to ascend to the presidency. During his time in office (1934–1940), Cárdenas not only implemented progressive agrarian and social reforms but also consolidated his control over the country. The first significant distribution of land occurred under his government. In what some view as the high point of the revolution, in 1938 Cárdenas used the provisions of the 1917 constitution to nationalize Standard Oil and establish the state oil company Petróleos Mexicanos (PEMEX, Mexican Petroleum). By the time Cárdenas handed power to his conservative successor Manuel Ávila Camacho, the governing party had formed a corporate state that held more absolute control than even Díaz had at the height of his power.

Although the government introduced successful reforms in education and healthcare and created political stability, for many marginalized peoples the revolution brought few changes. Indigenous peasants were still confronted with authoritarian political structures and rampant racial discrimination. For all the effort women put into the Mexican Revolution, as soldaderas as well as in other roles, they ultimately had little to show for their involvement. The military expelled women from the army at the end of the war and in 1925 banned them from their barracks altogether. Soldaderas engaged in a protracted battle for the recognition and pensions that their male counterparts enjoyed. Women had long been seen as a conservative force in society who were under the undue influence of the Catholic Church. As a result, in the anticlerical atmosphere of the postwar period, women did not receive suffrage rights on a federal level until 1953 (although the franchise came sooner on a local level, particularly in frontier regions). Even with these limitations, the revolution fundamentally changed the lives of many women. The disruptions of war provided women with a perspective of a society that extended beyond their family, village, and church. Some women emerged more empowered, which led to rebellions against arranged marriages and for access to more educational and economic opportunities. Although the revolution delivered little in terms of tangible gains for women, it did contribute to growing demands for equality.

The failures of the 1910 Mexican Revolution led to ongoing social protest, most notably as exhibited in a neo-Zapatista revolt in the impoverished southern state of Chiapas. On January 1, 1994, as the North American Free Trade Agreement (NAFTA) that was to eliminate trade barriers between Canada, the United States, and Mexico came into force, the launch of the guerrilla war caught the world by surprise. The Ejército Zapatista de Liberación Nacional (EZLN, Zapatista Army of National Liberation) announced their opposition to neoliberal economic policies that favored the wealthy to the detriment of marginalized Maya farmers. Under the leadership of the charismatic, masked Subcomandante Marcos, the EZLN conceptualized the struggle as a continuation of that which their namesake, Emiliano Zapata, had launched at the beginning of the twentieth century.

INTERPRETING THE REVOLUTION

Scholars disagree on when the revolution ended, or whether it is still an ongoing process. For some, the drafting of the 1917 constitution marks the revolution's culmination. Those who view revolution as a military action rather than the consolidation of an ideological agenda consider the cessation of hostilities in 1920 as the endpoint. Others point to 1940, when, after a period of deep social reforms, Cárdenas passed power to Ávila Camacho. The new government largely ended revolutionary social policy, though not necessarily its populist rhetoric. For others, a massacre of protesting students at Tlatelolco in Mexico City on the eve of the 1968 Summer Olympics demonstrated that Mexico had left its revolutionary heritage behind. In political terms, the electoral defeat of the ruling PRI at the hands of the conservative Partido Acción Nacional (PAN, National Action Party) in 2000 brought an end to the hegemonic legacy of the early revolutionaries. Nonetheless, some contend that Mexico continues to be shaped by various legacies of the 1910 popular uprising against Porfirio Díaz's dictatorship and that the revolution is an interrupted or still-ongoing process. The revolution was a seemingly chaotic, incoherent series of events, leading scholars to interpret it in a myriad of ways. They have long debated whether it was a social revolution, a peasant revolt, a civil war, a nationalist movement, a struggle for unrealized liberal ideals, or a mindless bloodletting.

Liberal Movement

Those who see the revolution as a liberal bourgeois reform movement emphasize Madero's initial goals of democracy, an embrace of individual liberties, and the positive outcomes of social reforms such as expanded access to education. Many of these liberal aspects were embodied in the 1917 constitution, particularly its anticlerical provisions, which were the most restrictive in a historically Catholic region. Another liberal reform was to professionalize and depoliticize the military and place it under civilian control. The government curtailed military expenditures to the point where Mexico had one of the smallest militaries in Latin America. In contrast to Porfirio Díaz, after Cárdenas's presidency no military leader would leverage personal renown gained from military exploits into a position of political power.

Great Rebellion

Historian Ramón Eduardo Ruiz refuses to call the events a revolution but instead labels it a "great rebellion" that pitted rebel factions against each other for control of the country. Leaders including Madero, Villa, Zapata, Obregón, and Carranza fought each other because they did not have a unified plan. The result was a disorganized rebellion rather than a revolution with a coherent ideology. At best, one faction of the bourgeoisie simply replaced another as the owners of the means of production. The winners only wanted a larger share of the spoils rather than the outright destruction of capitalism. As evidence that it failed to rise to the level of a revolution, Ruiz points out that the 1917 constitution is best understood as codifying nineteenth-century liberal ideals that stressed continuity over radical change. It merely affirmed the principles of private property and the sacred rights of the individual that were already present in Juarez's 1857 liberal constitution. The great expenditure of lives ultimately accomplished or changed little.

Civil War

The level of violence and a seeming lack of ideology that led parties to change sides to gain the upper hand have led some to interpret the events as little more than a civil war that devolved into a particularly senseless bloodbath. During the fighting, novelist Mariano Azuela published *Los de abajo* (*The Underdogs*), which became the most famous novel of the revolution. The story is based on the author's experiences with Villa and paints a rather dismal picture of the lack of changes that came out of these events. Toward the end of the novel, Azuela writes, "If a man has a rifle in his hands and a belt full of cartridges, surely he should use them. That means fighting. Against whom? For whom? This is scarcely a matter of importance." His protagonist proclaims, "Villa? Obregón? Carranza? What's the difference? I love the revolution like a volcano in eruption; I love the volcano because it's a volcano, the revolution because it's the revolution! What do I care about the stones left above or below after the cataclysm? What are they to me?" Although Azuela captures the brutality of the war, those who would argue it was a peasant revolt, nationalist movement, or a failed socialist revolution would disagree with his nihilistic portrayal of events.

Nationalist Movement

Some scholars see the revolution as a nationalist movement and point to attacks on foreign economic ownership as evidence of its anti-imperialist aspects. From this perspective, the high point of the revolution came in the 1930s with Cárdenas's nationalization of Standard Oil—well after the fighting had ceased. The March 18, 1938, decree that expropriated seventeen companies became a cause célèbre throughout Latin America. Many scholars and activists embraced the confiscation as a declaration of economic independence from the United States that they wished to replicate in their own countries.

Peasant Revolt

Anthropologist Eric Wolf interprets the Mexican events as a peasant revolt. A key question is whether the protagonists were looking forward to positive social changes or gazing back to an idyllic and highly romanticized past that never existed. For agrarianists such as Zapata, a key demand was that rural communities regain control over their communal ejido territories. Was this an attempt by Indigenous communities to cling to a quickly disappearing past? Or was it an effort to define a better future that would benefit the masses rather than a small number of wealthy landholders? Many disagree on whether Mexico's economy on the eve of the revolt was feudalist or capitalist, and whether the necessary objective economic conditions were present for a socialist revolution.

Failed Socialist Revolution

Others argue that Mexico indeed did experience a revolution, although it was a bourgeois democratic revolution that some Marxists argue is a necessary precondition for a socialist revolution. Unlike those who see it as a peasant revolt, Marxists

portray Porfirio Diáz's regime as leading to the consolidation of bourgeois capitalism, and not as a period of semifeudalism. The revolution represented the victory
of the middle-class bourgeoisie and the development of capitalism. Alternatively,
the events could be interpreted as an aborted or unfulfilled proletarian revolution
because the workers and peasants lacked an advanced class consciousness necessary
to achieve positive social changes. In this case, it was a failed socialist revolution
in which a class struggle attempted but failed to alter the mode of production.
Through this lens, the progressive aspects of land and labor reforms in articles
27 and 123 of the 1917 constitution are seen as attempts to advance a socialist
agenda, rather than to codify liberal ideals or embrace nationalist sentiments. The
scholar Adolfo Gilly retains an optimistic tone in that he interprets the events as an
interrupted but ultimately not defeated revolution. He presents Zapata's peasant
army as the vanguard of socialism and argues that his assassination in 1919 did
not end but merely delayed a longer political process. Eventually, the peasant and
worker masses will break free and conclude the revolution.

SUMMARY

Even though the Mexican Revolution has been commonly included in the pantheon
of significant twentieth-century revolutions, historians continue to debate interpretations of what these events mean. The revolution began as a revolt against an
authoritarian government and ended with an entrenched one-party state that held
more power than Porfirio Díaz ever could have imagined. The revolution expressed
the aspirations of peasants who had lost their land base, but they failed to achieve
a socialist transformation of society. Women and others made great sacrifices but
received little reward for their efforts. The violence killed one million people and
resulted in extensive destruction, but the fighting also led to the birth of a modern
Mexican identity. Heroes such as Emiliano Zapata emerged out of the war, even
though few of his goals had been achieved. Nevertheless, the revolution, and particularly its codification in the 1917 constitution, created a model that subsequent
revolutionaries throughout Latin America sought to emulate.

DISCUSSION QUESTIONS

Was it necessary to use violence to remove Díaz from power?
Was mass discontent or charismatic leadership more important in determining the
    direction of the Mexican Revolution?
Was the Mexican Revolution a peasant reaction against the modernizing en-
    croachment of capitalism, or a social revolution envisioning a better future?
Was the Mexican Revolution a democratic or social revolution?
In what ways was the Mexican Revolution a true revolution?

FURTHER READING

More historical works have been published on Mexico than on any other Latin American country, and many of these focus on the Mexican Revolution. Newer works continue to challenge interpretations presented in older works. Below are classic works on which subsequent interpretations build.

Azuela, Mariano. *The Underdogs: A Novel of the Mexican Revolution*. New York: Penguin, 1963. Based on the author's experiences fighting with Pancho Villa and originally published during the war, this novel paints a vivid but dismal picture of the revolution.

Flores Magón, Ricardo. *Land and Liberty: Anarchist Influences in the Mexican Revolution*. Montreal: Black Rose Books, 1977. A collection of writings of the leading anarchist in the Mexican Revolution.

Gilly, Adolfo. *The Mexican Revolution*. New York: New Press, 2005. A stirring, bottom-up account that argues that the revolution was interrupted and failed to achieve its socialist goals.

Joseph, G. M., and Jürgen Buchenau. *Mexico's Once and Future Revolution: Social Upheaval and the Challenge of Rule since the Late Nineteenth Century*. Durham, NC: Duke University Press, 2014. A broad introductory survey of the revolution.

Katz, Friedrich. *The Life and Times of Pancho Villa*. Stanford, CA: Stanford University Press, 1998. Lengthy and masterful biography of one of the main peasant leaders of the revolution.

Knight, Alan. *The Mexican Revolution*. 2 vols. Cambridge: Cambridge University Press, 1986. An ambitious, comprehensive, excellent synthesis of the Mexican Revolution.

Ruiz, Ramón Eduardo. *The Great Rebellion: Mexico, 1905–1924*. New York: Norton, 1980. Argues that the events in Mexico did not rise to the level of revolution.

Salas, Elizabeth. *Soldaderas in the Mexican Military: Myth and History*. Austin: University of Texas Press, 1990. Fascinating study that challenges the stereotypes of the roles women played in the Mexican Revolution.

Wolf, Eric R. *Peasant Wars of the Twentieth Century*. New York: Harper & Row, 1969. Includes a chapter that presents the Mexican Revolution as a peasant revolt.

Womack, John, Jr. *Zapata and the Mexican Revolution*. New York: Vintage, 1968. A classic work that examines the Mexican Revolution from the perspective of Emiliano Zapata and the peasants of Morelos.

FILMS

And Starring Pancho Villa as Himself. 2004. The story of how Mexican revolutionary Pancho Villa allowed a Hollywood crew under the leadership of D. W. Griffith (of *Birth of a Nation* fame) to film him in battle, altering the course of film and military history in the process.

Mexico in Flames. 1982. A chronicle of the Russian and Mexican revolutions in the early twentieth century.

Mexico, Part 1: Revolution, 1910–1940. 1989. A PBS/WGBH documentary that provides a narrative overview of the Mexican Revolution.

Viva Villa! 1934. An early Hollywood depiction of Pancho Villa in the Mexican Revolution.

Viva Zapata! 1952. Marlon Brando stars as Emiliano Zapata in a classic Cold War–era Hollywood film on the Mexican Revolution.

MEXICO

BELIZE

Usumacinta R.

Pasion R.

Gulf of
Honduras

L. Izabal

Coban

Huehuetenango   Negro R.

Polochic R.

SIERRA MADRE   SIERRA DE LAS MINAS

Quezaltenango

Motague R.

HONDURAS

GUATEMALA CITY

L. Atitlan

Antigua

EL SALVADOR

PACIFIC OCEAN

0   50   100
Miles

Guatemala

3

Guatemalan Spring, 1944–1954

KEY DATES

1820	Atanasio Tzul crowned king of the K'iche'
1821–1838	Guatemala made capital of the United Provinces of Central America
1838–1865	Conservative Rafael Carrera rules Guatemala
1872–1885	Liberal Justo Rufino Barrios rules Guatemala
1898–1920	Liberal Manuel Estrada Cabrera rules Guatemala
1902	United Fruit Company arrives in Guatemala
1931–1944	Liberal Jorge Ubico rules Guatemala
July 1, 1944	Ubico resigns, opening the way to the Guatemalan Spring
October 20, 1944	October Revolution establishes a progressive provisional government
March 11, 1945	Promulgation of new constitution
March 15, 1945	Inauguration of Juan José Arévalo as president
February 8, 1947	Promulgation of labor code
November 11, 1950	Jacobo Arbenz Guzmán elected president
June 17, 1952	Land reform (Decree 900) redistributes large landholdings
December 1953– July 1954	CIA operation PBSUCCESS to remove communist influence from Guatemalan government
June 16, 1954	Colonel Carlos Castillo Armas launches military coup against Arbenz's elected government
June 27, 1954	Arbenz resigns presidency, bringing revolutionary changes to an end

Similar to Porfirio Díaz in Mexico, Guatemala's pro–United States dictator Jorge Ubico (1878–1946) appeared to be deeply entrenched in power (1931–1944) but quickly fell when the public withdrew its support of his government. That political opening led to the election of Juan José Arévalo (1904–1990), who governed for six years (1945–1951). During that time he implemented moderate labor, social security, and agrarian reforms. Jacobo Arbenz Guzmán (1913–1971) won the 1950 presidential election and dramatically increased the pace of reforms. Most notably, a 1952 land reform program known as Decree 900 expropriated unused United Fruit Company (UFCo) land. In response, U.S. secretary of state John Foster Dulles (1888–1959) and CIA director Allen Dulles (1893–1969), both of whom had close relations with UFCo, authorized a 1954 military coup that overthrew Arbenz and implemented a long and bloody military dictatorship that undid most of the previous decade's progressive reforms. The extreme measures taken to stop and reverse those policies indicate that a fundamental shift threatened to take hold that would have transformed Guatemala's archaic socioeconomic structures.

MAYA

Guatemala is home to one of the highest concentrations of Indigenous people in Latin America. Most of these people speak one of twenty-two Maya languages and are descendants of the builders of the classic Maya civilization that flourished a thousand years ago. That civilization had largely disappeared by the time the Spanish conquistadors arrived in the early sixteenth century.

Few European immigrants came to Guatemala during the Spanish colonial period, and most wealthy landholders and political leaders had some Maya heritage. In most of Latin America, those of mixed European and Indigenous descent are called *mestizos*, but in Guatemala they are known instead as *ladinos*. The term generally refers to those who have abandoned a Maya ethnic identity and assimilated into a Western culture. The Maya primarily lived in rural areas and engaged in subsistence agriculture while ladinos resided in cities and worked in a cash economy. The Maya had little access to education, healthcare, and proper nutrition, and as a result had much higher infant mortality rates and shorter life expectancies than ladinos. At the beginning of the twentieth century, illiteracy rates hovered around 90 percent in rural Maya communities, with an infant mortality rate of 50 percent and life expectancies of less than forty years. These socioeconomic indicators were even lower for women.

Throughout the colonial period and even after independence, the Maya launched repeated uprisings against Spanish efforts to subjugate them as a labor force. The largest and best known of these uprisings came in 1820 on the eve of independence from Spain. The Maya evicted the Spanish governor and instead crowned Atanasio Tzul as king of the K'iche', one of the largest Maya groups. Tzul's independent kingdom did not last long, and the following year the Spanish empire collapsed.

Nevertheless, that revolt highlights the persistence of a Maya identity and aspirations for autonomous control over their own affairs.

NINETEENTH CENTURY

For almost three hundred years, the Spanish administered Guatemala as part of its viceroyalty of New Spain. When Mexico gained its independence in 1821, the rest of viceroyalty separated as the United Provinces of Central America, with Guatemala as its capital. A small, powerful, and wealthy class dominated the newly independent federation's political and economic systems. A liberal government implemented reforms that reduced the power of the Catholic Church and privatized communal Indigenous land holdings. In 1838, the conservative Rafael Carrera led a revolt that reversed these reforms and in the process tore the Central American federation apart into five separate countries. Carrera became the first of only four presidents who dominated the first century of Guatemala's existence. These leaders had a tendency to come to power legally and then stay in office through fraudulent means in a process known as *continuismo*.

As the first president of an independent Guatemala, Carrera implemented conservative policies that revived the authority of the Catholic Church, returned church and Indigenous-held lands to their previous owners, reintroduced Indigenous forced labor, and reinstated colonial political offices. In 1854, he had the congress name him president for life and attempted to exert control over the rest of Central America. Carrera died in 1865, and an 1871 liberal revolt defeated the conservatives and the liberals resumed their earlier efforts at modernization.

The liberal Justo Rufino Barrios assumed office in 1872. He was a positivist who came to be known as "Little Porfirio Díaz," his contemporary counterpart in neighboring Mexico who implemented similar types of policies. During Barrios's government, Guatemala became a coffee republic. By the end of his time in office in 1885, coffee comprised 75 percent of the country's exports.

In 1898, after a period of unrest Manuel Estrada Cabrera succeeded Barrios in office. Estrada Cabrera also ruled as a liberal who attempted to modernize Guatemala's economy by integrating it into the global capitalist system. Foreign owners, particularly Germans, dominated coffee production and by 1914 controlled half of the country's exports. In an attempt to balance the coffee economy and to move away from a monoculture export economy, in 1902 Estrada Cabrera invited the United Fruit Company to begin banana production in Guatemala. His plan to lure the company away from Colombia and Cuba where it already had established production faced no serious organized opposition in Guatemala. In fact, his supporters championed the benefits of his plan. The government was located in Guatemala City in the highlands, but since bananas were a tropical crop UFCo would economically develop lowland regions of the country. In addition, the scheme would personally benefit members of his government.

Turning Guatemala into a banana republic caused a dramatic change in labor relations. Highland Maya migrated to the lowlands to toil on the banana plantations. They often worked on a seasonal basis and returned to their homes in the highlands to engage in subsistence agriculture when there was no work on the plantations. They provided cheap labor that ensured high profits for the foreign-owned banana company. Estrada Cabrera was famous for his cruelty to his opponents and eventually alienated even his own handpicked legislative assembly. In 1920, the congress declared him insane and removed him from office. Political unrest plagued the decade that followed, but it was also a period critical to the formation of intellectual and political ideas that emerged after 1944 in the Guatemalan Spring.

JORGE UBICO

In 1931, Jorge Ubico was elected president and soon consolidated his control over the country. He abolished labor unions, persecuted workers, and embraced a rigidly patriarchal society. Similar to Barrios and Estrada Cabrera before him, Ubico ruled as a liberal and implemented a series of modernizing reforms. He rejected the Catholic Church's control over society in favor of the scientific administration of the country. These reforms included the secularization of education in a society in which the Catholic Church had previously dominated instruction. A lack of funding, however, restricted his efforts, and 86 percent of the country's inhabitants remained illiterate. Ubico also limited the control of the Catholic Church in other realms, including nationalizing church lands, ending the special privileges the church enjoyed, and establishing freedom of religion and civil marriage.

Despite these traditional liberal anticlerical stances, similar to Porfirio Díaz in Mexico, Ubico slowly moved toward a position of greater reliance on the Catholic Church. The president shared conservative political and social ideologies with the archbishop Mariano Rossell y Arellano, who was installed in 1939. Both hated communism and favored an authoritarian government, social stability, and respect for a hierarchal society. The government also permitted the return of religious orders, including the Jesuits, who had previously been expelled. Ubico's admiration of Spain's fascist leader Francisco Franco earned him the support of conservative Spanish priests, which further helped bolster his authoritarian rule.

While Ubico was not particularly concerned with human rights or the economic exploitation of Maya workers, he was fascinated with their folklore and traditions. He was the first president to visit Maya villages and celebrate their cultures. Ubico liked anthropologists and encouraged scholars to come to Guatemala to study Maya societies. In this aspect, he was influenced by his counterpart Lázaro Cárdenas (1934–1940) in Mexico, who implemented similar types of *indigenista* policies that celebrated native cultures. In 1934, Ubico ended debt peonage structures that trapped rural workers in a system of semislavery on large landed estates. At the same time, however, he implemented a vagrancy law that required people to work 150 days each year or face a threat of jail. Ubico intimidated his opposition and manipulated constitutional bans on reelection with a fraudulent **plebiscite** to maintain himself in power.

Ubico assumed a very strong pro–United States political position. Particularly with the Boston-based UFCo firmly planted in the country, the U.S. government gained a large degree of control over the country's economic and political decisions. Previously Ubico had openly identified as a fascist and expressed admiration for Adolf Hitler, Benito Mussolini, and Francisco Franco, but in the midst of the Second World War he altered his professed political preferences to match the prevailing winds. Guatemala was one of the first Latin American countries to join the Allies in the fight against Germany. Ubico exploited the war as an opportunity to confiscate German-owned coffee lands, not to benefit the Allied cause but to sell them at a profit to his friends. His government remained repressive and tolerated no outspoken opposition. Ubico executed labor leaders, students, political dissidents, and others who dared to challenge his hold on power. The Guatemalan president embodied an irony found elsewhere in the region in that he was a dictator allied with democratic powers in a war against dictators. The contradictions of fighting fascist military governments in Europe while supporting authoritarian administrations in Latin America eventually led to a loss of support from the U.S. government.

REVOLUTIONS OF 1944

In 1944, civilian pressure, especially from students and professionals as well as younger disgruntled army officers, led to Ubico's fall from power. In June 1944, students started a nonviolent *huelga de brazos caídos*, or sit-down strike, to demand autonomy for their university. Ubico refused to concede to their demands, and their protest spread to a general strike. Ubico declared a state of siege, which led prominent Guatemalans to petition for a return of constitutional guarantees. The president sent in troops to suppress the nonviolent demonstrations, who killed María Chinchilla Recinos in the process. The death of this young woman, and the injuring of four others who were participating in a teachers' march dressed completely in black as if in mourning, shocked the country and undermined the ruler's legitimacy. Soldiers fired on other protesters, injuring or killing dozens. In response, shopkeepers closed their establishments despite government orders to remain open. External factors, including the economic disruption of the war and a deterioration in Ubico's health, contributed to a weakening of his power. But more than anything, a withdrawal of popular support for his government led to its collapse. Finally, this growing movement forced the president to resign on July 1.

The toppling of Ubico's government was part of a broader regional phenomenon in Latin America, as the public's refusal to support strong-armed leaders forced their resignations. This movement began in neighboring El Salvador in May with a general strike that removed the military dictator Maximiliano Hernández Martínez. His fall on May 9 had repercussions throughout the region, with these events inspiring uprisings in Honduras, Nicaragua, Costa Rica, and Ecuador. Student strikes in Nicaragua attempted but ultimately failed to remove Anastasio Somoza García from power. In Ecuador, a May 28 general strike ushered in a period of progressive reforms known as the Glorious May Revolution. Protest in one country encouraged uprisings in others.

Support for these antigovernment movements extended beyond the small leftist political parties and labor unions that advanced working-class interests. Instead, these strikes appealed to students, professionals, shopkeepers, and white-collar workers who formed part of a growing urbanized population. They occurred during a period of economic crisis combined with a repressive government that had closed off possibilities for constitutional solutions. Commonly, the public had a fear that current leaders would establish themselves as permanent fixtures in power. Furthermore, these strikes lacked an individual charismatic leader who set an ideological agenda and became the public face of the movement. Instead, representatives from a broad coalition made decisions that influenced the direction of the movement. Although the strikes appeared to emerge spontaneously, in reality they followed months or even years of underground organizing that was largely hidden from public view.

Even though governments employed violence to repress these strikes, the activists did not employ armed force as their principal strategy to topple the governments. Rather, activists relied on mass demonstrations, marches, sit-ins, petitions, letter-writing campaigns, and work stoppages. Subsequently, governments fell not so much as a result of external pressure but rather as a loss of popular support and legitimacy that caused them to implode. An organized movement could then take advantage of the power vacuum to advance an alternative political project. These massive civic strikes are part of a rich but largely neglected Latin American tradition of nonviolent political struggles. In a region and at a time where change was commonly assumed to result only from armed struggle, these events illustrate the relevance of nonviolence as a means of political action.

The most famous and longest lasting of these civic strikes was the one in Guatemala. As with other uprisings in 1944, the movement in Guatemala was mostly a middle-class affair that emerged in response to a specific crisis. It had little unifying ideology beyond removing Ubico from office, and the movement lacked clear leadership. Generally, its goals resembled those of nineteenth-century liberalism rather than expressing the aspirations of a socialist revolution. The leading middle-class reformers wanted greater personal liberty, a political voice in society, more economic opportunities, and improvements in their social status. They also wanted more respect from the United States and Great Britain on the world stage. They were tired of Guatemala being kicked around and wanted global powers to treat it as an independent, sovereign power rather than a banana republic. Their efforts opened a path toward more radical reforms.

OCTOBER REVOLUTION

When Ubico resigned the presidency, he left a military triumvirate under the leadership of General Federico Ponce Vaides in control. Those military officers promised to hold presidential elections, but they never materialized. Ponce continued Ubico's repressive policies, including assassinating the newspaper editor Alejandro Córdova, who had become an outspoken critic of the government. His death and funeral revitalized revolutionary sentiments. Opposition groups began to conspire with sympathetic and reform-minded military leaders to launch a coup and remove Ponce from office.

On October 20, 1944, Colonel Jacobo Arbenz and Major Francisco Javier Arana led a force that captured a military base, distributed weapons to workers and students, and attacked the National Palace in what became known as the October Revolution. Hundreds of workers joined the movement that stormed military garrisons and police barracks. They tore up paving stones to create barricades. During the brief but intense fighting, women provided food and emergency medical care to the insurgents and opened their houses to those fleeing the fighting, including defecting soldiers who were hungry and terrified. Women also exploited gendered stereotypes that they were apolitical to facilitate passing messages surreptitiously among the insurgent forces.

Two days later, the revolutionaries defeated the remnants of the military that had remained loyal to Ubico. Arbenz and Arana established a provisional junta that wrote a new, progressive constitution and prepared for general elections. The new constitution curtailed executive power and granted greater autonomy to the judiciary. It also ended censorship, outlawed racism, legalized labor unions, required equal pay for equal work, and provided for civil equality for men and women.

Opposition leaders selected the educator and scholar Juan José Arévalo as their presidential candidate for the December 1944 elections. Arévalo had spent the last decade in exile in Argentina and over the years had fallen out of touch with Guatemala. Rather than returning immediately he slowly and cautiously traveled north from South America, testing the waters. Along the way he talked to Guatemalans about the political changes currently under way in the country and consulted with opposition leaders about the feasibility of a presidential run. The public warmly welcomed the outsider as a breath of fresh air, and he easily won the election with 85 percent of the vote. He took office in March 1945 under the new constitution.

Arévalo was not a charismatic leader, but his campaign launched a process of social change. He had social-democratic tendencies and embraced an ideology of "spiritual socialism" that was closer in nature to the utopian socialism of the nineteenth century than a Marxist call for class struggle. His goal was not a revolutionary transformation of society or a redistribution of wealth but rather psychological liberation. His government, however, did usher in a climate of political freedom, economic opportunity, and social justice.

Arévalo's political platform included three main programs that championed labor, social security, and agrarian reform. Influenced by Mexico's 1917 constitution, in 1947 Arévalo implemented Guatemala's first modern labor code. The reforms encouraged the organization of labor unions in both rural and urban areas, implemented an eight-hour workday, established a minimum wage, guaranteed social security payments, provided for vacations for workers, and allowed for collective bargaining. Arévalo also abolished Ubico's vagrancy laws and outlawed racial discrimination in the workplace. The new labor code spurred on worker organization in urban areas, banana plantations, and the railroads. Comparatively, however, the labor code was quite moderate. It forbade, for example, rural organizations on farms with fewer than five hundred people out of fear that such organizations would foster ethnic conflicts. The limitations of the labor code highlighted the persistence of racism among the governing upper class and the isolation of the country's majority Maya population.

The more controversial policies in Arévalo's government included a shift from private to public enterprises, including nationalization of the insurance industry and the creation of a social security institute. Arévalo's social security program emphasized the construction of schools, hospitals, and houses, as well as a national literacy campaign that increased educational opportunities. He expanded suffrage rights to all men and literate women, although illiterate women were still excluded from the franchise. Many of the moderate reforms primarily benefited the middle and upper classes.

The new government implemented a land reform program that embraced agrarian capitalism as a path to modernizing Guatemala's economy. Overall, the desire was to diminish the control UFCo held over the economy, with an ultimate goal of ending economic **dependency** and feudalism. Again, Mexico's example was present in the Guatemalan path to agrarian reform. Despite ample talk, Arévalo's government did not engage in much concrete action, and existing landholding patterns largely remained intact.

Women played an important but largely unrecorded role in this process of political change. University students who had mobilized against Ubico formed the Unión de Mujeres Democráticas (UMD, Union of Democratic Women) to continue a fight for women's rights. In the context of optimism that these political openings fueled, the UMD sponsored an inter-American women's congress in Guatemala City in 1947. Arévalo's wife, Elisa Martínez, welcomed delegates to a country that she proclaimed was a shining example of expanded citizenship rights and civil liberties that allowed for a free discussion of ideas. The congress advocated for greater democracy and human rights, and declared a woman's right to speak on these and other political issues. Although educated upper-class women organized the congress, working-class women participated as representatives of trade unions and the educational profession.

Notwithstanding the aspirations emerging out of the 1944 revolution that removed Ubico and the promises of Arévalo's new government, the resulting reforms were more moderate than radical. Economic policies emphasized regulation rather than the nationalization of the means of production. Government policies attempted to assimilate the majority Maya population into the political and social life of the country. This goal was achieved in part through the establishment of schools in rural communities. In 1945, the government founded an indigenist institute within the ministry of education. Although active with cultural programs, the institute remained largely ineffective at solving the persistent structural problems of racial discrimination and economic marginalization that the Maya people faced. Middle-class urban fears of rural ethnic revolts slowed the pace of more radical reforms.

Arévalo did not draw on an organized political party or a mass movement as his base of support. He did, however, allow more political space for the communist party that Ubico had banished during his dictatorial regime. That party became Arévalo's most dependable ally, in part because their rigidly controlled hierarchical structure resulted in it being the least corrupt political grouping in the country. Arévalo also took this action in the context of the Allies cooperating with the Soviet Union in the Second World War against the fascist powers. Since 1935, the Comintern had followed a moderate popular front policy of setting aside an agenda of a revolutionary class struggle. Instead, they collaborated with other liberal and left groups to work on a common reform agenda. In 1943, the Soviet Union had closed the Comintern to emphasize that communism would not present a threat to capitalist powers. In this context, the communist party no longer appeared as dangerous to the established order as it had previously.

The Arévalo administration encouraged urban workers and rural peasants to work together on common objectives. Conflicting agendas and identities made that elusive goal a constant struggle. In rural areas, Maya ethnic identities and a history of intense racial discrimination clashed with the rationale of a peasant class struggle for economic development. Politicized Maya communities formed new organizations to change their lived realities under systems of structural oppression. In urban areas, the working class was divided between those who adhered to their ladino identities and others who favored a more explicitly revolutionary agenda that incorporated the demands of Maya communities.

Arévalo's reform agenda triggered significant resistance from the wealthy upper class and others who benefited from the previous oligarchical system of government. This reaction led to thirty coup attempts against his government, primarily from liberal military officers. Despite those odds, he finished his term in office and for the first time in the country's history peacefully passed power on to another elected leader.

BIOGRAPHY: JACOBO ARBENZ GUZMÁN, 1913–1971

Guatemalan president Jacobo Arbenz rose to national prominence through the military. He was born in the provincial town of Quetzaltenango to a wealthy Swiss German pharmacist who in 1901 had immigrated to Guatemala. Arbenz took advantage of a scholarship to attend a military academy in the capital, Guatemala City, where he excelled as a student. After graduating with high honors, he

Jacobo Arbenz Guzmán campaigning for the presidency with his spouse, María Cristina Vilanova, about 1948–1949

Source: Government of Guatemala, María Cristina Vilanova

steadily rose through the military ranks and taught in the academy for several years. Although traditionally the military formed part of the bedrock of Latin America's conservative society, Arbenz is an example of a dissident leftist tradition within that institution. His wife, María Cristina Vilanova, introduced him to Marxist writings, including *The Communist Manifesto*, that influenced his socialist ideas and the policies he subsequently implemented as president.

As a soldier, Arbenz observed how Jorge Ubico's dictatorship in the 1930s used the military to repress agrarian workers. This experience radicalized him, and he began to form links with the labor movement. He became deeply involved in military conspiracies against Ubico and in 1944 helped lead the revolution that removed Ubico from power. He served as defense minister in the subsequent elected government of Juan José Arévalo, which provided him with broad public exposure and growing popular support. He leveraged that position to election to the presidency in 1950 with 65 percent of the vote.

In 1952, Arbenz implemented a new agrarian reform program that redistributed land to the peasants who worked it. The program particularly targeted the United Fruit Company, which led its supporters in the United States to encourage the Central Intelligence Agency to overthrow his government. Arbenz worked closely with Guatemala's small communist party, although he was not a member of the party and had only minimal relations with the Soviet Union. In June 1954, Colonel Carlos Castillo Armas launched a military coup that forced Arbenz to seek political asylum in the Mexican embassy and finally go into exile. His family wandered from one country to another as they sought an amenable political environment. Arbenz eventually joined the Guatemalan communist party in 1957, three years after he had been deposed from power. By that time it was too late to solidify the types of reforms he envisioned for the country.

In 1960, after the triumph of the Cuban Revolution, Fidel Castro invited Arbenz to move to Cuba. In exile, his family fell apart, his daughter developed a drug addiction and eventually committed suicide, and Arbenz descended into alcoholism. In 1970, Arbenz moved to Mexico City, where a year later he drowned in his bathtub. In 1995, Arbenz's remains were returned to Guatemala. In 2011, Guatemalan president Alvaro Colom publicly apologized for the government's role in ousting him from power. In retrospect, the reforms that Arbenz had launched were the best possibility that Guatemala had to address the country's deep-seated problems.

DOCUMENT: "DECREE 900," 1952

On June 17, 1952, the Guatemalan congress promulgated a wide-ranging agrarian reform law known as Decree 900 that provided the base for the expropriation of large estates, including foreign-owned banana lands. These excerpts of the law demonstrate its roots in the revolution's determination to modernize the country's economy in a way that would benefit small local farmers rather than wealthy individuals or multinational corporations.

The Congress of the Republic of Guatemala,

WHEREAS that one of the fundamental objectives of the October Revolution is the need to make a substantial change in the relations of ownership and in the forms of exploitation of land as a measure to overcome Guatemala's economic backwardness and to improve significantly the standard of living for the large masses of the population;

WHEREAS that the concentration of land in a few hands not only undermines the social function of property but produces a considerable disproportion between the many peasants who do not possess it, despite their ability to produce, and a few landowners who own excessive amounts, without cultivating it to its full extent or in proportion that justifies its tenure;

WHEREAS that according to article 90 of the constitution, the state recognizes the existence of private property and guarantees it as a social function, with no more limitations than those determined in the law, for reasons of public necessity or utility or national interest;

WHEREAS that the expropriation and nationalization of the German ions as compensation for war must be the first step to modify the relations of agricultural property and to introduce new forms of production in agriculture;

WHEREAS that the laws passed to ensure the forced leasing of idle land have not fundamentally satisfied the most urgent needs of the vast majority of the Guatemalan population;

BE IT THEREFORE RESOLVED that based on articles 67, 88, 90, 91, 92, 93, 94, 96, and sections 15 and 25 of article 137 of the republic's constitution, that the following agrarian reform law be decreed.

TITLE I: General disposition

ARTICLE 1. The agrarian reform of the October Revolution aims to liquidate feudal property in the countryside and the relations of production that originate in it to develop the form of exploitation and capitalist methods of production in agriculture and prepare the way for Guatemala's industrialization.

ARTICLE 2. All forms of slavery are abolished, and therefore the gratuitous personal benefits of the rural settlers and agricultural workers are prohibited, payment for labor in the form of land leases, and the division of Indigenous labor in whatever form it exists.

ARTICLE 3. The essential objectives of the agrarian reform include:

A) Development of the peasant capitalist economy and of the capitalist agriculture economy in general;

B) To give land to peasants, colonists and agricultural workers who do not own it, or who own very little;

C) Facilitate the investment of new capital in agriculture through the capitalist lease of nationalized land;

D) Introduce new forms of cultivation, providing livestock, fertilizer, seeds and necessary technical assistance, especially to the less wealthy peasants; and

E) Increase agricultural credit for all peasants and capitalist farmers in general.

ARTICLE 5. The expropriation referred to in this law decreed by social interests shall be consummated prior to indemnification, the amount of which shall be covered by "agrarian reform bonds" redeemable in the manner determined by the law.

ARTICLE 6. The amount of compensation shall be established based on the declaration of the fiscal registration of rural lands on May 9, 1952, and shall be paid in proportion to the expropriated land.

In case the property does not have a tax return, the compensation will be calculated according to the average of the declared value in tax registrations of adjoining or nearby land.

ARTICLE 8. For the purposes of this law, different rural estates registered under different numbers in the property registry but in the name of the same owner shall be considered a single property.

TITLE II: Adjudication, Usufruct, and Lease

CHAPTER I: Affected Goods

ARTICLE 9. Affected by the agrarian reform:

A) Wasted land;

B) Land that is not cultivated directly or at the owner's expense;

C) Land leased in any form;

D) Land necessary to form the urban populations to which the present law refers;

E) State farms denominated "national farms" or the national rural real estate, except for exceptions as established by law;

F) Municipal lands as established in the law;

G) Excesses from previous denunciations of private and municipal private property; and

H) Surplus water that the owners do not use in the irrigation of their lands or for industrial purposes, as well as those that surpass the rational volume necessary for their crops.

ARTICLE 10. Notwithstanding the provisions of the previous article, the following properties are not affected by the agrarian reform:

A) Rural properties up to ninety hectares whether cultivated or not.

B) Rural properties greater than ninety hectares and less than two hundred hectares with two thirds cultivated;

C) Lands of agricultural communities commonly called Indigenous or peasant communities;

D) Owned or leased land on which agricultural enterprises with technical or economic crops such as coffee, cotton, citronella, lemon tea, banana, sugarcane, tobacco, rubber, quinine, fruit, pasture, beans, cereals, or other articles whose production is destined to satisfy needs of the internal or external market.

E) Industrial or commercial installations or establishments of agricultural enterprises of private individuals, of the state, of the nation, or of a municipality as well as the model farms determined by the National Agrarian Department;

F) Pasture land used by cattle companies, provided that the permanent and rational use of the same for that purpose is verified;

G) Lands within five kilometers of the capital city, or of departmental and municipal capitals if entered into mutual agreement with the National Agrarian Department and the corresponding municipality, taking into account its absolute and relative population. Exceptions are national or municipal land that may be disposed of in accordance with the Law; and

H) Forest reserves.

ARTICLE 12. For the purposes of this law, as far as affectability is concerned, there shall be no difference between natural or juridical persons who own or lease land, even if they have entered into contracts with the state previous to the date of the promulgation of this law.

CHAPTER IV: Feudal latifundios and municipal lands

ARTICLE 32. Privately owned land holdings larger than two hundred hectares that are not cultivated by or on behalf of their owners or that have been leased in any way or exploited for personal benefit or to replace or supplement deficient wages during any of the last three years shall be considered latifundia and shall be expropriated in favor of the nation or in favor of the peasants and workers referred to in this article. Once expropriated, agricultural workers, farm laborers, or peasants without land will be granted the land as private property, if the majority of them so decide, or if once nationalized if a majority makes that decision in a democratic matter.

Once the needs mentioned in the previous paragraph are fulfilled, and if there is still land available on such farms, they may be leased to peasants, farm laborers, or agricultural workers, or to Guatemalan capitalist farmers under the conditions and proportions that this law established.

The usufructuaries will pay 3 percent of the value of each harvest to the National Agrarian Department, but the owners will pay 5 percent of the value of each harvest.

ARTICLE 33. If there are land conflicts between municipalities and agrarian communities, they will be adjudicated to the latter, in the place that the communities choose, in perpetual usufruct and to the extent that they need it.

If the conflict is between individuals and agrarian communities on uncultivated land, it will be resolved in favor of the latter.

CHAPTER V: Leases

ARTICLE 34. Any person, whether or not a farmer, who has access to capital has the right to request the lease of nationalized lands, provided they guarantee a percentage of the investment necessary to exploit them, which will be fixed by the National Agrarian Department, and in no case will the percentage be less than 15 percent or more than 25 percent.

ARTICLE 35. Also, if they so request, peasants, settlers, and agricultural workers may acquire the right to rent small parcels of land nationalized under this law, provided that they have not obtained any others in usufruct.

ARTICLE 36. No natural or juridical person may lease more than two hundred and seventy-nine hectares, and will not pay more than 5 percent of the annual crop for it. The payment to the state must always be made in money. It is the responsibility of the National Agrarian Department to grant the contracts referred to in this chapter.

ARTICLE 37. The term of the lease shall not be less than five years nor more than twenty-five and may be extended at the end of each period. Tenants are prohibited from entering into sublease agreements. If, at the end of the second year, the tenant did not produce crops that demonstrate the proper use of the land, the National Agrarian Department may terminate the contract, without liability, by awarding it to another applicant.

CHAPTER VI: Provisions in common to the previous chapters

ARTICLE 38. Lands granted in accordance with articles 4 and 32, may not be alienated or embargoed for a term not greater than twenty-five years, from the date of the award; but their owners can lease them.

    The usufructuaries of national or nationalized lands will lose their right if within two years they do not dedicate themselves to the cultivation of the parcels awarded. The claimed lands may be given in usufruct to other applicants.

ARTICLE 39. The usufructuaries cannot assign their rights to a third party, but they can lease the lands provided they have the approval of the National Agrarian Department. The usufruct of the national or nationalized lands granted in favor of private individuals expires upon death. Children, widows, or others who depended economically on the usufructuary will have preferential right to acquire the same lands in usufruct.

TITLE III: Agrarian Debt

CHAPTER III: Technical support, credits, and spare parts

ARTICLE 49. The National Agrarian Department may, in consultation with the National Agrarian Council, dispose of a portion of the agrarian debt fund to provide the necessary economic or technical assistance to the usufructuaries and tenants of article 34 and to the agrarian communities. The economic aid may consist of awarding livestock, seeds, implements, or agricultural machinery at a fair price and with as favorable conditions of payment as possible. In order to provide technical assistance, the Ministry of Agriculture must be consulted and supported. The Institute for the Promotion of Production and other analogous institutions, autonomous of the State, must provide all kinds of facilities for this purpose.

ARTICLE 50. In due course, in accordance with available resources and as demand so requires, the National Agrarian Bank will be created, with the primary purpose of authorizing and granting credits mainly for the small peasant economy and supplies and spare parts for the farmers, to the extent determined by the law.

    Guatemala, June 17, 1952, eighth year of the Revolution.

Source: *Ley de reforma agraria: Decreto número 900* (Guatemala: Departamento Agrario Nacional, 1952) (translation by author).

JACOBO ARBENZ GUZMÁN

In the 1950 elections, Colonel Jacobo Arbenz Guzmán was elected president without significant opposition. As minister of defense in Arévalo's government, he had put down a military coup in 1949 that led to the death of Colonel Francisco Javier Arana in an ambush near Guatemala City. Arévalo had placed Arana at the head of the armed forces and promised that he would be the official candidate in the next presidential elections. Arbenz and Arana had collaborated in the 1944 revolution, but political divisions between the two leaders highlighted the different visions for the direction that revolutionaries wanted to take the country. Conservative forces favored Arana while the left grouped around Arbenz. The removal of Arbenz's chief rival fed rumors that he had played a role in his assassination, although such a conspiracy was never proven. In any case, the ascendancy of Arbenz to power opened a path for more radical reforms.

Arbenz took office on March 15, 1951. In a dramatic change from Arévalo's administration and under the influence of his wife, María Cristina Vilanova, Arbenz spent less time talking about spiritual socialism and placed more emphasis on concrete material reforms. Vilanova was a strong feminist who was not content to be confined to the traditional ceremonial role of First Lady. Some observers compared her to her contemporary Eva Perón in Argentina who similarly assumed an unusually public role in advancing social policies. Arbenz's government significantly sped up the pace of reforms, including expanding voting rights, extending the ability of workers to organize, and legalizing political parties. More than anything, he pursued a goal of ending neocolonial relations with the United States and converting Guatemala into an economically independent country.

In the mid-1940s in the context of Soviet collaboration with the Allies in the Second World War, Arévalo had been able to work with Guatemala's small communist party with a minimum of political fallout. By the 1950s, however, relations between the United States and the Soviet Union had cooled significantly as the Cold War heated up. In this international context, charges of communist influence in Arbenz's government came to be seen as much more of a menace. In 1952, Arbenz formally legalized the communist party, which had adopted the less threatening name of the Partido Guatemalteco del Trabajo (PGT, Guatemalan Workers Party) in order to gain more public support. The PGT advocated for quite moderate policy objectives. Rather than attempting to move directly to socialism, it focused its struggle on the country's backward feudal economic situation. Party leaders believed that capitalism first must be more fully developed in the country before conditions would be right to move on to socialism.

The PGT remained tiny, with fewer than two hundred active members. The party failed to gain much influence in the army, workers' unions, or student organizations. They held no cabinet posts in government and only five of fifty-eight seats in the congress. Nevertheless, the well-known communist José Manuel Fortuny was one of Arbenz's main advisers and exercised a strong influence over government policy. Fortuny was a staunch nationalist who sought to improve living conditions in Guatemala. In short, the communist influence on Arbenz's government was small, but because of the party's disciplined structure and connections with international communist movements some analysts believed it represented a significant threat. Others in the oligarchy opposed the government because popular support for social reforms extended well beyond the confines of a small leftist party and thereby challenged their sociopolitical power.

Women in the communist party formed an Alianza Femenina Guatemalteca (AFG, Guatemalan Feminine Alliance) that supported Arbenz's leftist turn. In contrast to the established, upper-class women who had supported Arévalo, the women in the AFG were younger and often the first in their families to gain a university education and aspire to professional careers. They were also effective labor organizers and reached beyond the urban borders of Guatemala City to include agricultural and textile workers from the rural periphery in their movement. The AFG championed agrarian reform and Indigenous rights, and challenged the traditional gender roles that women were expected to play in Guatemala. Their gains in part fueled a conservative backlash against the Arbenz government.

Land reform became the Arbenz administration's signature issue. The president hesitated for a year after taking office to implement broad-ranging reforms because he was unable to obtain funding from the United States or the World Bank. Finally, on June 17, 1952, Arbenz enacted a groundbreaking land reform program known as Decree 900 (included as the primary source with this chapter). The legislation faced stiff resistance from the Catholic Church and opposition political parties, including a large number of urban ladinos. Despite this hostility, on August 7 the government began to redistribute land as part of an ambitious program to remake rural Guatemalan society. In a highly unequal society, 2 percent of the population owned 72 percent of all arable land, whereas 88 percent of the population was crowded onto only 14 percent of the land. The legislation expropriated land holdings over ninety hectares in size and compensated the previous owners with twenty-five-year bonds. Under this program, even revolutionary leaders, including Arbenz, lost land. In two years, one hundred thousand peasants received land as well as credit and technical assistance. Despite its reach, the program was not particularly radical. U.S. development officials considered the land reform program to be relatively moderate, similar to programs the United States was currently sponsoring in Japan and Taiwan.

The agrarian program faced controversies over whether to redistribute expropriated land into cooperatives or whether to give peasants private titles to their individual plots. A concern was that small subsistence farms would aggravate agrarian problems in the country, including failing to produce food efficiently for urban markets. At the same time, the liberal supporters of Ubico's former government did not want to lose their control over labor in the export economy if peasants were given their own land to farm. Arbenz faced significant challenges in shifting production to a sustainable domestic agricultural model.

To win support for his program, Arbenz built a base of support in the rural population. His government encouraged the formation of peasant unions and legally recognized hundreds of them. The ministry of agriculture assisted in the creation of hundreds of credit and marketing cooperatives that dramatically expanded agrarian opportunities. Arbenz's radicalization of the agrarian reforms begun under Arévalo entrenched peasant support for his government, alienated some middle-class moderates, and weakened the power of wealthy conservative landowners. Speeding up the pace of reforms solidified lower-class support for Arbenz and the PGT, especially since many farmers with smallholdings now owed their ownership of land and livelihood to the PGT's influence in the government.

As Arbenz consolidated his revolutionary gains, he began to take on UFCo. In particular, the government expropriated large, unused estates that hindered the expansion of agricultural production. When UFCo moved operations to Guatemala, it had banked land so that when the intensive cultivation of bananas exhausted the soil's fertility or a disease swept through a plantation the company would not have to move operations to another country, as had previously been the case. UFCo only used 15 percent of its extensive landholdings while many Guatemalan farmers lacked access to sufficient land to earn a living.

In 1953, the government expropriated one hundred thousand hectares of UFCo land and almost an equal amount the following year. In total, the land the government took from UFCo represented a seventh of all arable land in Guatemala. The government reimbursed UFCo with bonds equal to the value that the company had declared on Guatemala's public tax rolls rather than a much higher privately assessed value listed in the company's internal records. In response, UFCo cried foul and called on the U.S. government to intervene on its behalf. UFCo, however, was already under Justice Department investigation in the United States over antitrust issues. The State Department called off an overt intervention into UFCo's internal affairs because of the foreign policy implications of doing so. A larger consideration of containing a perceived expansion of communism in the hemisphere won out over domestic policy concerns or respect for the internal affairs of another sovereign country.

Guatemala's agricultural production rose as a result of Arbenz's reforms. At the same time, corruption flourished in the distribution of land. Some large landholders attempted to avoid expropriation of their estates by breaking them up into smaller plots so that they would fall under the ninety-hectare threshold. Nevertheless, the success of the agrarian reform program led to significant opposition to Arbenz's government from wealthy conservative individuals.

Arbenz's opponents condemned his policies as communist inspired, but his supporters declared that fears of ties to the Soviet Union were highly exaggerated. In fact, the Soviet Union had no formal relations with the Guatemalan government. The only contact the Soviets had made with Arbenz was an attempt to buy bananas, but the deal fell through when the Guatemalan government could not arrange for transportation without the help of UFCo, which controlled the shipping infrastructure. In the Cold War era, fear rather than reality drove perceptions.

Compared to other revolutions, the reforms that Arbenz implemented were not all that radical. Arbenz's social programs were not very extreme, and communists had only a very small influence in his government. An open and unknown question is whether Arbenz was an opportunist who attempted to play the current environment in a way that would consolidate his own personal position of power, or whether he was a dedicated revolutionary with much larger plans for a radical transformation of society. Although by 1954 the Guatemalan revolution had not taken that radical of a turn, Arbenz's domestic and international opponents feared the potential expansion and deepening of his reforms. If he had remained in office, what kind of policies might he have implemented in the future?

U.S. GOVERNMENT INTERVENTION

Worried about the direction that Arbenz was taking Guatemala, in April 1952 the strongly pro–United States ruler of Nicaragua, Anastasio Somoza García, proposed to U.S. president Harry Truman that they work together to overthrow Arbenz. They made an initial attempt in October 1952, but their cover was blown and they abandoned their efforts.

In August 1953, newly installed U.S. president Dwight D. Eisenhower authorized a $2.7 million budget for a psychological warfare and political action plan known as Operation PBSUCCESS. The plan called for a propaganda campaign against Arbenz, the recruitment of members of the Guatemalan military, and the "disposal" or assassination of fifty-eight leftist leaders. Together with secretary of state John Foster Dulles and Central Intelligence Agency (CIA) director Allen Dulles, Eisenhower authorized a military coup against Arbenz's government. In the context of the Cold War, the declared justification was Soviet influence on the Guatemalan government. An immediate trigger was that in the face of a U.S. arms **embargo** and confronting a growing military threat to his government, in May 1954 Arbenz had secretly arranged an arms shipment from Czechoslovakia.

Not coincidentally, John Foster Dulles was part of a law firm that represented UFCo in Central America, and his brother, Allen, also did legal work for UFCo and sat on its board of directors. These flagrant conflicts of interest have led to charges that they were not motivated by honorable and high-minded foreign policy objectives but rather by crass and personal economic concerns directly related to their financial interests in the banana company. Critics charge that the Eisenhower administration responded in a heavy-handed fashion to what in reality was a rather moderate nationalist reform movement in order to advance U.S. corporate interests.

MILITARY COUP

With U.S. backing that included provision of supplies and training, on June 16, 1954, Colonel Carlos Castillo Armas launched a military coup against Arbenz's constitutionally elected government. The coup was not a popular reaction to Arbenz's policies but a military action that was planned and executed in the United States. Radio propaganda and political subversion were more effective tools in overthrowing the government than direct military force. The CIA launched an effective psychological campaign that undermined Arbenz's ability to rule. U.S. pilots flew CIA planes over Guatemala City that struck fear in the hearts of the residents of the capital. In a completely fictitious action, CIA operatives taped radio programs in the United

States and beamed them into Guatemala from a transmitter across the border in Honduras that declared that they were Guatemalan patriots broadcasting live from liberated Guatemalan territory. This "Voice of Liberation" radio station engaged in a disinformation campaign with false reports of popular unrest and military rebellions. Right-wing military regimes in Nicaragua, Venezuela, and the Dominican Republic also actively conspired against the Arbenz government, with the collaboration of the CIA and the State Department.

The Guatemalan military refused to defend Arbenz because leading officers opposed him. Other factors also played a role in their decision. With all of the saber-rattling coming from Washington, military officers did not want to face a direct U.S. invasion that would easily overwhelm their small force. The military also had its own economic interests. It wanted more arms, and with Guatemala isolated with the U.S. embargo it was difficult to procure weapons. Their failure to protect Arbenz was not so much an issue of ideological opposition to a progressive government as a practical defense of their institutional concerns.

Some of Arbenz's supporters advocated arming workers and peasants to defend his government. The plan encountered several problems. The army prevented the distribution of weapons to militias, and some supporters did not want to take on a much better armed military. To do so would have very likely resulted in a bloodbath with little hope of success. Wishing to avoid such an outcome, Arbenz refused to arm workers and peasants to defend his government. In the face of what initially appeared to be overwhelming opposition, on June 27 Arbenz resigned the presidency, denounced U.S. involvement in the coup, and took refuge in the Mexican embassy.

After a brief period of turmoil, Castillo Armas assumed office. The new regime engaged in an all-out campaign of terror against Arbenz's supporters. Seven hundred people sought refuge in the Mexican and Argentine embassies. Castillo Armas outlawed political parties and labor unions and drove their operations underground. The repression was particularly fierce in the countryside, with massacres claiming the lives of as many as eight thousand people. The military promptly reversed all of the revolution's reforms and reverted landholding patterns back to the earlier Ubico period. The new government restricted voting rights to those who knew how to read and write, once again disenfranchising the vast majority of Guatemalans. It also reopened the country to foreign corporations, with the wealth pouring outward rather than leading to internal development.

Castillo Armas and his allies in UFCo, however, were not entirely successful in turning the clock back to the Ubico regime. Antitrust cases in the United States led to legal action that broke up the company. The coup had stirred right-wing nationalist sentiments with the result that, unlike other domestic private landowners, UFCo was not able to regain control over its land. Nevertheless, even though UFCo lost direct ownership of much of its property, it still effectively controlled the international market and price of bananas. In 1970, UFCo became United Brands and after 1984 did business as Chiquita Brands International.

At the time of the Guatemalan coup, it had been two decades since the United States had last intervened in an overt and military fashion in the internal affairs of another American republic. Franklin Delano Roosevelt declared a so-called Good Neighbor policy at the start of his presidential administration that included a withdrawal of the marines from countries that the United States had occupied for decades, including Haiti, the Dominican Republic, and Nicaragua. Roosevelt was not an anti-interventionist, but he did think an economic penetration of the hemisphere was a more effective foreign policy tool than placing boots on the ground. U.S. support for the 1954 military coup in Guatemala was a dramatic reversal of that policy and came at a cost to democratic forces across the hemisphere.

The military coup was not a passing period of intense violence but introduced a long and bloody series of military dictatorships. Castillo Armas's own competitors assassinated him three years later, and decades of militarization and civil strife followed in his wake. Right-wing administrations with fascist tinges that were antagonistic to the United States ruled the government for decades. Intense repression led to the emergence of leftist guerrilla movements in the 1960s and one of the bloodiest counterinsurgency campaigns in Latin American history to suppress them. The military engaged in a scorched-earth policy that sought to deprive the guerrillas of their base of support. Soldiers moved rural dwellers into "model villages" that resembled concentration camps where the military could monitor the civilian population. Peasants were forced into civil defense groups, and **paramilitary death squads** targeted those who refused to cooperate. The result was a highly militarized society that ensured the continuance of an extremely unequal and exclusionary society that led to the genocide of as many as 250,000 Maya. It was not until 1985 that Guatemala returned to civilian rule, but even then it remained apparent (as it is today) that the military calls the shots in the country. The country still suffers from a high degree of illiteracy, low life expectancies, and high infant mortality rates. The 1954 coup provides a cautionary tale as to the negative consequences of an outside imperial intervention in the internal affairs of another sovereign country.

WHY DID THE GUATEMALAN REVOLUTION FAIL?

Scholars have long debated why after a brief political opening the Guatemalan Spring came to a tragic end in 1954. Stephen Schlesinger and Stephen Kinzer argue in *Bitter Fruit: The Untold Story of the American Coup in Guatemala* that the decision to collapse Arbenz's government was made in Washington, D.C. U.S. policy makers feared Arbenz's move to economic and foreign policy independence, as well as his growing reliance on communist supporters. Some scholars question whether, given the history of U.S. domination of the region, Castillo Armas would have dared to revolt without overt U.S. support and approval. They point to UFCo's commercial enterprises in the country and its close alliance with the Dulles brothers to explain the Eisenhower administration's actions. In addition to economic interests, Cold

War ideological concerns also drove the CIA's intervention. Washington's bipolar foreign policy led officials to depict all reformist elements as communists and thereby greatly exaggerate the threat that Guatemala posed to the international order. Those sympathetic to this perspective seek to portray Eisenhower and the Dulles brothers as noble minded but misguided anticommunists who overreacted to a perceived danger with unforeseen and undesirable consequences.

Other scholars, such as Jim Handy in his book *Revolution in the Countryside*, highlight domestic rather than international factors as leading to Arbenz's fall. Instead of pointing to the role of UFCo and the CIA, Handy emphasizes the conservative opposition of Guatemalan landholders and how agrarian reform legislation undermined their economic investments. From this perspective, Arbenz's principal failure was not integrating the Maya peasants fully into his revolution since they could have provided his most solid and steadfast base of support in the face of conservative reaction. The country was predominantly agricultural and lacked a large urban working-class movement that was properly positioned to introduce political, social, and economic changes. The base of the movement needed to be found elsewhere.

The revolution also lacked a clear and strong political ideology, such as that the communist party could have provided had not a fear of communism been so pervasive. In addition, Arbenz failed to provide strong leadership in the face of Castillo Armas's coup. At the time, it appeared that Arbenz was confronting overwhelming opposition, but later it became apparent that most of that was bluster. The country faced deep divides, with most of the opposition based in the capital city. The ladino middle-class and market women launched numerous demonstrations against the president. Limiting the vote to literate women who tended to vote conservative reinforced the power of antirevolutionary politicians on a municipal level.

With more willpower, and a willingness to rely on the peasants and workers as his base, Arbenz probably could have survived the coup and continued his reform program. On a strategic level, in hindsight it was a mistake not to destroy the army that formed the base of the previous regime and provided an institutional framework of opposition to his reforms. Cuban revolutionaries only five years after Arbenz's fall were determined not to repeat this same mistake. Rather than working within the confines of existing institutions, the Cubans decided to abolish the army, close congress, decapitate the landholding class, and expel foreign-owned corporations. Unlike in Guatemala, that decision ensured the longtime survival of the Cuban Revolution.

Highlighting internal factors does not mean that external factors did not play a role in the development of events. Obviously a foreign military power could guide and determine the nature and direction of events. Given a fear of communism and hostility to agrarian reform policies, however, Arbenz's domestic foes had enough reason to oppose him and try to remove him from power whether or not an antagonistic foreign imperial power existed. It does a disservice to Guatemalans to remove agency from their actions and assume that they acted only at the behest of a foreign power, even if for a time their interests did align with those of an external imperial agent.

SUMMARY

Guatemala was the home of the second great social revolution in Latin America, but it also provides a cautionary tale of the difficulties and liabilities of attempting profound transitions in an underdeveloped and marginal economic situation. A history of strong and repressive leaders seemingly would make Guatemala an unlikely location for a social revolution. The collapse of Jorge Ubico's dictatorship in the midst of the Second World War that relied on the rhetoric of fighting for democracy, however, opened up the possibilities for deep reform.

Jacobo Arbenz assumed the presidency in 1951 and dramatically accelerated the pace of reforms begun under his predecessor Juan José Arévalo. At first the new governments made significant progress in expanding access to resources for the majority of the country's marginalized population. Arbenz, however, encountered significant difficulties when he attempted to expropriate United Fruit Company property to provide land to peasants. Those redistributive policies ran him afoul of wealthy individuals in Guatemala and the U.S. government, both of which charged him with pursuing communist-influenced policies. The Guatemalan Spring ended with a military coup and a reconcentration of wealth and power into the hands of a small and privileged group of people. A more thorough deconstruction of the previous regime, stronger leadership in the face of opposition to the reforms, and a reliance on grassroots support might have ensured the revolution's success.

DISCUSSION QUESTIONS

Why did Jorge Ubico's government fall?

Why is it so difficult to unify workers and peasants in a common struggle for social justice?

Why was the military's support so important for Arbenz to remain in power?

What was the relative importance of domestic as opposed to international opposition to the Arbenz government?

Does land reform inherently present a threat to capitalism?

Did the Cold War justify the anticommunism that brought down the Arbenz government?

What would have been the logical result of Decree 900 had Arbenz not been overthrown?

In retrospect, what could Arbenz have done differently to prevent the overthrow of his government? Was the collapse of his government inevitable?

FURTHER READING

Almost all of the writing on the Guatemalan Spring has been sympathetic to the Arbenz government. The great divide is between authors who focus on domestic opposition to his reforms and those who point the finger at the CIA for intervening in the country.

Arévalo, Juan José. *Anti-Kommunism in Latin America: An X-ray of the Process Leading to New Colonialism*. New York: L. Stuart, 1963. Former Guatemalan president attacks U.S. policy in Latin America as myopic and misguided.

Cullather, Nick. *Secret History: The C.I.A.'s Classified Account of Its Operations in Guatemala, 1952–1954*. Stanford, CA: Stanford University Press, 1999. Declassified CIA history of its covert operations in Guatemala.

Doyle, Kate, and Peter Kornbluh, eds. *CIA and Assassinations: The Guatemala 1954 Documents*. Electronic Briefing Book 4. Washington, DC: National Security Archive, 1997. http://nsarchive.gwu.edu. Declassified CIA documents on covert operations in Guatemala.

Forster, Cindy. *The Time of Freedom: Campesino Workers in Guatemala's October Revolution*. Pittsburgh: University of Pittsburgh Press, 2001. Examines Guatemala's revolution from the peasants' perspective.

Gleijeses, Piero. *Shattered Hope: The Guatemalan Revolution and the United States, 1944–1954*. Princeton, NJ: Princeton University Press, 1991. Defends Arbenz's reforms, though he argues that Arbenz moved too quickly in implementing them.

Grandin, Greg. *The Last Colonial Massacre: Latin America in the Cold War*. Chicago: University of Chicago Press, 2004. A probing examination of rural organizing during and after the Guatemalan Spring.

Handy, Jim. *Revolution in the Countryside: Rural Conflict and Agrarian Reform in Guatemala, 1944–1954*. Chapel Hill: University of North Carolina Press, 1994. Outstanding study of Guatemala's 1952 land reform program.

Immerman, Richard H. *The CIA in Guatemala: The Foreign Policy of Intervention*. Austin: University of Texas Press, 1982. Critique of CIA-inspired overthrow of Arbenz.

Schlesinger, Stephen C., and Stephen Kinzer. *Bitter Fruit: The Untold Story of the American Coup in Guatemala*. Garden City, NY: Doubleday, 1982. Passionate story of the CIA's involvement in the overthrow of Arbenz's government.

Schneider, Ronald M. *Communism in Guatemala, 1944–1954*. New York: Praeger, 1958. An extensively documented Cold War history that argues that communists played a significant role in the Arbenz administration.

FILMS

Devils Don't Dream! 1995. In 1950, Guatemalans elected Jacobo Arbenz president. When he began to give farmers their own land the CIA helped overthrow his government.

Men with Guns. 1998. A fictional depiction of villagers caught between guerrilla fighters and military violence, broadly based on Guatemala in the 1980s.

El Silencio de Neto (The Silence of Neto). 1994. Discusses the 1954 coup in Guatemala from the point of view of a young boy.

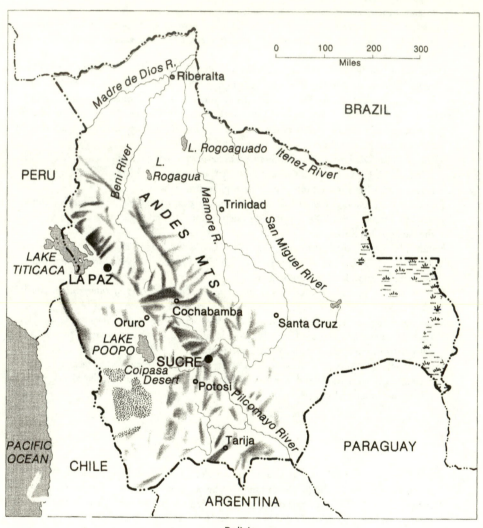

Bolivia

4

Bolivia's Nationalist Revolution, 1952–1964

KEY DATES

1932–1935	Bolivia loses Chaco War with Paraguay
1941	Formation of the Revolutionary Nationalist Movement (MNR)
1942	Strike at the Catavi tin mine leads to massacre
1943	A civilian-military coup brings Major Gualberto Villarroel to power with cooperation of the MNR
1945	National Indigenous Congress
1946	Popular protest leads to the hanging of Villarroel
1946	The Union Federation of Bolivian Mine Workers (FSTMB) drafts "Pulacayo Theses"
1951	Electoral fraud appears to close MNR's constitutional path to power
April 9–11, 1952	An insurrection brings MNR to power
October 31, 1952	MNR government nationalizes tin industry
August 3, 1953	Agrarian reform breaks up old hacienda system
November 4, 1964	General René Barrientos Ortuño leads military coup that ends MNR rule
October 9, 1967	Ernesto Che Guevara killed while leading a guerrilla uprising in Bolivia
1971–1978	Hugo Banzer Suárez holds power as military dictator
1985	Víctor Paz Estenssoro returns MNR to office through electoral victory
2005	Leftist labor leader Evo Morales elected president

During Easter week in 1952, a popular uprising brought a new government to power in Bolivia that turned the poorest country in South America upside down, obliterated traditional landholding structures, and modernized the economy. The urban middle class formed the base of support for the Movimiento Nacionalista Revolucionario (MNR, Revolutionary Nationalist Movement) that took over the reins of government. Workers and peasants exploited this political opening to demand radical structural changes. Popular pressure led to the nationalization of tin mines, an agrarian reform that broke up large landed estates, and the elimination of restrictions on suffrage rights. The 1952 revolution opened space for some of the most militant labor and peasant unions in Latin America.

Notably, the MNR's radical reforms did not trigger U.S. military intervention, as had Jacobo Arbenz Guzmán's policies in Guatemala. Historians have debated these contrasting responses, with explanatory factors including Bolivia's greater distance from the U.S. sphere of influence, domestic rather than foreign ownership of the nationalized commodities, and the MNR's willingness to adjust its policies to U.S. demands. Accommodation, however, did not ensure long-term survival. A military coup brought the MNR's rule to an end in 1964. When the MNR returned to office through electoral means two decades later, it was a much more conservative political force.

Many scholars regard the MNR as a failed or unfinished revolution. For a brief period in the 1950s, it unleashed social forces that appeared to be positioned to transform society in favor of previously dispossessed miners and peasants. Its failure to bring these aspirations to completion provides an important example of the limitations of realizing revolutionary changes in a poor and marginalized country.

LANDLOCKED BOLIVIA

Bolivia was Spain's most valuable colony during the European power's almost three-hundred-year presence in the Americas. Europeans extracted immense wealth from the silver mines at Potosí, yet today Bolivia is South America's poorest country. This contrast is not coincidental but provides a key example of how extractive enterprises underdevelop an economy and leave it worse off than if it had no natural resources at all.

Bolivia is currently the fifth largest country in Latin America, yet it lost every war it fought and today is only half the size it was when it gained independence from Spain in 1825. In the War of the Pacific (1879–1882), Bolivia forfeited its coast and nitrate fields to neighboring Peru and Chile. Half a century later, the country suffered another humiliating defeat, to Paraguay in the Chaco War (1932–1935), and in the process lost much of its population, territory, and oil fields. The result is that Bolivia is one of only two of the thirty-five republics in the Americas that do not have a coastline (the other is neighboring Paraguay). Although located in the heart of South America, it has few connections with its five neighboring countries. These losses combined with geographic isolation contributed to Bolivia's impoverishment.

Like Guatemala, many of Bolivia's inhabitants are of Indigenous descent. Present-day Bolivia was once known as Qullasuyu, a region that made up the southern quadrant of the Inka Empire (or Tawantinsuyu). In the 1950s, many people still primarily spoke the Indigenous languages of Quechua, Aymara, or Guaraní. Most lived in rural areas and worked in agriculture. They suffered the lowest life expectancies, highest infant mortality rates, and highest illiteracy rates in South America. Bolivia was a large country, but it was also one of the least densely populated countries in the Americas—its poverty was not the result of overpopulation.

Bolivia is one of the most politically unstable countries in the Americas. Since gaining independence from Spain, it has averaged about one irregular and extra-constitutional change of government per year. Most were palace coups with little corresponding change in wealth and power relations. Instead, the struggles were between rival conservative and liberal factions, with both representing wealthy economic interests far removed from the majority of the population. The conservatives were rooted in silver mining in the southern part of the country as well as in large landed estates on which they held peasants in servile and feudalistic relationships. During the nineteenth century, wealthy landowners seized much of the land from autonomous Indigenous communities. By 1950, 6 percent of landowners held 92 percent of the land. They only worked a very small part of it, and even that they farmed inefficiently. As a result of this unequal distribution of land, Bolivia imported one-fifth of its food.

By the end of the colonial period, Bolivia's silver deposits had largely been exhausted, leaving the country with a stagnant economy. In the 1880s, the country's economic focus shifted away from the silver mines at Potosí and the conservative stronghold at Sucre and toward new tin mines at Oruro and their corresponding economic center at La Paz. The liberals won an 1899 civil war against the conservatives and used their newfound dominant position to set the country on a course of economic development and modernization based on the exploitation of tin. Soon, the Bolivian economy became almost exclusively dependent on tin exports, leaving it extremely vulnerable to international fluctuations in demand and price. Three corporations controlled 80 percent of the tin trade, and the owners acquired much more power than the Bolivian government. Tin barons imposed policies that played to their personal benefit but functioned to the detriment of the country as a whole and particularly hurt rural communities.

Bolivia had a dual and polarized society, its aggregate parts rarely intersecting with each other. About one-third of the population lived in urban areas and was dependent on the tin economy. During the first half of the twentieth century, an increase in access to education in urban areas led to a jump in literacy from 17 to 31 percent. This contributed to rising middle-class expectations, but with the twentieth-century decline of the tin industry and an almost total lack of industrialization, they had few possibilities to improve their economic situation. In contrast, rural peasants working on traditional haciendas with few political rights comprised two-thirds of the population. Formally, Bolivia was a democracy, but literacy and property requirements excluded the rural Indigenous masses and urban working class from political participation.

Of the three tin barons, Simón Patiño (1862–1947) was the wealthiest and most powerful (the other two were Mauricio Hochschild and Carlos Victor Aramayo). Patiño came to be known as the "Andean Rockefeller." By the Second World War, he was one of the five richest men in the world. His annual income exceeded that of the country's budget, and his son's allowance was larger than the allotted funding for education. Even though he was Bolivian, he extracted wealth from the country to live opulently in Europe. Economic development did little to benefit the country. By the 1930s, the tin barons dedicated little new investment in mining. At the same time, the quality of the ore dropped, production declined, and profit margins shrank. The 1929 Great Depression hit the industry particularly hard, leading to a collapse of the tin-based export economy. The oligarchy that had formed around tin interests began to lose its grip on the country.

CHACO WAR

In 1932, as Bolivia was sinking into an economic crisis, the country became involved in a protracted war with neighboring Paraguay over the arid and sparsely populated Chaco region that lay between the two countries. Some attribute the conflict to a dispute between oil companies for access to petroleum in the Chaco, with Royal Dutch Shell backing Paraguay and Standard Oil supporting Bolivia. By the time the fighting ceased in 1935, tens of thousands of soldiers lay dead on each side. Bolivia was the loser, both in terms of the number of dead and territory ceded to Paraguay. Most soldiers died from natural causes such as dehydration and dysentery, and many more were captured or deserted. The devastating loss caused Bolivians to reflect critically on their society and ponder who was to blame for the country's failures. A seemingly corrupt and self-interested civilian administration lost credibility in the eyes of the public as well as the military. Political leaders engaged in a self-serving form of government in which they gained power only to benefit themselves rather than to improve society. Economic and political leaders led institutions that were in a process of fragmentation and collapse.

The Chaco War introduced isolated rural communities to a broader political system with which they had not previously interacted. Drafting peasants into the military brought them into contact with an urban working class that was also impoverished and dispossessed. The organizational structure of the army re-created the caste structure of society and contributed to the growth of a class consciousness among the Quechua and Aymara combatants. Those of European descent populated the upper-level officer corps, while the lower-level officers were mostly mestizos. The rank-and-file soldiers who bore the brunt of deaths in the war were from rural

Indigenous communities and had the least to gain from a war that was not fought in their interests. After the war, many of these involuntary recruits refused to return to their previous serf-like lives. They wanted change.

In this context, Indigenous activists organized grassroots movements to advocate for their rights. A complex network of communal authorities known as the *cacique* (or local chiefdom) movement bargained with government authorities to seek justice for their communities. They demanded a return of their land and appealed for aid for Indigenous schools. Their activism led to the formation of state-funded rural schools, in addition to private and religious institutions. Scholars previously interpreted these early movements as prepolitical, meaning they did not fundamentally challenge the structure of society. In reality, they provided the roots for later political actions. These activists formed the first peasant **syndicates** or labor unions. These new organizational structures gained support from leftist political parties, miners, workers, and anarchists. They learned new forms of struggle from these external contacts, such as the sit-down strike. As their strength grew, they demanded abolition of compulsory feudalistic service relations on haciendas. The syndicates attacked oppressive hacienda structures, which increased pressure for agrarian reform and profound changes in society.

SOCIALISM

The economic and political crises resulting from the Great Depression and the Chaco War led to a proliferation of political parties and a growth in socialist ideologies. The Falange Socialista Boliviana (FSB, Bolivian Socialist Falange) used the word socialist but was a far-right fascist party that appealed to chauvinistic nationalism. Leftist parties included the Trotskyist Partido Obrero Revolucionario (POR, Revolutionary Workers Party) and the pro-Soviet Partido de la Izquierda Revolucionaria (PIR, Party of the Revolutionary Left). Their emergence reflected popular aspirations for systemic change (see table 4.1).

Military leaders David Toro and Germán Busch capitalized on leftist sentiments to implement self-styled socialist regimes that combined progressive labor policies with resource nationalization policies. The most significant move was Toro's March 1937 decree that nationalized Standard Oil's holding. His action was the first major nationalization of a natural resource in Latin America, and it happened a full year before Lázaro Cárdenas took a similar but much better known step in Mexico. Toro and Busch's economic and labor policies responded to popular pressure for change, but they also ruled in an authoritarian fashion that sought to maintain control over society. Their reformist policies reflected widespread discontent with liberal capitalist ideas but also co-opted support for more radical alternatives from leftist political parties.

The Movimiento Nacionalista Revolucionario (MNR, Revolutionary Nationalist Movement) was the largest and most important of the new political parties. At

Table 4.1. Political Groups

COB	Central Obrera Boliviana (Bolivian Workers Confederation). Founded in 1952 following the MNR revolution. Under the control of FSTMB secretary-general Juan Lechín Oquendo, the COB became Bolivia's chief trade union federation.
COMIBOL	Corporación Minera de Bolivia (Bolivian Mining Corporation). State mining corporation created in 1952 when the MNR nationalized the country's tin mines. Controlled by organized labor.
FSB	Falange Socialista Boliviana (Bolivian Socialist Falange). Founded in 1937. A far-right political party that drew inspiration from Benito Mussolini's fascism and Francisco Franco's falangism. The FSB adopted a strongly anticommunist stance.
FSTMB	Federación Sindical de Trabajadores Mineros de Bolivia (Union Federation of Bolivian Mine Workers). The FSTMB was the first miners' federation in Bolivia. Formed in 1944 under MNR sponsorship, it continually provided the MNR with needed support. It rapidly became the most powerful union in the country. Juan Lechín Oquendo was the organization's secretary-general.
MNR	Movimiento Nacionalista Revolucionario (Revolutionary Nationalist Movement). Founded in 1941 by future presidents Víctor Paz Estenssoro and Hernán Siles Zuazo. The MNR was the leading force in the 1952 revolution. It moved sharply to the right and advocated neoliberal economic policies when it returned to power in 1985.
PIR	Partido de la Izquierda Revolucionaria (Party of the Revolutionary Left). Officially formed July 26, 1940. A party with Marxist-Leninist tendencies, it generally maintained that the Bolivian proletariat was weak in numbers and consciousness due to uneven economic development. It drew its support largely from the middle class. The party ascribed to Marx's historical determinism and rejected a permanent revolution on the grounds that before becoming socialist, Bolivia must pass through a capitalist stage. The PIR placed strong emphasis on the role of education in revolutionizing Bolivian society and connected with various artisan and labor groups. Its influence was strongest among railway workers. It also showed some interest in the situation of Indigenous peoples.
POR	Partido Obrero Revolucionario (Revolutionary Workers Party). The POR was the Trotskyite sector of the left. The party attacked the student left while pursuing connections with various labor groups. In the early 1940s, it consisted of a mixture of proletarian elements along with middle- and upper-class intellectuals. It gained considerable influence with miners and was deeply involved with mining syndicates. It was also somewhat interested in the situation of Indigenous peoples.

RADEPA   Razón de Patria (Homeland's Cause). The RADEPA was a secret
            military society that was influenced by nationalistic, corporatist,
            fascist, and statist doctrines from both Europe and Latin America.
            Many of its members were veterans of the Chaco War. The RADEPA
            wanted control of the government but lacked an organized platform
            and program. It generally favored direct military seizure of the state.

Republicans The party officially formed in 1914 when they split off from the ruling
            liberal party yet showed little differentiation from the original liberal
            party. The Republicans gathered together powerful groups, including
            the new wealthy mine owners and disgruntled members of the old
            landed aristocracy. It followed the same traditions of the liberals,
            drew its strength from the upper class, and was racist and oligarchic.
            It first took control in a coup in 1920 and ruled until the military
            takeover in 1936. After a brief decline in power, the Republicans
            reemerged in the late 1940s and won the 1947 and 1949 elections.
            They took a strong stand against the left and the labor movement.

---

the time of its formation in 1941, the MNR consisted largely of moderate-left, middle-class intellectuals, who at one point had supported the conservative government of General Enrique Peñaranda but had grown alienated with the general's increasing warmth toward the United States. The example of fascist leaders in Germany and Italy implementing policies to develop their country's basic industries influenced the MNR's proposed policy objectives. Despite its fascist origins, the MNR was also highly pragmatic. The party included mestizo and Indigenous members and leaders who were not particularly attracted to the German Nazi preoccupation with racial purity, or the supposed superiority of the Aryan "race." Tinges of anti-Semitism grew largely out of resentment toward the economic challenges that an influx of Jewish refugees from Nazi Germany represented for local Bolivian merchants. The MNR was more nationalistic and anti-imperialist in its outlook than totalitarian or militarist in its proposed governing strategies. Party leaders resented U.S. and British wealth and power, and that imperial presence made those with an underdeveloped political consciousness susceptible to Nazi criticism of Western allies. The MNR also made common cause with leftist mine workers who likewise criticized imperialism, although for quite different reasons. Broader populist actions in Latin America, particularly Juan Perón's mobilization of workers in Argentina, also influenced the MNR leadership.

In 1942 the political climate of Bolivia shifted when the country officially joined the Allies in the Second World War. The MNR retained its fascist policies, but the close ties with Germany were broken and the MNR subsequently focused instead on national issues. Eventually, the MNR, and Bolivians in general, abandoned Germany when it became obvious that the Nazis were losing the war. In the 1942 congressional elections, nontraditional, largely leftist parties gained more votes than did the established liberal and conservative parties. This outcome launched a trend toward the radicalization of Bolivian society, a process that continued until the elections of 1951. The radicalization of the middle class bled over into the working class, and popular discontent with the oligarchy acquired characteristics of a mass movement.

Repeated attempts to organize the working class bred several conflicts between the government and the laborers, particularly in Patiño's mines. The most important clash occurred in December 1942 when miners from Patiño's Catavi mine went on strike to demand better working conditions. The miners' wives were upset when the company closed stores on which they relied for food supplies. With María Barzola in the lead, the women supported the miners in their strike. The government declared the strike illegal and sent in troops to repress the action. They opened fire on the unarmed miners and their families, killing hundreds, including Barzola, who became a symbol of their struggle. The MNR capitalized on the slaughter and, under the leadership of Víctor Paz Estenssoro (1907–2001), attacked the Peñaranda government and supported the miners, thus gaining key labor backing for their party. The added pressure further reduced popular support for the government as the left continued to grow stronger.

As the government weakened, the military became restless with the lack of progress at addressing societal problems. A number of secret societies formed within the military, the most important being Razón de Patria (RADEPA, Homeland's Cause) that materialized as part of a longer tradition of progressive, nationalist military leaders in Latin America. In 1943, RADEPA allied with the MNR in a successful civilian-military coup against the Peñaranda government. The previously unknown Major Gualberto Villarroel (1908–1946) emerged as the leader of the new military junta that implemented reformist policies. The United States and the majority of other Latin American countries refused to recognize the new regime until the extremist leaders of the MNR were removed, but despite the official displacement of these leaders the actual ties between the Villarroel government and the MNR remained close. The MNR's influence largely defined governmental policies.

For the first time in Bolivian history, Villarroel's government worked to draw the Indigenous masses into national politics. In 1945, the government organized a National Indigenous Congress that gathered one thousand delegates to discuss rural problems and to improve the lives of people in peasant communities. The regime issued a decree abolishing labor service obligations for Indigenous workers. This could have been a revolutionary act and would have destroyed the large landholding system (known as **latifundia**), but it was never enforced.

The Villarroel regime also continued to support the mine workers' movement. The MNR worked closely with Juan Lechín Oquendo, a mine leader and member of the Trotskyist POR. Miners formed the Federación Sindical de Trabajadores Mineros de Bolivia (FSTMB, Union Federation of Bolivian Mine Workers), with Lechín as its head. The FSTMB took over leadership of the labor movement and provided the MNR with essential support.

BIOGRAPHY: JUAN LECHÍN OQUENDO, 1914–2001

Juan Lechín Oquendo was Bolivia's foremost labor leader. He worked in the Catavi and Siglo XX tin mines, where he gained awareness of the desperate conditions under which the majority of workers suffered. He became involved in the labor movement and joined the Trotskyist Revolutionary Workers Party (POR). In 1944, Lechín organized a miners' congress that led to the formation of the Union Federation of Bolivian Mine Workers (FSTMB). Members elected him as the federation's executive secretary, a position he held until 1987.

Even as Lechín continued to work with the leftist POR, he also became involved with the more moderate MNR. After the 1952 revolution, Lechín was named minister of mines and petroleum. He also led the founding congress of the Bolivian Workers Confederation (COB) in 1952 and remained its executive secretary until 1987.

Lechín was the most radical of the central MNR leadership. He advocated arming the workers' militias to prevent a conservative backlash against the revolution's progressive reforms. He was a charismatic leader who became popular with the working class. His leftist positions led him into conflict with the more moderate

Juan Lechín Oquendo
Source: Revista Gente y la actualidad, Buenos Aires, Argentina, September 15, 1970

leadership of Víctor Paz Estenssoro and Hernán Siles Zuazo. Militants, however, complained that he compromised the interests of labor in favor of consolidating the MNR's hold on power, including supporting austerity measures as the economy began to spin out of control.

In order to reduce tensions within the MNR, Paz Estenssoro returned to the presidency in 1960 and named Lechín vice president, a position he held until 1964. Lechín initially was to be the MNR's presidential candidate in 1964, but he split with the party when they passed over him for the nomination. Instead, he joined a coup that toppled the MNR, mistakenly thinking that the military would let him share power. Rather than keeping its promise, the military government forced the labor leader into exile.

When Bolivia returned to civilian rule in 1982, Lechín resumed his previous position as leader of the FSTMB and COB. As a labor leader, he opposed the economic measures of his former colleagues in the MNR Hernán Siles Zuazo (1982–1985) and Víctor Paz Estenssoro (1985–1989), who now introduced draconian neoliberal policies that privatized tin mines and undermined the livelihoods of miners and other members of the working class.

In 1987, Lechín left his positions as head of the FSTMB and COB. He had never risen to the position of president of Bolivia, but he did represent the most significant left-wing political force in the country.

DOCUMENT: THE UNION FEDERATION OF BOLIVIAN MINE WORKERS (FSTMB), "PULACAYO THESES," 1946

Mine workers adopted this document at a November 1946 meeting in the city of Pulacayo. Because of Bolivia's economic backwardness, no national bourgeoisie was present to carry forward a revolutionary movement, so this responsibility would fall to a proletarian vanguard. It is based on the Trotskyist concept of permanent revolution and became the most important expression of the demands of Bolivia's labor movement.

I. Basic principles

1. The proletariat, in Bolivia as in other countries, constitutes the revolutionary social class par excellence. The mineworkers, the most advanced and the most combative section of this country's proletariat, determine the direction of the FSTMB's struggle.

2. Bolivia is a backward capitalist country; within its economy different stages of development and different modes of production coexist, but the capitalist mode is qualitatively dominant, the other socio-economic forms being a heritage from our historic past. The prominence of the proletariat in national politics flows from this state of affairs.

3. Bolivia, even though a backward country, is only one link in the world capitalist chain. National peculiarities are themselves a combination of the essential features of the world economy.

4. The distinctive characteristic of Bolivia resides in the fact there has not appeared on the political scene a bourgeoisie capable of liquidating the latifundia system and other pre-capitalist economic forms, of achieving national unification and liberation from the imperialist yoke.

   These unfulfilled bourgeois tasks are the bourgeois democratic objectives that must unavoidably be realized. The central problems facing the semi-colonial countries are: the agrarian revolution, that is, the elimination of the feudal heritage, and national independence, namely, shaking off the imperialist yoke. These two tasks are closely inter-linked.

5. The specific characteristics of the national economy, important as they may be, are more and more becoming an integral part of a higher reality known as the world economy. This is the basis for proletarian internationalism. Capitalist development is characterized by a growing interlinking of international relations, expressed in the growing volume of foreign trade.

6. The backward countries are subjected to imperialist pressure. Their development is of a combined character. These countries simultaneously combine the most primitive economic forms and the last word in capitalist technology and

civilization. The proletariat of the backward countries is obliged to combine the struggle for bourgeois democratic tasks with the struggle for socialist demands. These two stages—democratic and socialist—are not separated in struggle by historic stages; they flow immediately from one another.

7. The feudal landowners have linked their interests with those of world imperialism and have become unconditionally its lackeys.

    From this it follows that the ruling class is a veritable feudal bourgeoisie. Given the primitive level of technology, the running of the latifundia would be inconceivable if imperialism did not support them artificially with scraps from its table. Imperialist domination is inconceivable without the aid of the national governments of the elite. There is a high degree of capitalist concentration in which three firms control mining production, the heart of the country's economic life. The class in power is puny and incapable of achieving its own historic objectives, and so finds itself tied to the interests of the latifundists as well as those of the imperialists. The feudal-bourgeois state is an organ of violence destined to uphold the privileges of the landowners and the capitalists. The state, in the hands of the dominant class, is a powerful instrument for crushing its enemies. Only traitors or imbeciles could continue to maintain that the state can rise above the classes and paternally decide what is due to each of them.

8. The middle class or petit bourgeoisie is the most numerous class, and yet its weight in the national economy is insignificant. The small traders and property owners, the technicians, the bureaucrats, the artisans and the peasantry have been unable up to now to develop an independent class policy and will be even more unable to do so in the future. The country follows the town and there the leading force is the proletariat. The petit bourgeoisie follow the capitalists in times of "class peace" and when parliamentary activity flourishes. They line up behind the proletariat in moments of acute class struggle (for example during a revolution) and when they become convinced that it alone can show the way to their own emancipation. In both these widely differing circumstances, the independence of the petit bourgeoisie proves to be a myth. Wide layers of the middle class obviously do possess an enormous revolutionary potential—it is enough to recall the aims of the bourgeois democratic revolution—but it is equally clear that they cannot achieve these aims on their own.

9. What characterizes the proletariat is that it is the only class possessing sufficient strength to achieve not only its own aims but also those of other classes. Its enormous specific weight in political life is determined by the position it occupies in the production process and not by its numerical weakness. The economic axis of national life will also be the political axis of the future revolution.

The miners' movement in Bolivia is one of the most advanced workers' movements in Latin America. The reformists argue that it is impossible for this country to have a more advanced **social movement** than in the technically more developed countries. Such a mechanical conception of the relation between the development of industry and the political consciousness of the masses has been refuted countless times by history.

If the Bolivian proletariat has become one of the most radical proletariats, it is because of its extreme youth and its incomparable vigor, it is because it has remained practically virgin in politics, it is because it does not have the traditions of parliamentarism or class collaboration, and lastly, because it is struggling in a country where the class struggle has taken on an extremely war-like character. We reply to the reformists and to those in the pay of La Rosca that a proletariat of such quality requires revolutionary demands and the most extreme boldness in struggle.

II. The type of revolution that must take place

1. We mineworkers do not suggest we can leap over the bourgeois democratic tasks, the struggle for elementary democratic rights and for an anti-imperialist agrarian revolution. Neither do we ignore the existence of the petit bourgeoisie, especially peasants and artisans. We point out that if you do not want to see the bourgeois democratic revolution strangled then it must become only one phase of the proletarian revolution. Those who point to us as proponents of an immediate socialist revolution in Bolivia are lying. We know very well that the objective conditions do not exist for it. We say clearly that the revolution will be bourgeois democratic in its objectives and that it will be only one episode in the proletarian revolution for the class that is to lead it.

2. The proletarian revolution in Bolivia does not imply the exclusion of the other exploited layers of the nation; on the contrary, it means the revolutionary alliance of the proletariat with the peasants, the artisans and other sectors of the urban petit bourgeoisie.

3. The dictatorship of the proletariat is the expression at state level of this alliance. The slogan of proletarian revolution and dictatorship shows clearly the fact that it is the working class who will be the leading force of this transformation and of this state. On the contrary, to maintain that the bourgeois democratic revolution, as such, will be brought about by the "progressive" sectors of the bourgeoisie, and that the future state will be a government of national unity and concord, shows a determination to strangle the revolutionary movement within the framework of bourgeois democracy. The workers, once in power, will not be able to confine themselves indefinitely to bourgeois democratic limits; they will find themselves obliged—and more so with every day—to making greater and greater inroads into the regime of private property, in such a way that the revolution will take on a permanent character.

Before the exploited, we, the mineworkers, denounce those who attempt to substitute for the proletarian revolution, palace revolutions fomented by various sections of the feudal bourgeoisie.

III. The struggle against class collaboration

1. The class struggle is, in the last analysis, the struggle for the appropriation of surplus value. The proletariat that sells its labor power struggles to do this on the best terms it can and the owners of the means of production (capitalists) struggle to seize the product of unpaid labor; both pursue opposite aims, which makes their interests irreconcilable.

   We must not close our eyes to the fact that the struggle against the bosses is a fight to the death, for in this struggle the fate of private property is at stake.

   Unlike our enemies, we recognize no truce in the class struggle.

   The present historical stage, a period of shame for humanity, can only be overcome when social classes have disappeared and there no longer exist exploiter and exploited. Those who practice class collaboration are playing a stupid game of words when they maintain that it is not a question of destroying the rich but of making the poor rich. Our goal is the expropriation of the expropriators.

2. Every attempt to collaborate with our executioners, every attempt to make concessions to the enemy in the course of the struggle, means abandoning the workers to the bourgeoisie. Class collaboration means renouncing our own objectives. Every conquest by the workers, even the most minimal, is obtained only at the price of a bitter struggle against the capitalist system. We cannot

think about reaching an understanding with our oppressors because, for us, the program of transitional demands serves the goal of proletarian revolution.

We are not reformists, even when putting before the workers the most advanced platform of demands; we are above all revolutionaries, for we aim to transform the very structure of society.

3. We reject the petit bourgeois illusion according to which the state or some other institution, placing itself above the social classes in struggle, can solve the problems of workers. Such a solution, as the history of the workers' movement, nationally and internationally, teaches us, has always meant a solution in accord with the interests of capitalism at the expense of the impoverishment and oppression of the proletariat.

Compulsory arbitration and legal limitations of workers' means of struggle, in most cases mark the onset of defeat. As far as is possible, we fight to destroy compulsory arbitration.

Social conflicts should be resolved under the leadership of the workers and by them alone!

4. The realization of our program of transitional demands, which must lead to proletarian revolution, is always subject to the class struggle. We are proud of being the most intransigent when there is talk of making compromises with the bosses. That is why it is a key task to struggle against and defeat the reformists who advocate class collaboration, as well as those who tell us to tighten our belts in the name of so-called national salvation. There can be no talk of national grandeur in a country where the workers suffer hunger and oppression; rather we should really talk of national destitution and decay. We will abolish capitalist exploitation.

War to the death against capitalism! War to the death against the reformist collaboration! Follow the path of class struggle towards the destruction of capitalist society!

Source: Excerpt from the Union Federation of Bolivian Mine Workers (FSTMB), "Pulacayo Theses," 1946, Oxford University Press, http://global.oup.com.

The Villarroel regime lasted from 1943 until 1946 and collapsed largely as a result of extreme police violence and repression. In 1944, the government responded to opposition electoral gains by jailing and assassinating their leaders. In July 1946, a popular protest march turned into a revolt, and a mob hanged Villarroel. The pro-Soviet PIR opportunistically participated in the government that followed Villarroel's death. Unions took advantage of the political unrest to organize numerous strikes for better wages and working conditions over the next several months in the Patiño mines. Indigenous workers in alliance with urban leftist activists also led strikes on haciendas for their rights. Ideological divisions among the MNR, POR, and PIR prevented their coalescence into one powerful political force, even though they generally shared policies of opposition to the traditional oligarchy and support for labor reforms.

Following the collapse of the Villarroel government, the MNR spent the six-year period between 1946 and 1952 (called the *sexenio*) in exile. It spent this time engaged in clandestine activity, re-creating its image, and searching for its future as a political party. Women were crucial in organizing resistance during this period, including supporting political prisoners, sheltering dissidents, and building communication networks. The MNR rid itself of all its remaining fascist elements and adopted a nationalist program that advocated a program of strong economic stabilization. Under the guiding hand of Paz Estenssoro and a new leader, Hernán Siles Zuazo, the son of a previous president of the same name, the MNR attempted to broaden its base of support, particularly among the middle class. Through rooting itself in different sectors of society, it sought to emulate the success of Mexico's Institutional Revolutionary Party (PRI) that had ruled in that country since 1929. In a period of rising rightist forces, continual labor unrest, and repression, the MNR became the left's best hope for social justice.

Three factions emerged in the MNR. One continued with its traditional rightist, protofascist program that emphasized national dignity, harmony, and anti-Semitism. Walter Guevara Arze became the primary leader of the MNR's conservative wing. A second, centrist tendency with pragmatic nationalists formed the core of the MNR. Paz Estenssoro and Siles Zuazo, with their national-developmentalist values, led this faction. Their leadership was more reformist than radical. Labor leader Lechín led a third faction that advocated a leftist program of political, social, and economic change. This group supported universal suffrage, the nationalization of the tin industry, and agrarian reform to dismantle the latifundia system. The broad and diverse coalition led to an awkward and fragile alliance. The MNR was not organized on the basis of a class struggle, but as a broad multiclass movement of middle-class activists with young people, and especially university students, in the lead. Workers with tenuous ties to leftist unions and some organized peasant communities joined them as well.

The PIR made a tactical error in ignoring rampant popular demand for change in Bolivian society, siding instead with the country's traditional parties. In the elections of 1947 and 1949, the PIR lost to the Republicans but refused to relinquish power. The two parties, however, became political bedfellows, with the Republicans slowly replacing the PIR in power. They relied heavily on military force in an attempt to contain demands for change and in the process created a repressive situation much like that under the Villarroel regime. The PIR used violence to suppress the mine workers and fraud to reduce the number of electoral votes the MNR received. The pressure for change became so strong that the FSTMB publicly called for a violent, armed struggle. This demand came out of the POR wing of the FSTMB, but the MNR desired to keep control of the labor movement and as a result was forced to move their position even further to the left. Finally, international tin prices declined drastically, leaving the country in dire economic straits. All of these episodes combined to lead the MNR to commit itself to an armed overthrow of the PIR regime.

In September 1949, the MNR organized a civilian revolt under the leadership of Siles Zuazo. After two months of fighting, the Bolivian army firmly defeated the MNR. Despite the former cooperation between the RADEPA and the MNR, the military supported the PIR government in the rebellion. In 1951, the MNR tried for the last time to take control of the government through electoral means. Paz Estenssoro and Siles Zuazo ran for the presidency and vice presidency, respectively, on a political platform that emphasized the labor/left's central issues of universal suffrage, nationalization of the tin mines, and agrarian reform. Their goal was to destroy the oligarchy, open up the country's resources for economic development, and advance social justice. They sought to nationalize the tin mines with a goal toward diversifying the economy and breaking the country's dependence on a single export product.

The MNR ticket won a plurality of the vote in the 1951 election, and congress should have confirmed their victory. Military leaders and the established political oligarchy, however, voided the outcome and prevented the MNR from taking power. Conservative political leadership declared the MNR to be communist and dangerous, and turned power over to the military. Facing this reality, the MNR leadership considered its alternatives. First, they attempted to organize another civil-military coup as they had done in 1943, but the military was unwilling to join them. Tensions intensified until Paz Estenssoro and other MNR leaders decided that civilians must be armed in order to defeat the army. The final revolt of the MNR began on April 9, 1952, and lasted only three days. The old regime fell with the miners marching into La Paz, the Bolivian capital.

INSURRECTION

The brief but bloody armed insurrection from April 9 to April 11, 1952, brought the MNR to power. The MNR enjoyed support from part of the army, but their victory was due in large part to the tin miners who, fueled with revolutionary rhetoric, had stepped into the political vacuum that the old system's collapse had created. MNR militants distributed arms to urban and rural militias, and together they overwhelmed the police power of the state. About six hundred people died in the fighting, but the old regime collapsed due more to its lack of popular support than to the military blow that the insurgents were able to deliver. The insurrection opened the way to a social revolution, although one that middle-class reformers rather than the working class led. The MNR leaders' ideology remained more nationalist than socialist in its outlook.

Despite leading the revolt, the MNR quickly began to lose control over the political process that it had set in motion. The creation of new and open political spaces led to the popular mobilization of workers and peasants who demanded more radical structural changes than the moderate MNR leadership had originally proposed. Paz Estenssoro and Siles Zuazo were reluctant leaders who attempted to engage in a legal and constitutional process, but leftist revolutionaries took the movement in a much more radical direction. Working-class and peasant pressure had been building since the Chaco War, and their efforts contributed to the slogan "mines to the state and land to the people." Those aspirations came to characterize the movement and quickly outpaced what the moderate MNR leadership had originally proposed.

The political establishment at the time of the insurrection presented limited organized resistance to the MNR. The tin mines, which provided the vast majority of Bolivia's national income, were unproductive and expensive to run. As the mines' once-rich veins ran out of ore, the owners failed to invest in new development. Most years, the mining industry barely covered its own costs. For this reason, with sufficient compensation, the tin barons did not complain about a national takeover of their industry. Likewise, absent hacienda owners offered little opposition to land confiscation if provided with sufficient compensation. In short, the traditional ruling class was economically weak and offered little opposition to the MNR's program.

The MNR quickly instituted a program of profound changes that altered the social, economic, and political realities of the country. The three most important reforms were in line with the political program that the radical wing of the party had pressed: nationalization of the tin mines, agrarian reform, and universal suffrage. The overall goal of these reforms was to modernize the economy, with a resulting downward redistribution of income and wealth from the upper to the lower class. The new government also curtailed the power of the armed forces by closing the national army college and purging five hundred members from the officer corps. As a result, the civilian militias were better armed than the police and military, and therefore helped determine the direction of the country.

Women played important economic and social roles in Bolivian society, but the revolution did little to change their status. The MNR never drafted a program or statement on women's rights. Leaders organized a women's branch of their party but with the goal of advancing the government's interests rather than addressing gender issues or changing women's domestic status. Even so, the women's branch did help create political space for women. Poor urban women formed a grassroots group called the Barzolas, named after the leader of the 1942 Catavi strike, to mobilize support for the revolution. The women's involvement included participation in the armed militias that solidified MNR control over the country, and Lydia Gueiler Tejada was one of the commanders. The Barzolas denounced antigovernment activity, particularly that of upper-class members of society, in whose houses they worked as domestic servants. On a level of policy, however, the government conducted reforms along class rather than gender lines, and women remained dependent on men. The revolution failed to deliver on promises of a more thoroughgoing social transformation of society.

Nationalization of Tin Mines

The most import reform to come out of the revolution was an October 31, 1952, decree that nationalized 80 percent of the tin mines, Bolivia's key industry. With this legislation, the new MNR government nationalized the big three tin companies. The MNR created a state mining corporation called the Corporación Minera de Bolivia (COMIBOL, Bolivian Mining Corporation) that administered tin production under joint labor-government management. Radicals demanded confiscation of the mines without indemnification, but in the end more moderate forces prevailed. The owners received twenty million dollars from the proceeds of subsequent tin sales for their former properties.

The nationalization of the mines provided opportunities for popular organizations to flourish. Under Lechín's leadership, the Central Obrera Boliviana (COB, Bolivian Workers Confederation) formed within a week of the MNR triumph. The COB demanded a system of co-government with the MNR and became one of the strongest labor movements in Latin America. The COB gained an increase in wages for the miners, better working conditions, a social security system, and subsidies for goods that laborers purchased in company stores. In addition, workers who were fired in the 1942 strike returned to their jobs. The COB also assisted highland Aymara and Quechua Indigenous communities to organize peasant unions in order to agitate for land reform.

Unfortunately, the workers inherited a costly and run-down industry, and at the same time the price of tin fell on the world market. Furthermore, MNR leaders were more interested in mobilizing miners, peasants, and women in support of the government than in liberating and transforming their lives. The Trotskyists soon lost control of the COB to moderate sectors of the MNR, and in the process the facade of co-governance contributed to an erosion of radical worker expressions. The MNR revolution was intensely nationalist, but it did not lead to a socialist revolution that envisioned a more equitable society with workers directly in control of the means of production. Nevertheless, conservatives viewed the extensive nationalization program as a threat and denounced the labor activists as communists. All of these limitations hindered the effectiveness of the nationalization program.

Agrarian Reform

The second significant MNR reform was an August 2, 1953, decree that broke up the old hacienda system and redistributed land to the Aymara and Quechua peasant masses. Rural communities previously had been largely excluded from the MNR movement, but with the agrarian reform decree, the 1952 revolution spread to the countryside. Rural workers destroyed work records on the estates and killed and expelled landowners and the abusive overseers they employed to maintain order on the estates. The result was the forcible seizure of land through the occupation of haciendas and the division of large estates (latifundia) into very small individual holdings (minifundia). The confiscation of land was relatively easy because many of the wealthy owners were absentee landlords who lived in the cities. Only later did legislation formalize the expropriations.

Peasants organized syndicates and militias to advance their agenda. Rural unions formed armed militias to press for the redistribution of land. The COB attempted and failed to direct the process under way in the country. Instead, peasant leaders pushed aside government officials and came to control entire regions of the country. Despite the relatively moderate reforms, conservatives and moderates in urban areas viewed the mobilized rural masses with alarm. A good deal of racism toward Aymara and Quechua peasants heightened that level of fear.

The redistribution of land from large and inefficient estates led to an expansion of local internal markets and a corresponding slow rise in peasant living standards. The agrarian reform initiatives, however, failed to change traditional farming techniques. Government programs to educate peasants in modern technologies floundered, and agricultural production lagged. Farmers lacked access to financing and credit that would have increased their levels of production. Administration of the program was slow, irregular, and underhanded. Nevertheless, government policies did transform rural peasants into active participants in the country's political life.

The rapid pace of land seizures quickly overwhelmed the MNR government's ability to administer the process. The redistribution of land was not a gift from the government but the result of the organized pressure of rural syndicates that pushed hard for it. Conservative MNR members condemned the unauthorized seizures of land and urged officials to crack down on rural militants in order to stop the violence against wealthy estate owners. The government succeeded in co-opting some Indigenous leaders and communities. Paz Estenssoro used these local leaders to maintain his power, including inducing rural communities to side with his administration against labor unions. These pressures led the radical reform process in the countryside to moderate and shrink in size and significance by the 1960s. Once some peasants gained access to land, they became extremely conservative and no longer wished to engage in political organizations. Rather, they wanted to be left alone to live their own lives. Providing peasants with their primary demand—land—effectively neutralized them as a political force.

Universal Suffrage

Until 1952, literacy and gender restrictions limited the vote to wealthy, landowning males and left the vast majority of the country's population outside of the country's formal political process. In the 1920s, upper-class women began to organize for their civil and political rights. The Catholic Church held a conservative influence over society and opposed women participating actively in the public realm. Feminist movements had little appeal for working-class and peasant women. Men in their communities did not enjoy the rights for which the feminists fought, which made their participation in such battles meaningless. For them, the struggle was against racial discrimination and economic exploitation rather than for gender equality.

The new government eliminated literacy requirements and in the process granted voting and other citizenship rights to Indigenous peoples for the first time. In contrast, such political changes did not occur in the neighboring Andean republics of Peru and Ecuador until the late 1970s. Although this decree was intended to mobilize poor peasants and miners, women were also unintended beneficiaries of the expansion of the franchise. The provision of a universal vote brought the women's suffrage movement to a rapid and unexpected conclusion. Only 7 percent of the population had voted in the 1951 election, and as a result of this reform the number of voters jumped from two hundred thousand to more than one million. Providing women and Indigenous peoples with the vote converted them into an important political force that could influence the outcome of electoral contests. Almost all candidates, however, still came from the male, upper-class, European-descent sectors of society. Women and Indigenous peoples did not gain a significant direct political presence in government for another half century.

CONSOLIDATION

Once in control of the government, the MNR attempted to emulate the PRI in Mexico to maintain themselves in power. They created political spaces where power could be negotiated between the new forces that had been brought to the forefront: workers, peasants, the middle class, and a new civilian-controlled military. Still, historical divisions persisted within the MNR. The more traditional and conservative wing of the party resisted social and political changes. Moderate pragmatists attempted to achieve economic development through the fostering of state capitalism. Those on the left, particularly the COB, pushed for more radical changes such as a system of state socialism.

The MNR's patriarchal leadership never expressed much interest in women's rights or their social agenda. They excluded women from government leadership and decision-making positions. Gueiler was the only woman to lead a militia group during the insurrection, but afterward she was marginalized from political power. The male leadership converted the Barzolas from a grassroots movement into a secret police and shock troop to support government interests, including attacking protesters who fought independently for working-class interests. The Barzolas gained control over marketplaces and excluded those who were not part of their group.

The four main MNR leaders represented separate power bases, and they agreed to a pact to rotate terms in office. The primary leader and 1951 presidential candidate Paz Estenssoro assumed the presidency for the first four-year period from 1952 to 1956. His vice president, Siles Zuazo, was elected for the second term from 1956 to 1960. Both wanted to develop a state capitalist system, but nevertheless, passing the presidency from Paz Estenssoro to Siles Zuazo in 1956 represented one of very few peaceful transfers of political power in Bolivian history.

The MNR struggled to deliver on promises of redistributing wealth and power more equally across society. The revolution's early years had triggered high expectations from lower-class peasants and workers. Facing a dire economic situation, MNR leaders first swung left in their policy decisions and then after 1956 toward the right. Rather than favoring redistributive programs, the government now pursued policies that benefited the middle class and U.S. creditors. In the process of consolidating power, the MNR failed to break the country's dependency on tin exports or build a strong domestic economic base. Tin still provided Bolivia with its major source of revenue. Declines in the mining industry meant that annual per capita income fell from US$118 in 1951 to US$99 in 1959. In addition, agricultural and mineral production fell. Manufacturing rose during the first years of the MNR government but fell after 1957. With the heavy dependence on mining, half of the country's imports were food, which led to skyrocketing food prices and increases in the overall cost of living. The result was 900 percent inflation, with corresponding losses in wage gains.

The MNR appealed to the United States for financial support and eventually became dependent on foreign aid, with the United States providing 30 percent of the country's budget. In retrospect, some scholars have argued that the foreign aid successfully preserved some of the achievements of the revolution such as land reform. Others point out that International Monetary Fund (IMF) conditions reduced the MNR's ability to govern the country on behalf of Bolivian interests. A consequence of these economic and social compromises was that the MNR lost the support of the miners who originally had placed it in power. Furthermore, the MNR increased its persecution of political opponents, and as a result the labor unions lost even more influence over the direction of governmental policy decisions.

According to the original pact, the relatively conservative MNR cofounder and the party's third-highest leader Walter Guevara Arze was to serve from 1960 to 1964. Paz Estenssoro, however, violated their power-sharing agreement and returned to office instead. His goal was to prevent the collapse of the MNR government, but the result of his actions was a fracturing of the MNR coalition. In his second term, Paz Estenssoro offered generous compensation to former mine owners. He also invited new foreign investment into the country on favorable terms. He ended the participation of labor unions in the management of the governmental tin company and reduced welfare benefits to miners. Paz Estenssoro also restored the U.S.-trained army to offset peasant and worker militias, and in the process gained the support of the military, which helped him maintain his hold on power. What could have become a socialist revolution instead emphasized a nationalist agenda, which ironically included increased dependence on the United States. By the end of Paz Estenssoro's second term, the revolution had experienced a reversal of its initial radical orientation.

ROLE OF THE UNITED STATES

The Guatemalan and Bolivian revolutions emerged at the same time and with similar nationalist agendas, but the U.S. government responded in diametrically opposed ways to the two events. At the same time that the CIA was undermining Jacobo Arbenz's administration in Guatemala, the State Department provided funding to prop up the MNR government in Bolivia. On July 6, 1953, the State Department announced a one-year contract to purchase tin from Bolivia's nationalized mines. On October 14, 1953, it followed with an assistance package of $9 million for food, $2 million for emergency technical assistance, and $2.4 million for road construction. By

1954, the United States had contributed $18.4 million to support Bolivia's nationalist reformers while it had spent $20 million to overthrow Guatemala's reformist government. Why would it support one revolutionary experiment but simultaneously pour an equal amount of funds and resources into ending another?

The political processes in Bolivia and Guatemala shared several similarities. Both advanced a modernizing reform program. Leaders in the two countries drew on support from coalitions of the urban middle class, workers, and peasants. Both rejected the traditional oligarchies for their elitism, Eurocentrism, and export-oriented economic liberalism. Instead, they used state power to redirect economic development toward a domestic focus. Finally, the two countries had the highest concentration of Indigenous peoples in the Americas, and both attempted to integrate them into mainstream society.

Still, Bolivia and Guatemala had very significant differences. The Bolivian MNR represented a more successful case of accommodation, due to the country's history, the personalities of the leaders, their skill at engaging in diplomacy, and differences in perceived national interest. In short, Bolivian leader Paz Estenssoro was willing to collaborate with the United States, while in Guatemala, Arbenz was not. U.S. diplomats excelled at drawing the MNR's pragmatic leadership to their side and in the process suppressed more radical working-class tendencies.

Communists played a small but crucial role in both countries. Their ideology in both cases could be described as Marxism filtered through a nationalist perspective. Opponents greatly exaggerated the degree of communist influence in the two revolutions, but local leaders responded to those to their left in different manners. Some in the United States called the MNR fascist or communist (and sometimes both at the same time), but communists had only a small presence in both governments and did not hold any significant positions of leadership. Early on, Paz Estenssoro maintained fascist affiliations, and Stalinists opposed the MNR. Paz Estenssoro was apprehensive of a powerful left, and as a result the United States did not have as much fear of the MNR. In contrast, in Guatemala, Arbenz needed communist support to counter right-wing opposition to his government. In fact, had he relied more heavily on the communists, he may have been able to withstand both domestic and U.S. opposition and maintain himself in office.

Geography also plays a role in explaining the difference in U.S. response to the two revolutionary movements. Guatemala is located on the Caribbean basin that the United States has long considered to be at the heart of its geopolitical sphere of influence. In contrast, as a landlocked country deep in the heart of South America, Bolivia was more distant and had less strategic significance for the United States.

Economic concerns cannot be overlooked, and they provide a compelling explanation for the contrasting responses to reform movements in the two countries. The Dulles brothers and others in the Eisenhower administration had significant financial and personal interests in the United Fruit Company, whose lands Arbenz had expropriated in Guatemala. On the other hand, the Bolivian tin mines that the MNR nationalized were the property of Simón Patiño and other Bolivians. Furthermore, the

United States had a surplus of tin and did not have an immediate concern with supply. As a result, the expropriation of the tin mines did not have as much of an impact on U.S. economic interests as did Arbenz's policies in Guatemala.

Bolivia also had the advantage of witnessing U.S. actions against Arbenz as he launched a reform program in Guatemala. As a result, in the context of the 1950s Cold War, the MNR was careful not to alienate the United States, and in fact they actively sought out diplomatic recognition from the colossus of the north. The MNR deliberately did not move against medium-sized U.S.-owned mines and other economic interests that were not related to the key tin mining sector.

Unlike Guatemala, the MNR significantly reduced the size of the military and allowed the growth of militias—a force that perhaps could have kept Arbenz in office in the face of a military coup. A weak military meant the United States could not turn to it to remove the MNR from office. The alternatives to the MNR were more radical Marxist groups, and none of them were preferable to the United States over the MNR. A return of U.S. military aid after 1957 allowed a strengthening of the armed forces to the point where in 1964 they were able to overthrow the MNR government and retake power. An important lesson for a successful revolution is to dismantle elements of the previous regime that present a threat to the new regime's hold on power.

In the end, however, explaining varying U.S. foreign policy actions is not always an exercise in evaluating a rational thought process. U.S. policy-making officials had a limited understanding of Latin America, and they failed to develop a clear, logical, or consistent policy toward the region. Those policy shortcomings were evident in Cuba after the triumph of their revolution in 1959 and most directly led to the failure of the Bay of Pigs invasion in 1961.

COUP

The original 1952 MNR pact called for the Trotskyist labor leader Lechín to assume the presidency in 1964. Unlike Paz Estenssoro and Siles Zuazo, who favored a capitalist model, Lechín advocated taking Bolivia in a socialist direction. Neither the United States nor the Bolivian military wanted an avowed Marxist as president. In response, Paz Estenssoro sought to retain power so that financial aid from the United States would continue to flow to the country. When Paz Estenssoro attempted to change the constitution so that he could be reelected, the military stepped in and brought the MNR's twelve years in government to an end. Paz Estenssoro's desire to keep everyone happy led to no one being satisfied and his eventual downfall.

Coup leader General René Barrientos Ortuño (1919–1969) had been one of the original supporters of the MNR revolution. In power, a now more conservative Barrientos decapitated worker and peasant organizations through the imprisonment and exile of their leadership. The army occupied the mines, fired many workers, and slashed the wages for those who remained, although not for the administrators. The MNR had turned to moderate reformist policies to head off more profound, transformative revolutionary changes, but the result was a repressive military dictatorship that emphasized export-oriented trade at a detriment to internal economic development that would favor workers' interests. The left's failure to mobilize and empower the peasants as part of a revolutionary movement's popular base opened them to manipulation first by the MNR and then by Barrientos for their own political ends.

In 1966, the famous guerrilla leader Ernesto Che Guevara arrived in Bolivia to launch a hemispheric revolution, but he failed to connect with leftist miners or rally peasants to his cause. Barrientos brought in a U.S.-trained military force that captured and executed Guevara in October 1967. Barrientos was killed in a plane crash in 1969, and a series of other military dictators followed him in power. The most significant, and the most brutal, was Hugo Banzer Suárez (1971–1978), who repressed labor and peasant organizations and tripled Bolivia's foreign debt. In 1979, Gueiler was appointed as the interim head of state, the first and only woman in Bolivia to have that role and only the second in Latin America, before being overthrown in a right-wing military coup. Despite her previous affiliation with the progressive wing of the MNR, her short time in office did not result in any lasting changes.

Bolivia did not return to a civilian government until 1982 with the election of Siles Zuazo. The former MNR leader had broken with Paz Estenssoro in 1964 when he had attempted to maintain himself in power. Siles Zuazo took office at the head of a leftist alliance, but Bolivia descended into significant economic difficulties. Reversing his earlier political stances, Siles Zuazo responded with neoliberal economic measures that weighed most heavily on the working class. Society was deeply fragmented, and a tiny minority of politicians and business people made policy decisions that would benefit their own economic interests.

In 1985, Paz Estenssoro once again won election to the presidency and returned the MNR to power. He was now older and more conservative than during his first terms in office. He implemented harsh neoliberal austerity measures that slashed government subsidies for public services and privatized the mines and state-owned companies that he had helped nationalize thirty years earlier. The government understated the value of the industries and then sold them at fire-sale prices to politically connected members of the upper class. One economic objective was to stop hyperinflation through the destruction of labor unions that could advocate for working-class interests. The result was a decline in living standards for most Bolivians, an increase in the country's indebtedness, an upward redistribution of wealth, and an accompanying rise in socioeconomic inequality.

A series of MNR and other conservative governments ruled Bolivia for the next twenty years. Their neoliberal economic policies undermined working-class interests, which led to powerful protests that rocked the country. Critical observers note that democracy requires much more than elections; it also requires broad public participation. Although the MNR had implemented universal suffrage during their first time in power, they subsequently ruled against the economic interests of the majority of the country's population. The MNR that held power in the 1980s and 1990s was distant from that which had led the 1952 insurrection.

In 2005, leftist labor leader Evo Morales rode waves of protests against the MNR's neoliberal policies to a successful campaign for the presidency. In office, Morales redirected Bolivia's natural resources to meet local needs rather than to benefit foreign economic interests. His government began to fulfill the long-delayed and betrayed promises of the 1952 MNR revolution.

SUMMARY

Some scholars point to the 1952 MNR revolution as the second great revolution in Latin America after the Mexican Revolution. Observers debate to what extent it was a social or political revolution. Some describe it as an unfinished or incomplete process, and in particular emphasize the failures of leadership to consolidate a progressive political process. It followed a path similar to that of revolutionaries in Guatemala and initially appeared to have learned from some of the shortcomings that their counterparts in Central America had experienced. The MNR was more successful in dismantling previous political structures and courting the support of the U.S. government. After about a decade in power, however, both experiments ended in military coups.

Moderates in Bolivia co-opted the socialist promises of the 1952 revolution, and the 1964 military coup terminated any hopes for additional progressive changes to benefit the country's impoverished and marginalized populations. Continual problems of fragmentation and division plagued the MNR during its twelve years in office. The party suffered from a legacy of vertical forms of leadership that failed to consolidate popular participation in the revolutionary project. At the same time, radicals failed to consolidate their revolutionary agenda to press for the creation of a new society. Once workers and peasants gained their immediate goals of better salaries, working conditions, and access to land, they stopped fighting for more profound transformations of society and the revolution stalled and eventually reversed course.

DISCUSSION QUESTIONS

How did the Chaco War spark the MNR revolution?

Was the MNR conservative, centrist, or leftist?

Was the MNR revolution a grassroots movement, or one based in the middle class?

Was U.S. involvement in Bolivia significant in determining the direction of MNR policies?

How do the Guatemalan and Bolivian revolutions compare?

FURTHER READING

Bolivia's is the most understudied of the Latin American revolutions. The best works focus on broader issues rather than the MNR revolution itself. We still need a good contemporary synthetic overview of the revolution.

Alexander, Robert J. *The Bolivian National Revolution*. New Brunswick, NJ: Rutgers University Press, 1958. An early study by a leading political scientist while the MNR was still in power.

Barrios de Chungara, Domitila. *Let Me Speak! Testimony of Domitila, a Woman of the Bolivian Mines*. New York: Monthly Review Press, 1978. Story of a woman who became politically active through her work in the mines.

Gotkowitz, Laura. *A Revolution for Our Rights: Indigenous Struggles for Land and Justice in Bolivia, 1880–1952*. Durham, NC: Duke University Press, 2007. An important study that examines how Indigenous peasants shaped the MNR revolution.

Grindle, Merilee, and Pilar Domingo, eds. *Proclaiming Revolution: Bolivia in Comparative Perspective*. Cambridge, MA: Harvard University David Rockefeller Center for Latin American Studies, 2003. Collection of essays on the causes of the MNR revolution on its fiftieth anniversary.

Hylton, Forrest, and Sinclair Thomson. *Revolutionary Horizons: Popular Struggle in Bolivia*. London: Verso, 2007. Highly readable overview of Bolivia's history with a particular emphasis on an Indigenous perspective.

John, S. Sándor. *Bolivia's Radical Tradition: Permanent Revolution in the Andes*. Tucson: University of Arizona Press, 2009. An analysis of the origins, internal dynamics, and trajectory of Bolivia's Trotskyist Revolutionary Workers Party (POR).

Lehman, Kenneth. *Bolivia and the United States: A Limited Partnership*. Athens: University of Georgia Press, 1999. Expert synthesis of U.S.-Bolivian relations.

Lora, Guillermo. *A History of the Bolivian Labour Movement, 1848–1971*. Cambridge: Cambridge University Press, 1977. A classic examination of Bolivian labor written by Bolivia's leading Trotskyist leader.

Malloy, James. *Bolivia: The Uncompleted Revolution*. Pittsburgh: University of Pittsburgh Press, 1970. A standard study of the MNR that argues that the 1952 revolution has yet to be completed.

Young, Kevin A. *Blood of the Earth: Resource Nationalism, Revolution, and Empire in Bolivia, 1927–1971*. Austin: University of Texas Press, 2017. Examines role of popular mobilizations in determining government resource-extraction policies.

FILMS

Blood of the Condor (*Yawar Mallku*). 1969. A dramatization of an incident in which foreign development workers sterilized Quechua women without their consent as part of a birth-control program.

The Courage of the People. 1971. This film reenacts a 1967 miners' strike in the company town of Siglo XX, using many of the original strikers and their families.

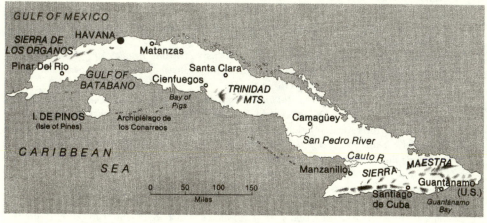

Cuba

5

Cuban Revolution, 1959–

KEY DATES

1898	Cuban independence from Spain
1934–1944	Fulgencio Batista in power
March 10, 1952	Batista returns to power in military coup
July 26, 1953	Fidel Castro leads failed attack on Moncada Barracks
August 1955	Founding of the 26th of July Movement
November 25, 1956	Castro returns to Cuba on the *Granma* with eighty-two fighters
March 13, 1957	Failed Revolutionary Directorate attack on presidential palace in Havana
January 1, 1959	Batista leaves for exile in Miami
January 8, 1959	Guerrillas enter Havana
May 17, 1959	Agrarian reform law
April 15–19, 1961	Failed U.S.-backed Bay of Pigs invasion
April 16, 1961	Castro proclaims socialist character of revolution
December 2, 1961	Castro publicly embraces Marxism-Leninism
February 4, 1962	Organization of American States (OAS) expels Cuba
October 1962	Cuban Missile Crisis
1965	Refounding of Cuban Communist Party
1970	Ten-million-ton sugar harvest
1975	Family Code
1980	Mariel boatlift
July 31, 2006	Fidel Castro temporarily transfers powers due to illness
February 24, 2008	Raúl Castro replaces brother Fidel as Cuban president
December 17, 2014	Cuba and United States reestablish diplomatic relations
November 25, 2016	Fidel Castro dies after long illness

The 1959 Cuban Revolution was the most successful, longest lasting, and furthest reaching of the twentieth-century revolutions in Latin America. On July 26, 1953, Fidel Castro led an attack on the Moncada Barracks in Santiago in eastern Cuba that he hoped would spark a popular uprising against the corrupt Fulgencio Batista (1901–1973) dictatorship. The assault was timed to coincide with the centennial of independence hero José Martí's (1853–1895) birth and designed to appeal to nationalist sentiments. After the uprising failed, Castro went into exile in Mexico where he met the Argentine Ernesto "Che" Guevara who had just witnessed the coup against Jacobo Arbenz in Guatemala. Guevara, who subsequently became the Americas' most renowned guerrilla leader and theoretician, argued that revolutionaries should arm the masses and not hesitate to execute their opponents who had repressed the population. His policies ensured Cuba's survival even as the new revolutionary government's extensive land reform program and expropriation of foreign industries led to the failed 1961 U.S.-backed Bay of Pigs invasion.

As revolutionary leaders consolidated their control over the island, they radicalized and extended reforms, often with dramatic results. Gains in education and healthcare led to socioeconomic indicators that rivaled those of the industrial world, sometimes surpassing the United States. Critics complained, however, that this was done at the cost of individual liberties. Although strong by developing world standards, Cuba failed to reach its goal of an industrialized economy.

INDEPENDENCE

Cuba has a perfect environment for sugar production, and this commodity has long provided a cornerstone of the island's economy. Sugar production began on the island during the Spanish colonial period, but it did not become an important export crop until the end of the eighteenth century. The dramatic growth of sugar in Cuba is intimately tied to the history of Haiti. A slave revolt (discussed in the first chapter) began on the neighboring island in 1791 and eventually destroyed its sugar economy. Before the Haitian Revolution, sugar production had made that island the most valuable colony in the world. With Haiti's independence from France in 1804, many French planters moved to neighboring Cuba in order to continue profiting from the sugar industry.

Cuba did not gain independence from Spain in the early nineteenth century together with its other colonial possessions. Unlike in the rest of the Americas, the increase in sugar exports from Cuba meant that it did not face economic pressure to separate itself from European colonial control. In addition, as Spain lost the rest of its American empire, its military and political infrastructure became entrenched on the Caribbean island. Various attempts to free Cuba from Spanish control throughout the nineteenth century all failed.

By 1850, Cuba produced one-third of all the sugar in the world. Even though it remained a Spanish colony, it became thoroughly dependent on the United

States. Seventy percent of Cuba's trade was with its neighbor to the north, and three-fourths of that was in sugar. Since large plantations were more economical than small ones, sugar production stimulated centralization of the industry. Sugar also required a large capital outlay, a small skilled managerial class, and a large unskilled labor force. These dynamics led to a reliance on African slave labor. As a result, slavery persisted in Cuba until 1886, more than twenty years after the Civil War in the United States and well after the institution's disappearance in most of the rest of the world.

The writer José Martí led the Cuban struggle for independence, both in a political sense from Spain and in an economic sense from the United States. He was the child of a Spanish colonial official but came to identify with Cuban nationalists. Martí spent much of his time in exile, including working as a journalist in the United States, where he was radicalized by the 1886 Haymarket Square massacre in Chicago that led to the execution of a group of anarchists. Martí returned to Cuba to fight for independence, only to be killed in battle on May 19, 1895. He was subsequently seen as revolutionary nationalist who worked against economic dependency and for political independence. Martí famously proclaimed, "Revolution is not what we begin in the jungle but what we will develop in the republic." Had he survived, he would have guided subsequent Cuban history in a more positive direction.

Martí's dream of a politically and economically independent Cuba was thwarted when the United States intervened in 1898 in order to ensure that the island remained within its sphere of influence. Although the United States pledged not to annex the island, as some territorial expansionists had long desired, the United States controlled Cuba's internal affairs through the addition of the Platt Amendment to its constitution. This legislation gave the United States "the right to intervene for the preservation of Cuban independence, the maintenance of a government adequate for the protection of life, property and individual liberty." The growth of radical student movements and leftist political parties eventually led to the abrogation of the Platt Amendment in 1934.

BATISTA REGIME

In 1934, Sergeant Fulgencio Batista assumed power in a military coup with the tacit support of the U.S. government. Batista largely ruled through puppet presidents and then as an elected leader from 1940 to 1944 before temporarily stepping down. The Partido Ortodoxo (Orthodox Party) campaigned in the 1952 elections against the massive corruption and political patronage of the previous two elected administrations. When the populist reform party appeared positioned to win, Batista once again took power in a military coup. Back in office, Batista oversaw a period of uneven modernization and growing social inequalities. His base of support was in the army, but he gradually lost backing from the broader public. Batista censored the media and executed thousands of political opponents to quell discontent with his corrupt and repressive administration. The United States provided Batista with financial, military, and logistical support in his battle against a perceived communist threat.

In the 1950s, Cuba was trapped in a sugar-based, monoculture export economy that was dependent on the cyclical nature of external, particularly U.S., markets. Furthermore, Cuba's sugar industry was stagnating. It suffered from structural unemployment and underemployment due to the nature of a four-month harvest that left workers without a steady income for the other two-thirds of the year. While many urban dwellers were fairly well off, those in rural areas suffered grinding poverty. The extreme inequalities in the country fueled a sense of social injustice.

The Cuban economy suffered from extreme U.S. corporate control. Foreigners owned more than 80 percent of the country's utilities, mines, cattle ranches, and oil refineries, as well as half of the public highways and 40 percent of the sugar industry. Similar to Mexico on the eve of its revolution, in 1958 U.S. investment on the island reached one billion dollars. The situation was ready to explode.

MONCADA BARRACKS

On July 26, 1953, Fidel Castro led an attack of mostly young people on the Moncada army barracks in the eastern Cuban city of Santiago. He had engaged in the audacious and arguably foolhardy action with the hope that it would spark a popular uprising across the island. Militarily, the attack was a miserable failure. Of the 160 participants, eighty, including Fidel and his brother Raúl, were captured within three days. More than sixty were killed, some in the attack and others after being brutally tortured in prison. The assault on Moncada took place on the centennial of José Martí's birth. Castro referenced the independence leader twelve times in his courtroom defense that supporters smuggled out of prison and published as *History Will Absolve Me*. He concluded the speech with the famous proclamation, "Condemn me—it does not matter. History will absolve me." He successfully turned his defeat into a clarion call for revolution.

The Cuban government sentenced Castro and his coconspirators to lengthy prison terms. For Castro, it was a time of reading, reflecting, and developing ideas. Castro argued that political independence was not sufficient for the island to realize its potential. Rather, as Martí had advocated, Cuba also needed to gain its economic independence from the United States. This led the revolutionary leader to examine issues of imperialism and colonialism. Castro's interpretation foreshadowed the 1960s dependency theory critique that the flow of natural resources from the periphery to an industrial core would underdevelop Latin America's economies. A political revolution was necessary to change this economic situation.

After an intense international campaign for Castro's release, the Cuban government freed him on May 15, 1955, along with the rest of his coconspirators. The revolutionary leader left for exile in Mexico,where he continued to develop his plans to overthrow Batista's government. Together with his brother Raúl and the Argentine

Ernesto Che Guevara, Castro founded the Movimiento 26 de Julio (M-26, 26th of July Movement), named after the date of the attack on the Moncada Barracks. The rebels began preparations for an armed revolution. Their ideology included an embrace of democracy, humanism, pluralism, anti-imperialism, and nationalism.

In December 1956, Castro returned to Cuba with eighty-two fighters on the yacht *Granma*. Frank País, a revolutionary leader of the urban underground in Santiago, led an uprising that was to coincide with the arrival of the boat. Unfortunately, the yacht did not arrive on time due to a rough sea and the sailors' inexperience. Without the coordinated activity, Batista's troops crushed País's uprising. When the guerrilla force finally landed, it came under intense fire from the Cuban military. It was almost defeated, and only eighteen of the original fighters survived. Those who did, however, took to the remote mountains of Sierra Maestra, where they gathered strength as local peasants joined their struggle.

The pro-Soviet Cuban Communist Party initially criticized Castro's guerrillas as misguided, adventurous, and lacking a theoretical cohesion and ideology. The communists did not believe that Cuba had the necessary level of capitalist economic development for a socialist revolution. They argued that launching an armed struggle in this context was irresponsible, was recklessly adventurous, and would inevitably result in futile bloodshed. Instead, they favored working within the system. In fact, some communists had accepted cabinet posts in Batista's first government in the 1930s, a fact that led to their being discredited in the eyes of the guerrillas. Many communists did not join forces with the guerrillas until it was clear they could militarily defeat Batista.

A parallel resistance to the Batista regime grew out of students and members of the middle class organized into an urban underground called the *llano*, or plains, in contrast to the rural guerrillas in the *sierra*, or mountains. A March 13, 1957, attack by the Directorio Revolucionario (Revolutionary Directorate) on the presidential palace in Havana, which mimicked the previous assault on Moncada on the other side of the island, failed to kill Batista. In response, Batista increased his repression of dissidents, including the murder of País on July 30, 1957. His death was a severe blow to the 26th of July Movement.

A planned general strike for April 1958 also failed, which shifted more attention to the rural guerrillas fighting in the eastern Sierra Maestra. As they gained strength, the guerrillas began a march toward Havana in the west with the goal of cutting the island in two. At the end of December 1958, Guevara defeated Batista's forces in the battle of Santa Clara in the middle of the island. In one of the war's most famous actions, the guerrillas derailed and captured an armored train with weapons and reinforcements that the regime had sent against the insurgents. For the first time the rebels controlled a major city, and this achievement signaled the end of Batista's regime. On January 1, 1959, Batista fled into exile in Miami. A week later, the rebel army rolled into Havana. They occupied key military posts, and the guerrillas called for a general strike to put down any remaining support for the dictatorship. Castro arrived in Havana to the cheers and open embrace of the general public that was ready to see Batista ousted from power.

The guerrilla army won due to their persistence and the disciplined nature of their forces. They had gained the sympathy of the masses, including the peasants, workers, and urban middle class, thanks in part to the corrupt and repressive nature of Batista's military. Although the military was brutal, naked force alone was not enough to maintain control over the country. Rather, the military disintegrated when it faced a well-organized opposition. Weak conservative institutions, including a Catholic Church that played less of a public role in Cuba than elsewhere in Latin America, meant fewer barriers to the revolution's success. The guerrillas enjoyed the advantages of strong, competent, and motivated leadership. In addition to being idealistic, capture would have meant certain torture and possible death. That potential fate made members of the guerrilla force even more determined to stand firm in their struggle.

BIOGRAPHY: FIDEL CASTRO, 1926–2016

Fidel Castro at a September 22, 1960, meeting of the UN General Assembly
Source: Photo by Warren K. Leffler, Library of Congress Prints & Photographs Online Catalog

Fidel Castro led the guerrilla 26th of July Movement that toppled the pro–United States Fulgencio Batista dictatorship in Cuba in 1959. He was born in 1926 to a wealthy Spanish farmer in northwestern Cuba. His childhood helped him see the vast differences between social classes. Castro attended a Jesuit school, where he received a fine education and excelled as an athlete. He studied law at the University of Havana in the 1940s, where he gained a reputation as a student activist. During his time as a student, he had his first taste of an armed revolution when he participated in an ill-fated invasion of the Dominican Republic in an attempt to remove the strongman Rafael Trujillo from power.

As a student in the 1940s, Castro studied the writings of Karl Marx and the Cuban communist party founder Julio Antonio Mella. Nevertheless, his political activities in the 1950s were those of a revolutionary nationalist and not a Marxist. Castro's justification for the July 26, 1953, assault on the Moncada army barracks highlights the native roots of the Cuban Revolution. In his courtroom defense *History Will Absolve Me*, Castro referred frequently to Cuban independence hero José Martí. Although Martí's social and political program of national reform is evident in this speech, Castro's ideology also shows the influence of other thinkers. Castro read the Peruvian

Marxist José Carlos Mariátegui, among others, while in prison from 1953 to 1955. Consistent with Mariátegui's thought, Castro approached Cuba's problems in a nondoctrinaire manner, with a flexible attitude as to how to foment a revolutionary consciousness in an underdeveloped country. Not only was Castro an anti-imperialist, revolutionary nationalist in the tradition of Martí, but also like Mariátegui he stressed the revolutionary potential of the peasantry and affirmed the value of African and Indigenous cultural expressions.

Despite these intellectual influences, Castro was better known for his organizing skills and charismatic leadership than his political theory or his strength as an ideological thinker. He studied and learned the military strategy that he carried out in his guerrilla warfare in the Sierra Maestra mountains from Augusto César Sandino's fight against the U.S. Marines in Nicaragua in the late 1920s. Like Sandino, Castro relied on a strategy of flexible organization that could adapt to changing conditions. Both guerrilla leaders depended on a sympathetic peasant base to support their fight.

Castro emphasized that the new Cuban Communist Party formed in 1965 would be built on Cuban ideas and methods. At the same time, the party drew on a mixture of both Latin American and European influences. Although Cuba developed close economic ties with the Soviet Union, it refused to submit political control of its communist party to a foreign ideology. In spite of parallel interests with Moscow, Cuba maintained an independent foreign policy.

DOCUMENT: "FIRST DECLARATION OF HAVANA," 1960

In August 1960, the Organization of American States (OAS) met in Costa Rica to declare that Cuba's revolutionary government presented a threat to the Americas because of its links with the Soviet Union. Several days later, more than a million people gathered in Havana's Revolutionary Square to demonstrate their approval of the following declaration in support of the revolution.

Close to the monument and to the memory of José Martí in Cuba, free territory of America, the people, in the full exercise of the inalienable powers that proceed from the true exercise of the sovereignty expressed in the direct, universal and public suffrage, has constituted itself into a national general assembly.

Acting on its own behalf and echoing the true sentiments of the people of our America, the national general assembly of the people of Cuba:

1. Condemns in all its terms the so-called "Declaration of San José," a document dictated by North American imperialism that is detrimental to the national self-determination, the sovereignty and the dignity of the sister nations of the continent.

2. The national general assembly of the people of Cuba energetically condemns the overt and criminal intervention exerted by North American imperialism for more than a century over all the nations of Latin America, which have seen their lands invaded more than once in Mexico, Nicaragua, Haiti, Santo Domingo, and Cuba; have lost, through the voracity of Yankee imperialism, huge and rich areas, whole countries, such as Puerto Rico, which has been converted into an occupied territory; and have suffered, moreover, the outrageous treatment dealt by

the marines to our wives and daughters, as well as to the most exalted symbols of our history, such as the statue of José Martí.

This intervention, based upon military superiority, inequitable treaties and the miserable submission of treacherous rulers throughout one hundred years has converted our America—the America that Bolívar, Hidalgo, Juárez, San Martín, O'Higgins, Sucre, and Martí wanted free—into an area of exploitation, the backyard of the political and financial Yankee empire, a reserve of votes for the international organization in which the Latin America countries have figured only as the herds driven by the "restless and brutal North that despises us."

The national general assembly of the people declares that the acceptance by the governments that officially represent the countries of Latin America of that continued and historically irrefutable intervention betrays the ideals of independence of its peoples, negates its sovereignty and prevents true solidarity among our nations, all of which obliges this assembly to repudiate it in the name of the people that echoes the hope and determination of the Latin American people and the liberating patriots of our America.

3. The national general assembly of the people of Cuba rejects likewise the intention of preserving the Monroe Doctrine, used until now, as foreseen by José Martí, "to extend the dominance in America" of the voracious imperialists, to better inject the poison also denounced in his time by José Martí, "the poison of the loans, the canals, the railroads. . . ."

Therefore, in the presence of a hypocritical **Pan-Americanism** that is only the dominance of Yankee monopolies over the interests of our people and Yankee manipulation of governments prostrated before Washington, the assembly of the people of Cuba proclaims the liberating Latin-Americanism that throbs in Martí and Benito Juárez. And, upon extending its friendship to the North American people—a country where Negroes are lynched, intellectuals are persecuted and workers are forced to accept the leadership of gangsters—reaffirms its will to march "with all the world and not with just a part of it."

4. The national general assembly of the people declares that the help spontaneously offered by the Soviet Union to Cuba in the event our country is attacked by the military forces of the imperialists could never be considered as an act of intrusion, but that it constitutes an evident act of solidarity, and that such help, offered to Cuba in the face of an imminent attack by the Pentagon, honors the government of the Soviet Union that offered it, as much as the cowardly and criminal aggressions against Cuba dishonor the government of the United States.

Therefore, the general assembly of the people declares, before America and before the world, that it accepts and is grateful for the support of the Soviet Union's rockets, should its territory be invaded by military forces of the United States.

5. The national general assembly of the people of Cuba categorically denies the existence of any intent whatsoever on the part of the Soviet Union and the Chinese People's Republic to "use Cuba's political and social situation . . . to break the continental unity and endanger the unity of the hemisphere." From the first to the last shot, from the first to the last of the twenty thousand martyrs who died in the struggles to overthrow the tyranny and win revolutionary control, from the first to the last revolutionary law, from the first to the last act of the revolution, the people of Cuba have acted with free and absolute self-determination, and therefore, the Soviet Union or the Chinese People's Republic can never be blamed for the existence of a revolution which is Cuba's firm reply to the crimes and wrongs perpetrated by imperialism in America.

On the contrary, the national general assembly of the people of Cuba maintains that the policy of isolation and hostility toward the Soviet Union and
the Chinese People's Republic, promoted and imposed by the United States
government upon the governments of Latin America, and the belligerent and
aggressive conduct of the North American government, as well as its systematic
opposition to the acceptance of the Chinese People's Republic as a member of
the United Nations, despite the fact that it represents almost the total population of a country of over six hundred million inhabitants, endanger the peace and
security of the hemisphere and the world.

Therefore, the national general assembly of the people of Cuba ratifies its
policy of friendship with all the peoples of the world, reaffirms its purpose of
establishing diplomatic relations with all the socialist countries and, from this
moment, in the full exercise of its sovereignty and free will, expresses to the government of the Chinese People's Republic that it agrees to establish diplomatic
relations between both countries, and that, therefore, the relations that Cuba
has maintained until now with the puppet regime, which is supported in Formosa
by the vessels of the Seventh Fleet, are hereby rescinded.

6. The national general assembly of the people reaffirms—and is certain of doing
   so as an expression of a view common to all the people of Latin America—that
   democracy is incompatible with the financial oligarchy, racial discrimination, and
   the outrages of the Ku Klux Klan, the persecutions that prevented the world from
   hearing for many years the wonderful voice of Paul Robeson, imprisoned in his
   own country, and that killed the Rosenbergs, in the face of the protests and the
   horror of the world and despite the appeal of the rulers of many countries, and
   of Pope Pius XII, himself.

The national general assembly of the people of Cuba expresses its conviction that democracy cannot consist only in a vote, which is almost always fictitious and manipulated by big land holders and professional politicians, but
in the right of the citizens to decide, as this assembly of the people is now
deciding, its own destiny. Moreover, democracy will only exist in Latin America
when its people are really free to choose, when the humble people are not
reduced—by hunger, social inequality, illiteracy, and the juridical systems—to
the most degrading impotence.

For all the foregoing reasons, the national general assembly of the people of
Cuba:

Condemns the latifundium, a source of poverty for the peasants and a backward and inhuman agricultural system; condemns starvation wages and the
iniquitous exploitation of human labor by immoral and privileged interests;
condemns illiteracy, the lack of teachers, of schools, of doctors and hospitals,
the lack of protection of old age that prevails in Latin America; condemns the
inequality and exploitation of women; condemns the discrimination against the
Negro and the Indian; condemns the military and political oligarchies that keep
our peoples in utter poverty and block their democratic development and the
full exercise of their sovereignty; condemns the handing over of our countries'
natural resources to the foreign monopolies as a submissive policy that betrays
the interests of the peoples; condemns the governments that ignore the feel-
ings of their people and yield to the directives of Washington; condemns the
systematic deception of the people by the information media that serve the
interests of the oligarchies and the policies of oppressive imperialism; condemns
the news monopoly of the Yankee agencies, instruments of the North American
trusts and agents of Washington; condemns the repressive laws that prevent

workers, peasants, students and intellectuals, which form the great majority of each country, from organizing themselves and fighting for the realization of their social and patriotic aspirations; condemns the monopolies and imperialistic organizations that continuously loot our wealth, exploit our workers and peasants, bleed and keep in backwardness our economies, and submit the political life of Latin America to the sway of their own designs and interests.

In short, the national general assembly of the people of Cuba condemns both the exploitation of man by man and the exploitation of under-developed countries by imperialistic finance capital.

Therefore, the national general assembly of the people of Cuba proclaims before America:

The right of the peasants to the land; the right of the workers to the fruit of their work; the right of children to education; the right of the ill to medical and hospital attention; the right of youth to work; the right of students to free, experimental, and scientific education; the right of Negroes and Indians to "the full dignity of Man"; the right of women to civil, social and political equality; the right of the aged to a secure old age; the right of intellectuals, artists, and scientists to fight, with their works, for a better world; the right of nations to their full sovereignty; the right of nations to turn fortresses into schools, and to arm their workers, their peasants, their students, their intellectuals, the Negro, the Indian, the women, the young and the old, the oppressed and exploited people, so that they may themselves defend their rights and their destinies.

7. The national general assembly of the people of Cuba proclaims: The duty of peasants, workers, intellectuals, Negroes, Indians, young and old, and women, to fight for their economic, political and social rights; the duty of oppressed and exploited nations to fight for their liberation; the duty of each nation to make common cause with all the oppressed, colonized, exploited peoples, regardless of their location in the world or the geographical distance that may separate them. All the peoples of the world are brothers!

8. The national general assembly of the people of Cuba reaffirms its faith that Latin America soon will be marching, united and triumphant, free from the control that turns its economy over to North American imperialism and prevents its true voice from being heard at the meetings where domesticated chancellors form an infamous chorus led by its despotic masters.

Therefore, it ratifies its decision of working for that common Latin American destiny that will enable our countries to build a true solidarity, based upon the free will of each of them and the joint aspirations of all. In the struggle for such a Latin America, in opposition to the obedient voices of those who usurp its official representation, there arises now, with invincible power, the genuine voice of the people, a voice that rises from the depths of its tin and coal mines, from its factories and sugar mills, from its feudal lands, where *rotos* [a member of the exploited labor force of Chile, generally of Indigenous and European descent], *cholos* [a member of the exploited labor force of Peru, generally of Indigenous and European descent], *gauchos* [Argentine cowboys, an exploited class that forms the backbone of the cattle industry of that country], *jíbaros* [a member of the much exploited agricultural labor force of Puerto Rico], heirs of Zapata and Sandino, grip the weapons of their freedom, a voice that resounds in its poets and novelists, in its students, in its women and children, in its vigilant old people.

To that voice of our brothers, the assembly of the people of Cuba answers:

"Present!" Cuba shall not fall. Cuba is here today to ratify before Latin America and before the world, as a historical commitment, its irrevocable dilemma: *Patria* [homeland] or Death!

9. The national general assembly of the people of Cuba resolves that this declaration shall be known as "The Declaration of Havana."

Havana, Cuba, Free Territory of America, September 2, 1960

Source: Fidel Castro, *The Declaration of Havana* (n.p.: 26th of July Movement in the United States, 1960).

ROLE OF WOMEN

Women have long been acknowledged for their important roles in in the Cuban Revolution. They participated in urban underground movements that challenged Batista's government even before the 1953 attack on the Moncada Barracks. In September 1958, the rebel army created an all-women's platoon named after Mariana Grajales, an icon of Cuba's independence struggles. Grajales's sons José and Antonio Maceo served as generals in the Ten Years' War (1868–1878) that had failed to free Cuba from Spanish control. During that war, Grajales ran field hospitals and provided provisions to the soldiers. She was hailed for her willingness to enter the battlefield to aid wounded soldiers, playing a role similar to the soldaderas in the Mexican Revolution. In the guerrilla insurrection, the Grajales platoon went beyond such support roles to engage in active fighting and in the process challenged the chauvinism of some of their male counterparts.

Two women, Haydée Santamaría and Melba Hernández, participated in the assault on the Moncada Barracks. Similar to Castro, Santamaría's parents were small-scale Spanish sugar planters, and she participated in almost every step of the revolutionary process. Santamaría was captured and imprisoned in the aftermath of the Moncada attack. She told her prison guards that if her brother Abel and fiancé Boris Luis Santa Coloma, who had been tortured and killed after their arrest, would not speak, neither would she. In May 1954, the government released Santamaría from prison and she continued her work on behalf of the revolutionary movement. She arranged for the publication of Castro's speech *History Will Absolve Me* as a pamphlet and assisted in its distribution as a propaganda tool.

In 1956, Santamaría helped organize the November 30 Santiago uprising with Frank País that was to correspond with the arrival of the *Granma* on the Cuban coast. Even though she had never before left the island, in 1958 revolutionary leaders sent her to Miami to organize on behalf of the M-26 and to buy guns for the guerrillas. Despite having only a sixth-grade education, after the triumph of the revolution Santamaría founded and ran the publishing house Casa de las Américas. She built it into one of the most important cultural institutions in Latin America, one that was renowned for its published literary works. When militants formed the Cuban Communist Party in 1965 she was selected as a member of its central committee and remained at the highest levels of leadership for her entire life. In 1967, she presided over the Organización Latinoamericana de Solidaridad (OLAS, Latin American Solidarity Organization). Until her death in 1980, she played a key role in fostering the development of the revolution.

Celia Sánchez was another key founder of the Cuban Revolution. Her father's occupation as a doctor provided her with the necessary cover and connections to work effectively as a member of the 26th of July Movement in her native province of Manzanillo. She helped make arrangements for the landing of the *Granma* and was responsible for organizing their reinforcements in Cuba. She helped supply the rebels with weapons, food, and medical supplies. In 1957, she was the first woman to join the guerrilla army and rose through the ranks to become a member of the rebel army's general staff.

Sánchez was Castro's closest companion. After the triumph of the revolution, she served as secretary to the presidency of the Council of Ministers and in the Department of Services of the Council of State. Together with Santamaría, in 1965 Sánchez was named to the communist party's central committee. With her death from lung cancer in 1980, Castro lost a close confidante. Some observers say he was never the same afterward.

GUERRILLAS IN POWER

The war ended when Batista fled in the face of the guerrillas closing in on Havana on New Year's Day 1959. That triumph was only the beginning of the revolution. The task of radically transforming the country's political and economic structures now lay before them. The guerrillas enjoyed enormous popular backing, but supporters had widely divergent views on what should happen next. Castro embraced a Pan-Americanist ideology, much like that which Latin American independence leaders Simón Bolívar and José Martí had previously expressed. In addition, he was an anti-imperialist. He argued that property should not be seen as a right but should serve a social function in society. This ideology led to a nationalization of subsoil rights and public services, as well as an agrarian reform that included the expropriation of large estates and the formation of cooperatives. The revolutionaries wanted to remake the country so that the island's resources benefited the people rather than foreign capitalist enterprises.

Destruction of the Old Regime (1959–1962)

The initial goal of the guerrillas once they took power was to consolidate their domestic political position. The leaders sought to centralize power, as well as to crack down on their political opposition and a conservative press that could challenge their hold on power. The guerrillas engaged in public trials and executed thousands of Batista's henchmen. They purged conservatives and strengthened their alliances with communists in order to fortify their political position. These moves created a polarized split between moderate and radical supporters of the revolution. Moderates only wanted to remove Batista from power and disagreed with implementing far-reaching social reforms based on a leftist ideology.

One of the first policy objectives of the new revolutionary government was to socialize the economy. Similar to the Guatemalan and Bolivian revolutions earlier in the decade, a centerpiece of the agenda was an expansive agrarian reform program that was designed to alter extreme inequalities in landholding. A May 1959 decree restricted the size of estates. Property holdings were so concentrated that the law affected 85 percent of the farms on the island. The government distributed the land in small plots to individual farmers for subsistence agriculture as well as creating agricultural cooperatives for commercial purposes. Much of this land distribution took place in Oriente (eastern) province, where the guerrillas had enjoyed early peasant support for their struggle.

The government kept some of the large estates intact and converted them into state farms. The same workers continued to work the land, but now they were paid better wages and labored under improved working conditions. The government sought to diversify agricultural production in the country. An elusive goal was to gain agricultural self-sufficiency through the transfer of farmland from sugarcane production to cotton, rice, soybeans, and peanuts.

The new revolutionary government prioritized a redistribution of income. They achieved this goal through lowering rents and utilities, and providing free social services to the public. As a result, wages rose 40 percent, purchasing power rose 20 percent, and unemployment disappeared as all members of society were assured of a job. The revolutionaries also sought to gain economic independence from the United States. They achieved this through the nationalization of foreign industries, including telephone companies, oil refineries, factories, utilities, sugar mills, banking, and urban housing. The redistributive policies later targeted Cuban-owned businesses.

The revolutionary government converted military barracks into schools and hospitals to liberate rather than oppress the population. They opened private beaches and social clubs to the general public. The Cuban revolutionaries developed new organizations to solidify support for their political project. The government founded neighborhood vigilance committees called Comités de Defensa de la Revolución (CDR, Committees for the Defense of the Revolution) to promote social welfare and report on counterrevolutionary activity. The Organizaciones Revolucionarias Integradas (ORI, Integrated Revolutionary Organizations), founded in March 1962, unified Castro's 26th of July Movement, the communist party, and the Revolutionary Directorate. At the end of 1963, revolutionaries formed the Partido Unificado de la Revolución Socialista (PURS, United Party of the Socialist Revolution) to replace the traditional communist party. Rather than a mass party, it had a selective membership and joining the party was a privilege. In 1965, PURS became the new Cuban Communist Party. Youth organizations also flourished after the triumph of the revolution. Founded in October 1960, the Association of Young Rebels grouped youth in the ORI. In April 1962, the association was changed to the Unión de Jóvenes Comunistas (UJC, Union of Young Communists).

In 1960, Vilma Espín, a wealthy chemist from the privileged sectors of society who was married to Raúl Castro, founded the Federación de Mujeres Cubanas (FMC, Federation of Cuban Women) with official government support. Early goals of the FMC included domestic programs, such as providing women with domestic skills. As with other early second-wave feminists, the FMC emphasized the importance of education and an eradication of misogynist ideas. As the revolution advanced, the FMC sought to involve women in society, on both an economic and a political level. The FMC drew women out of the home and into the workforce and also involved them in the political formation of a collective society. The FMC emphasized the importance of day care for children so that women could join the labor force.

The revolution provided many gains for women. Many young women left their homes to teach in the famous 1961 literacy campaign and for the first time experienced a broader world. More than half of those who learned to read and write in the campaign were women, and with these new skills they joined medical and biological fields in large numbers. Even so, women remained responsible for domestic labor in the house, the so-called second-shift work. This incentivized young and poor women to demand more, and they criticized the FMC leadership for approaching women's problems from the perspective of privileged sectors of society. They wanted mutual respect from their husbands and equally shared responsibilities in domestic tasks and the care of children. The FMC leaders wanted to preserve the nuclear family, but many poor women saw the traditional family structure as a cause of oppression. Furthermore, the FMC was organized from the top down to consolidate women's support for the revolution, rather than dedicated to transforming gender relations.

The revolutionaries established a new pattern of foreign relations. Some leaders saw the Soviet Union as their most logical ally and protector from their revolution's inevitable conflict with the United States. Cuba resumed diplomatic relations with the Soviet Union, and in turn the Soviets agreed to buy Cuban sugar, although they faced the liability of the long distance in shipping the commodity. In addition, Cuba actively pursued an internationalist foreign policy. The government supported guerrilla movements in Panama, Nicaragua, the Dominican Republic, and Haiti. Scholars have debated whether an idealist drive to spread a socialist revolution motivated support for other insurgencies, or whether more pragmatic considerations of gaining international allies and deflecting U.S. attacks away from Cuba inspired those policy decisions.

Cuba strongly supported anticolonial movements in Africa. In 1960, Cuba provided military aid and medical personnel to the Algerian National Liberation Front in its fight against French colonialism. The following year, military instructors arrived in Ghana to assist guerrillas fighting in Upper Volta, and in 1965 Che Guevara led a contingent of two hundred combat troops to join a revolutionary struggle in Congo. Most significant was Cuba's military support in the 1970s for Angolan independence and against the intervention of apartheid South Africa. Operation Carlota, named after the leader of an 1843 slave uprising, included a massive airlift of Cuban volunteer troops to assist in the defense of the Angolan capital of Luanda.

The new Cuban government's domestic and international policies soon strained relations with the United States. Some scholars view a confrontation as inevitable because of the United States' long-standing desire to control the island's destiny. Revolutionary show trials and the expropriation of large estates with the agrarian reform legislation, particularly those that U.S. citizens and corporations owned, only heightened these tensions. Relations spun downward when, in May 1960, the Cuban officials told Texaco, Standard, and Shell to process crude oil that the government had received from the Soviet Union in their refineries. The U.S. government instructed the companies to refuse, and in June the Cubans expropriated the refineries. In response, President Dwight Eisenhower ended Cuba's sugar quota, which only led the Cuban government to expropriate more U.S.-owned properties. In October, the United States placed a trade embargo on Cuba that included the banning of U.S. exports to the island. The action led to more Cuban expropriations, including Sears, Coca-Cola, and U.S.-owned nickel deposits. In January 1961, shortly before leaving office, Eisenhower broke diplomatic relations with the neighboring republic. It is unclear who started the diplomatic tit for tat between the two countries, but once the downward spiral began, it was very difficult to halt the deterioration of relations.

Soon after Batista's departure, the Central Intelligence Agency (CIA) initiated funding of exile groups to remove the revolutionaries from power. During the summer of 1960, the CIA set up training camps in Guatemala. In March 1961, the newly installed president John F. Kennedy granted approval for the CIA-created force to invade the island. The mercenaries entered at the Bay of Pigs on April 15, 1961, but the Cuban forces were waiting for them on the shore known as Playa Girón. The invasion was poorly planned and executed, and quickly turned into a rout. By April 19, the Cubans had defeated the invaders. The wealthy anticommunist exiles promised Kennedy that the locals felt betrayed by the direction the revolution had taken and would rise up against Castro's government. The common people, however, had benefited substantially from the revolution's social programs and redistributive policies. They had no desire to return to Batista's repressive and exclusionary regime that the invading mercenary force represented. The Bay of Pigs failure highlighted just how little policy makers in the United States understood Cuban realities.

The U.S. defeat at Playa Girón increased Castro's support and prestige in the country. This led to a quickened pace of reforms and a radicalization of the revolution. The failed invasion provided Castro with a convenient opportunity to announce the socialist nature of the revolution. On December 2, 1961, Castro proclaimed, "I am a Marxist-Leninist, and I will be a Marxist-Leninist until the last days of my life." Observers subsequently debated whether Castro had been a communist from the beginning of the revolution and as an astute politician had waited until the proper moment to make such a proclamation, or whether the irrational responses of the country's logical trade partner, the United States, had forced him to turn to the

Soviet Union. If this were the case, a declaration of the socialist nature of the revolution was merely a ploy to gain Soviet support.

On February 4, 1962, the United States convinced the Organization of American States (OAS) to expel Cuba from its membership. Over the course of the next several years, the U.S. government strong-armed most of the other American republics to break diplomatic relations with the Cuban government. A notable exception was Mexico, and its maintenance of relations with the communist island provided the United States with a convenient backdoor for secret talks with its adversary.

On October 22, 1962, Kennedy ordered a quarantine of the island and demanded the dismantling of missiles that the Soviets were installing on the island to protect the Cubans from a threatened U.S. invasion. The two governments disagreed whether the missiles were of a defensive or offensive nature. During the course of a tense period of thirteen days known as the Cuban Missile Crisis, the U.S. military pressed for an invasion of the island, but instead the two superpowers reached an agreement. The Soviet Union agreed to remove the missiles, and in exchange the United States pledged not to invade the island and to remove missiles they had installed in Turkey that were targeted at their adversary. For its part, the Cuban government wanted to be treated as an equal to the superpowers on the global stage, and they were bitterly upset when the two Cold War opponents negotiated behind their backs. Although the Cubans and Soviets would subsequently present a public face as warm allies, the betrayal permanently altered their diplomatic relations even as their economic ties strengthened.

After the Cuban Missile Crisis, the United States never again attempted to invade the island, but it did continue its attacks against the government, targeting the economy, infrastructure, and even civilians. The CIA repeatedly launched raids against the country's refineries and ports, and infiltrated enemy agents onto the island. Most famous were the assassination plots against government leaders. Operation Mongoose included such ludicrous plans as providing Castro with exploding cigars or powder that would make his beard fall off. Although these plots were not successful in overthrowing the Cuban government, fighting off the constant attacks made it more difficult for revolutionaries to advance their progressive social programs.

Period of Experimentation (1962–1966)

The Cuban revolutionaries enjoyed various advantages that allowed them to proceed quickly with the implementation of their socialist experiment soon after they had dismantled the previous regime. The revolutionary war had caused relatively little destruction of life and property, and so they did not need to put as much effort into reconstruction as would have been the case after a long and drawn-out civil war such as Mexico had faced. Cuba had a fairly well developed infrastructure, which provided a strong groundwork on which to build socialist programs. These factors helped offset the economic damage of the U.S. embargo.

A large portion of the Cuban workforce had been unionized before the revolution, and this provided them with a good deal of political consciousness. Even in the sugarcane fields, Cuba's proletarianized agricultural workforce had a high level of class consciousness. Workers had sympathy with the revolutionary changes sweeping the country, as well as motivation to participate actively in them. For the most part, rather than demanding land, an agrarian proletariat fought for better working conditions and wages. The government used idle farmland and increased industrial capacity to improve living standards. According to some Marxists, on the eve of the revolution Cuba had not a feudal mode of production but rather an advanced capitalist economy, albeit one based on rural sugar production rather than an urban industrial workforce. From this perspective, Cuba witnessed not a peasant revolt but precisely the type of proletarian revolution that resulted from working-class alienation, although in this case it was rooted in a rural rather than urban proletariat. If this were indeed the case, an additional but little-understood advantage that Cuba enjoyed was the presence of the proper, objective economic conditions that orthodox Marxists had long argued were necessary for a socialist revolution. Possibly for this reason Cuba experienced more success while other revolutions failed.

Despite these advantages, the Cuban revolutionaries faced a range of problems. Many of the economic experts and ablest technicians came from the professional class that identified with the previous capitalist system. The implementation of socialist policies led them to leave the country. The inexperience of the revolutionaries who replaced the trained professionals led to errors and caused disruptions in the economy and the smooth functioning of society. The revolutionaries pumped money and resources into rural housing and infrastructure, but poor planning led to a waste of scarce resources. The revolutionaries in their drive to socialize the economy ignored the private sector, which still comprised half of the country's economy. Government policies that favored affordable food for consumers forced farmers to sell their crops at low prices. Those farmers who were motivated by the marketplace had few incentives to increase their production.

The U.S. embargo also caused crippling shortages that damaged the economy. With a cutoff of trade with the United States, the Cubans shifted their trade relations to Eastern Europe, which introduced a series of problems. Their new trade partners were geographically more distant than their close neighbors to the north, which added significantly to shipping costs and logistics. Language barriers also introduced challenges. Shifting to new suppliers generated unforeseen problems with replacement parts as equipment aged, since the global metric-sized threads and tools were not compatible with the machinery produced in the United States.

Redistribution of resources from the upper to lower classes also created new challenges. A growth in disposable income led to increases in consumer demands. Before the revolution, meat consumption was largely limited to the wealthy, but now many more people had access to the wages necessary to buy meat. This demand led to the overkilling of cattle, which lowered their reproduction rates and soon resulted in scarcities. A lack of imports also caused shortages. A lack of consumer products forced the introduction of rationing in March 1962. The rationing was to be a short-term measure designed to ensure equal and democratic access to resources until production could rebound and make such distribution systems unnecessary. Half a century later ration booklets were an institutionalized aspect of the revolution and pointed to one of its major shortcomings.

Even with these limitations, a good deal of idealism motivated the revolutionaries. Che Guevara in particular emphasized what he called the "New Socialist Man" who would be motivated by moral rather than material incentives. Instead of working hard to improve an individual's economic situation, Guevara encouraged people to focus on the improvement of society. This goal required a significant shift away from the fundamentally liberal goals of improved wages and working conditions toward a class consciousness that instead fought for a change from a capitalist to a communist mode of production. Guevara set a personal example by sacrificing time with his family on weekends to participate in voluntary work projects. Despite his best efforts, the Cuban public did not respond entirely well to the emphasis on moral incentives. By 1969, the government moved to a more pragmatic mix of engaging both material and moral incentives.

The positive socioeconomic gains of the period of experimentation proved to be quite remarkable. The revolutionaries quickly built a strong education system. The 1961 literacy campaign sent out more than one hundred thousand workers to teach almost a million people to read and write, and became a model that other countries subsequently followed. The campaign was built on such slogans as, "If you know, teach; if you don't know, learn"; "Every Cuban a teacher; every house a school"; and "The people should teach the people." The literacy campaign followed in the footsteps of José Martí's statement, "To know how to read is to know how to walk." The campaign raised literacy levels from 76 percent before the revolution to 96 percent in 1962, the highest in Latin America and a level that equaled that of wealthy industrialized countries. This high percentage of people who could read and write indicated that the island was essentially free of illiteracy.

By mid-1961, all Cuban schools were public and free. The rapid growth of literacy and educational opportunities introduced a new set of challenges. The government could not keep up with the demand for schools and faced shortages of teachers and classroom materials. Increased access to educational opportunities contributed to a growth in social aspirations. Many people were no longer content to work in agriculture as unskilled laborers. Instead, they sought to put their new education to use in professional fields. Their upwardly mobile aspirations created shortages as previously unskilled workers moved away from productive sectors of the economy.

Government policies that shifted resources from the wealthy to the poor overcame class disparities and significantly shrank income inequalities. The difference in wages between the highest- and lowest-paid individual in a company could not be any greater than four to one. The revolution improved access to affordable and decent housing. By law, every family had the right to one—and only one—dwelling. While the law clamped down on speculation, the country could not meet the demand for housing. At the same time, housing conditions improved dramatically, particularly with access to running water, sewage systems, and electricity.

Revolutionary leaders struggled to overcome persistent social problems such as sexism and racism. Official government policy was to outlaw racial and gender discrimination, and to embrace the country's African cultural heritage as an important component of Cuban identity. The result was dramatically increased opportunities for those previously excluded populations. On an informal level, however, racism continued to be an issue, which showed the limitations of attempting to legislate moral attitudes. Even though discrimination was still a problem, it was not as pronounced as in other countries, such as Brazil. Significant advances were made to attack formal gender inequalities that created new opportunities for women in the public sphere, although, as with racism, those policies often did not reach into private household domains. Furthermore, government and military positions remained overwhelmingly in the hands of men of European descent—the same social class that had always run the country.

One of the greatest accomplishments of the Cuban Revolution was a dramatic expansion and improvement in the medical system. The government increased the healthcare budget tenfold, which allowed for free medical services for everyone. The healthcare system provided for one doctor for every two hundred people, and about half of these doctors were women. The revolution increased the number of nurses by a factor of ten and tripled the number of dentists. Many of these gains were in rural areas where communicable and preventable diseases were particularly devastating for the local population. As a result of these policies, many diseases such as tuberculosis, malaria, smallpox, diphtheria, and typhoid were eradicated or greatly reduced. Socioeconomic indicators improved dramatically, including lowering infant mortality and raising life expectancy rates to the highest levels in Latin America. Cuba's successes led to advances rivaling those of wealthy industrialized countries. Cuba's medical system achieved many of these gains because of a focus on preventative rather than curative medicine, which is a much more efficient, cost effective, and successful method of treatment.

Building on the gains in the field of medicine, Cuba subsequently became a leader in biotechnology research. Latin Americans turned to Cuba when they could not receive appropriate treatment in their own countries. The export of doctors and medicine became an important generator of hard currency for the country. At the same time, the U.S. embargo made access to some medicine difficult for common people on the island, even as Cuban technicians developed new treatments that could have saved lives in the United States had they been allowed to export them. The Cold War standoff hurt private citizens on both sides of the Florida Straits.

Return to Sugar (1966–1970)

In the 1960s, government experiments with a move to a socialist mode of production took Cuba through a series of policy reversals that ultimately hindered the island's economic development. At first, the country made steps away from dependency on an export market toward self-sufficiency, but that came at a cost. Because of favorable weather and because many of the perennial sugarcane stands had been at the peak of their production cycle, Cuba enjoyed good harvests in 1960 and 1961. With the move to experimentation and the push to diversify agricultural production, in 1962 Cubans plowed up the best cane land to plant other crops for domestic consumption. The resulting harvest was the worst since 1955.

In the mid-1960s, government planners reversed course and decided that it would be better to work with Cuba's historic strength as a sugar island. Their plan was to use the earnings from the export of that commodity to purchase needed goods as imports. They hoped that profits from sugar production could be used to fund a desired industrialization of the economy. In pursuit of that goal, the government announced a target of a ten-million-ton harvest in 1970. It was an audacious objective and if achieved it would be, by far, the largest harvest in the country's history. By the late 1960s, Cuba was realistically capable of producing only six million tons of sugar. The goal of ten million tons would be very difficult to meet.

The return to sugar production faced a series of significant challenges. The sugar industry now lacked the administrative and technical expertise that it had enjoyed in the 1950s before the revolution. Many professionals who were the most skilled at running the industry had left the country, and others now worked in different sectors of the economy. Much of the equipment necessary for a large-scale harvest had been abandoned, and a lack of proper maintenance rendered much of it useless. An absence of parts from the United States to repair the old mills meant bringing them back on-line would be expensive. Little had been invested domestically in maintaining or growing sugar production. For the most part, sugar stands had not been replanted and those fields that remained were well past their prime.

By 1968 the number of professional cane cutters from before the triumph of the revolution had fallen by about 80 percent. Cutting sugarcane required notoriously difficult and physically demanding manual labor, and, once given the educational and economic opportunities, many of those previously engaged in that backbreaking task left to explore better prospects. To replace this lost labor, the Cuban government redirected people and resources from other sectors of the economy to the sugar industry. Professionals with no skill or experience in cutting sugar were sent to the fields even as they continued to earn their normal salaries that were higher than what sugar cutters would typically have been paid. Not only did that prove to be an expensive way to harvest the crop, but also it caused significant disruption and turmoil in other sectors of the economy. One of the major failings of the sugar policy was the diversion of resources away from other productive industries.

In 1970, Cuba had its largest sugar harvest ever, but rather than a success, that attempt proved to be a significant failure for the government. Rather than producing 10 million tons, Cubans only harvested 8.5 million tons—well short of its goal. The process of reaching so high ruined the industry, and as a result subsequent harvests were poor. On July 26, 1970, at the annual commemoration of the assault on the

Moncada Barracks, Castro admitted defeat and took personal responsibility for the disaster. Even as the failure led to a loss of Castro's prestige, he vowed that the government would make the necessary changes to achieve success in the future. He reemphasized the need for sacrifice and the inevitability of hardships. He pledged that the revolution would go on.

Sovietization of Cuba (1970–1990)

With the bungled attempt to achieve economic self-sufficiency and industrial development through sugar production, Cuba turned to the Soviet Union for support. The island subsequently became heavily dependent on the Soviets. Among other support mechanisms, the Soviet Union increased its subsidies for the Cuban economy through running trade deficits with the island and paying above-market prices for its sugar.

In the 1970s, Cuba also depersonalized and institutionalized its revolution. The military was restructured along traditional hierarchical lines. The government emphasized an increased importance of popular organizations. Workers were more closely involved in the setting of production goals and other workplace policies. The implementation of work quotas helped raise production levels. These changes also meant a move away from Guevara's emphasis on moral incentives to material ones. But as a result of this shift, the growth of the **gross national product (GNP)** more than doubled to an impressive growth rate of 10 percent a year from 1971 to 1975.

The 1975 Family Code provided landmark legislation that dictated equality in the home, in addition to the workplace, in politics, and in access to educational opportunities. The code stipulated equality in marriage and declared that the husband must share 50 percent of household work and responsibility for raising children. The code's maternity law was the most far reaching in the world. It provided for an eighteen-week paid maternity leave and guaranteed that a woman could return to her previous job after taking a year without pay. The legislation contributed to an increase in access to childcare, educational levels, and opportunities for women in the labor force.

The 1975 Cuban Communist Party congress also engaged gender issues with a statement supporting full equality for women. Critics complained that these policy statements, as with earlier ones that outlawed racism, only had a limited effect on changing deeply ingrained cultural mores that were played out privately in the domestic sphere. To codify these gains, the party congress drafted the country's first socialist constitution. That document provided legal guarantees for equal rights both inside and outside the home, which led to an expansion of women's participation in the public sphere.

The new constitution also reorganized the country's administrative structures, including the creation of popularly elected assemblies at the municipal, provincial, and national levels. The national assembly elected a council of state that in turn named the head of government and the first secretary of the communist party.

Fidel Castro served in those roles for the next thirty years. Foreign critics complained that this system made little distinction between the government and the party, while supporters countered that it was a Cuban system that worked well in their domestic environment.

In the late 1970s, poor management and quality control led to a shrinking of the GNP from previously high growth rates to about 4 percent a year. Furthermore, consumer goods, such as shoes and TVs, declined in quality. Facing fewer economic opportunities, in 1980 ten thousand people crowded into the Peruvian embassy with the hope of being able to leave the island. After a period of tense negotiations, the United States agreed to admit those who wanted to leave en masse. The resulting exodus of 125,000 people came to be known as the Mariel boatlift, so called for the port from which they departed. The Cuban government took advantage of the opportunity to empty its prisons of criminals as well as to deport others with significant mental illnesses. The government learned to play crises to their benefit. In the 1980s, the government moved to attack economic problems through a diversification of exports. Cuba also gained access to hard currency by reexporting Soviet crude oil that had been brought into the country to be refined. As a result, the economy began to rebound.

Special Period (1990–Present)

The collapse of the Soviet Union in 1991 led to the most significant economic crisis in Cuba's history. The loss of the island's major trading partner meant that between 1989 and 1992, average income dropped by 45 percent. Government planners responded with what they denominated "a special period in peacetime" to confront the crisis. The revolution faced the liabilities of not achieving economic self-sufficiency. Many observers thought that the days of the socialists in power were limited, although the next quarter century demonstrated that these pundits had significantly underestimated the revolution's resilience.

In 1992, the Cuban national assembly made sweeping changes to government policies. The alterations included stating a respect for freedom of religion in what was a highly secular society. This opening to religion was a reflection of the influence of liberation theology among revolutionary movements in Central America that broke with the Catholic Church's traditional alliance with a conservative oligarchy. For the first time, the communist party would accept those professing a religious belief into its ranks. The assembly also made changes to its centrally planned economy, including permitting joint venture enterprises with foreign capital. In particular, this opened up the way for companies in Spain, Canada, and Mexico to invest in the Cuban tourist trade, which had grown into a significant generator of revenue for the government.

Meanwhile, the U.S. government continued to put pressure on Cuba even as the island moved toward a normalization of relations with the rest of the world. The original rationalization in 1960 for a blockade of the island was because of its ties to the Soviet Union. After the disappearance of the Soviet Union, Cuba's backing of revolutionary movements justified the policy, even though that support had ended decades earlier. The 1992 Torricelli Act and the 1996 Helms-Burton Act extended the trade embargo to U.S. subsidiaries in third countries and barred ships that had docked in Cuba from entering the United States for a period of 180 days. In essence, any country that wanted to trade with the United States had to boycott Cuba. Meanwhile, significant global diplomatic pressure grew against the extraterritorial reach of U.S. policies. Latin American leaders called for the embargo to end, and it was repeatedly condemned in the United Nations. In 1992, Cuba introduced a resolution that denounced the embargo as a violation of the UN Charter. That year, fifty-nine countries voted for the resolution, three opposed it, and the rest abstained. In 2015, 190 countries joined Cuba in opposition to the embargo, with only Israel aligning with the United States in support for a policy of isolation. The following year, both the United States and Israel abstained from the vote, with all other UN member countries supporting the resolution. Only Republican Party control over the legislative process in the United States kept the antiquated embargo in place.

Even with all of these changes, Cuba continued to be highly dependent on the production of sugar. The government attempted to modernize production but was hindered by a lack of oil imports that had largely reverted agricultural production back to animal traction. In the 1980s, the sugar harvest averaged eight million tons a year, but in 1992 it fell to less than five million tons, the lowest in twenty-five years. A monoculture export economy continued to be an albatross around the island's neck.

In July 2006, Fidel Castro temporarily passed power to his brother Raúl because of an illness. Almost two years later, Fidel formally stepped aside to allow Raúl to assume his offices of president and first secretary of the communist party. In February 2013, the national assembly reelected Raúl for another five-year term of office. At the same time, the younger Castro announced that he would not seek reelection in 2018. In office, Raúl liberalized many of the policies that his brother had followed. Supporters cheered the policies as necessary to come to terms with the realities of the contemporary world, whereas others worried that those steps would take the island back to capitalism with all of its associated problems of inequality and poverty.

In a stunning reversal of half a century of estrangement, on December 17, 2014, U.S. president Barack Obama and Cuban president Raúl Castro made simultaneous announcements that the two countries would reestablish diplomatic ties. That was a first step toward a full normalization of relations that included the removal of Cuba from the State Department's list of state sponsors of **terrorism** and an opening of embassies. In March 2016, Obama made a historic visit to the island. Ending the embargo, however, would require legislative action, and the Republican-dominated congress gave no indication that it would be willing to take such a step. Meanwhile, Cuba continued to insist that the United States end its embargo of the island and return the Guantánamo naval base that it had occupied since 1903. Although significant advances had been made, more work needed to be accomplished before Cuba would realize its long-standing goal of convincing the United States to recognize its rights as a sovereign and independent country.

After a long illness, Fidel Castro died on November 25, 2016. Cubans marked his death with solemn tributes, but after having largely been out of the public eye for a decade his passing had minimal effect on government policy. Perhaps the historic commander had become irrelevant, but more likely observers had overstated the personalized nature of the revolution. Before dying, the legendary leader had instructed that no monuments should be constructed in his honor. The profound social transformations that he had launched had been sufficiently institutionalized that they would survive in his absence, even in the face of an antagonistic Donald Trump administration in the United States.

ASSESSMENT

The Cuban Revolution is often considered a success, both because of its dramatic socioeconomic achievements and because of its ability to survive for more than half a century in the face of intense imperialist pressure from its giant neighbor to the north. Some criticize Cuba for its lack of freedoms, including shortcomings in democratic governance. The debates often revolve around issues of what should be a priority: national sovereignty, individual freedoms, or access to social guarantees such as education and healthcare. A perennial question is why individual freedoms and social rights seem to be mutually exclusive goals and whether they necessarily need to be so.

Opponents of the Cuban Revolution often frame their goals in terms of a return to democratic governance. Historically, however, political participation in Cuba, as in the rest of the Americas, had been limited to a very small base of wealthy, literate, male landholders of European descent. Until the mid-twentieth century, those enjoying full citizenship rights comprised less than 5 percent of the population. Democracy in a broader sense refers not only to elections but also more importantly to equal access to resources and a say in how those are used and distributed in society. By dramatically expanding access to education and healthcare, Cuba's revolutionary government increased people's ability to enjoy the country's wealth.

Opponents also criticize restrictions on freedom of speech in Cuba. In reality, all societies have parameters and ground rules by which people are expected to play. A common saying in Cuba was, "Within the revolution everything; outside the revolution nothing." Government leaders argue that social advances in the country were due to the revolution and that members of society should not bite the proverbial hand that feeds them. The revolution's supporters also contend that crackdowns on dissent were necessary because of the unceasing U.S. attempts to overthrow the Cuban government. Before the revolution, Cuba had neither individual freedoms nor social equality. Many of those opposed to the revolution want to return to a prerevolutionary situation in which they control everything. A dilemma for supporters was how to increase individual freedoms without strengthening a conservative opposition committed to a rollback of the revolution's progressive advances.

Economically, Cuba faced difficulties in breaking from its historic pattern of dependence on a monoculture sugar-export economy. Critics charged that Cuba simply moved from the orbit of the United States to that of the Soviet Union. After the fall of the Soviet Union, Cuba became increasingly dependent on the tourist trade for hard currency. As a result, foreigners enjoyed privileged access to resources, including better food and Internet access, that were largely not available to Cubans. While politically conscious Cubans acknowledged the need for sacrifices to ensure the survival of the revolution, others complained that this system of "tourist apartheid" was in essence a continued form of imperial domination over the island.

SUMMARY

The Cuban Revolution represents a watershed in twentieth-century revolutions in Latin America and forms a gold standard by which other movements are judged. Not only was it the most thoroughgoing of the revolutions, but also it was the most sustainable. Cuba was unique in many ways that would seem to make it an unlikely location for a revolution. It was the last Spanish colony to gain its freedom, and it was also close to the United States. Those same factors may also explain its success. As the target of imperialist powers, nationalism was a strong force in Cuba. The nationalist impulses also raise questions of how explicitly a *communist* revolution it was, and whether a turn to the Soviet Union was an opportunistic move in the face of U.S. opposition. In any case, the revolution confronted overwhelming odds to survive for more than half a century. It achieved remarkably high health, education, and other socioeconomic indicators that rivaled those of industrialized countries. In the eyes of many Latin Americans, Cuba's ability to survive and flourish in the face of imperialist pressures made it a model worthy of respect.

DISCUSSION QUESTIONS

What was the relative importance of the urban underground in the removal of Batista from power?

Was Fidel Castro a humanist, nationalist, socialist, or communist? Did his ideology change after he took power?

Why did the revolution succeed in Cuba?

How important was leadership to the success of the Cuban Revolution? Was it a people's revolution or one of individual leaders? What degree of credit should go to Fidel Castro and Che Guevara for its success?

Did women play a unique role in the Cuban Revolution?

Was the purging and execution of supporters of the old regime justified? Was this necessary for revolutionary success or contrary to the ideals of a revolution?

Did the USSR play an imperial role or one of international solidarity in Cuba?

What does democracy mean for Cuba?

FURTHER READING

A very large literature exists on the Cuban Revolution, most of it polemical rather than academic and explicitly partisan in either its support of or its opposition to the revolution. Given the divisive nature of the revolution, it may be impossible—and perhaps even undesirable—to write a neutral account of these events.

Chase, Michelle. *Revolution within the Revolution: Women and Gender Politics in Cuba, 1952–1962.* Chapel Hill: University of North Carolina Press, 2015. Emphasizes the role of women in the Cuban Revolution.

Chomsky, Aviva. *A History of the Cuban Revolution.* Malden, MA: Wiley-Blackwell, 2011. A highly readable and sympathetic survey of the Cuban Revolution.

Cushion, Steve. *A Hidden History of the Cuban Revolution: How the Working Class Shaped the Guerrilla Victory.* New York: Monthly Review Press, 2016. Argues that the working class played a larger role than the rural guerrillas in the Cuban insurrection.

Farber, Samuel. *Cuba since the Revolution of 1959: A Critical Assessment.* Chicago: Haymarket Books, 2011. Criticizes the Cuban Revolution from a leftist perspective.

Geyer, Georgie Anne. *Guerrilla Prince: The Untold Story of Fidel Castro.* 3rd rev. ed. Kansas City, MO: Andrews McMeel, 2001. One of many biographies of the Cuban leader.

Gott, Richard. *Cuba: A New History.* New Haven, CT: Yale University Press, 2004. A broad historical overview of Cuba.

LeoGrande, William M., and Peter Kornbluh. *Back Channel to Cuba: The Hidden History of Negotiations between Washington and Havana.* Chapel Hill: University of North Carolina Press, 2014. An important book about secret negotiations between Cuba and the United States.

Pérez, Louis A., Jr. *Cuba: Between Reform and Revolution.* 3rd ed. New York: Oxford University Press, 2006. Political survey by an eminent Cuban historian.

Pérez-Stable, Marifeli. *The Cuban Revolution: Origins, Course, and Legacy.* 3rd ed. New York: Oxford University Press, 2012. Presents a negative image of the Cuban Revolution.

Stout, Nancy. *One Day in December: Celia Sánchez and the Cuban Revolution.* New York: Monthly Review Press, 2013. Fascinating biography of Fidel Castro's closest companion.

FILMS

Bananas. 1971. Woody Allen as a fictitious and absurd Castro-esque revolutionary.

Cuba Va: The Challenge of the Next Generation. 1993. Young people born after the 1959 revolution discuss the challenge of Cuba's economic crisis in the 1990s.

El Che. 2009. Steven Soderbergh's two-part biopic based on the diaries of guerrilla leader Che Guevara, who led the Cuban Revolution and was later killed in Bolivia.

Fidel. 1969. Activist filmmaker Saul Landau's documentary about Fidel Castro portrays his revolution, his relationship with the people of Cuba, his school years, and the Bay of Pigs incident.

Fidel. 2001. Showtime biography of Fidel Castro's rise to power in Cuba, based on Georgie Anne Geyer's biography *Guerrilla Prince* and Robert E. Quirk's *Fidel Castro.*

Fidel: The Untold Story. 1999. Estela Bravo's documentary celebrates the life and political career of Fidel Castro through archival footage, interviews with Fidel, and commentary by family, associates, former guerrilla fighters, politicians, and historians.

IA—Kuba (*I Am Cuba*). 1964. Soviet film portrays four main stories that depict the rise of the communist revolution in Cuba, including Batista's Havana, the grinding poverty, and the oppression of the Cuban people.

Lucía. 1968. Follows the lives of three different women named Lucía during three different revolutionary periods of Cuba's history: the 1895 Cuban independence war, the 1930s Machado era, and 1960s revolutionary Cuba.

Maestra (*Teacher*). 2013. An examination of young women who taught in rural communities in the 1961 literacy campaign.

Memorias del Subdesarrollo (*Inconsolable Memories/Memories of Underdevelopment*). 1968. A study of Cuban society before and after the revolution as seen through the eyes of a man who is a landlord and self-styled writer.

Strawberry and Chocolate. 1993. A Cuban film that directly engages issues of homophobia.

Chile

6

Chilean Road to Socialism, 1970–1973

KEY DATES

1952	Salvador Allende campaigns for president for the first time
1958–1964	Presidency of conservative Jorge Alessandri
1964–1970	Presidency of Christian Democrat Eduardo Frei
1967	Land reform program
September 4, 1970	Allende wins presidential election
November 3, 1970	Allende takes office
July 17, 1971	Chilean government nationalizes copper mines
March 4, 1973	Popular Unity's vote increases in midterm congressional elections
September 11, 1973	General Augusto Pinochet overthrows Allende in brutal military coup
September 21, 1976	Car bomb kills Pinochet opponent Orlando Letelier in Washington, D.C.
October 5, 1988	Pinochet's loses a plebiscite that would have maintained him in power
March 11, 1990	Pinochet hands power to an elected civilian government
October 16, 1998	Pinochet arrested while recovering from back surgery in a London hospital

Chile is unique in many ways. The country appears as a geographic anomaly on maps. Hugging the western coast of South America, it is squeezed between the high Andean mountains and the Pacific Ocean. It averages less than two hundred kilometers wide, and it measures more than four thousand kilometers long. Henry Kissinger, the presidential assistant for National Security Affairs in the Richard

Nixon administration, once derogatorily described the country as a dagger pointing at the heart of Antarctica. The northern part of the country is the driest region on earth, with some areas never having received any recorded rainfall. That area also has the world's largest-known copper reserves. Most people live in the fertile central valley that enjoys a moderate Mediterranean-like climate. The cold southern regions are home to the Mapuche, who stopped first Inka and then Spanish encroachment into their territory.

In a part of the planet that has suffered through its share of military coups and extraconstitutional changes in administration, before 1973 Chile had long been seen as the most stable and democratic country in Latin America. Whereas governments in other countries often drafted new constitutions to suit their political needs, Chile had a single constitution from 1818 until 1925. Chile enjoyed the longest periods of continuous civilian rule of any Latin American republic. After gaining independence from Spain in 1818 until 1973, the only interruptions occurred in 1891 and between 1924 and 1932.

Chile was the first country in Latin America where an avowed Marxist came to power through constitutional means. Similar to the progressive president Jacobo Arbenz in Guatemala, Salvador Allende won election as president in 1970 and then dramatically accelerated reforms begun under his predecessor. Allende's goal to transform Chile from a capitalist and dependent country into a socialist and independent one within a democratic and constitutional framework delivered significant gains to the lower class at a cost to the upper class. Unsurprisingly, his policies quickly alienated the U.S. government. Nationalization of U.S.-owned copper mines, as with Arbenz's confiscation of the banana lands in Guatemala, prompted Nixon's support for Augusto Pinochet's brutal September 11, 1973, military coup.

The Pinochet military regime that stretched for seventeen long years from 1973 to 1990 brought interpretations of Chile's democratic traditions into question. Historically, the country's electoral process had been corrupt and dominated by a small, conservative minority of wealthy men. Although civilians led most governments, voting restrictions excluded the active participation of the majority of the population. An alternative interpretation pointed to Chile's political stability as a logical outgrowth of its heavy dependence on the export of a single commodity—first nitrate and then copper. A lack of conflict between competing internal economic interests meant that the country did not experience frequent and extraconstitutional changes in power as different power blocs struggled to control the central government, a phenomenon that commonly occurred in other countries. Particularly in the nineteenth century, political stability should not be confused with democratic rule. Instead, an impulse for democratic rule emerged out of leftist political parties and labor unions that fought against the exclusionary economic system that wealthy individuals had imposed on Chile.

Chile returned to civilian rule at the end of Pinochet's dictatorship in 1990, but a new 1980 constitution left significant power in the military's hands. Pinochet's neoliberal economic policies subjected the country to extreme social and economic inequalities. Even the 2000 presidential election of socialist Ricardo Lagos presented a limited challenge to these exclusionary policies. The Chilean experiment with a socialist revolution illustrates the restrictions on achieving profound and radical societal changes within an institutional and democratic framework.

LABOR MOVEMENTS

Chile developed an export-oriented economy that, by the latter part of the nine-teenth century, had become highly dependent on the export of a single product, nitrate, to British markets. Chile provides a classic example of the liabilities of an economy highly dependent on foreign capital and the export of a single commod-ity. Nitrate sales funded the development of state structures and enriched the ruling class while leaving the vast majority of the population economically impoverished, politically powerless, and subject to exploitation and repression. The nitrate industry dramatically expanded the working class, and along with its larger size came a pro-liferation of militant actions to improve their working, living, and social conditions. These workers came to understand that they had class interests distinct from those who owned the mines, controlled the infrastructure, and benefited financially from international trade. The workers became actors in a class struggle that moved beyond issues of pay and working conditions, to ones that dealt with ownership and modes of production. This realization was the setting for the emergence and growth of a working-class consciousness in Chile, especially among the workers in the northern nitrate fields, on the shipping docks at the port of Valparaíso, among the coal miners in southern Chile, and in factories in Santiago.

Workers suffered abject poverty and miserable working conditions that con-tributed to short life expectancies and high infant mortality rates. Miners worked twelve-hour days and were paid on a piecework basis in scrip that could only be used at the company store, where they were charged inflated prices. Companies actively recruited families because married men were less likely to revolt or leave the mines than single males, plus their children could be drafted to work in the mines. The miners suffered in a dangerous, unhealthy, and stressful environment that led to injuries and death from cave-ins and explosions. The miserable working conditions led to strike waves that the mining companies brutally repressed with the slaughter of thousands of protesting workers.

The worst massacre in Chilean history occurred in December 1907 among nitrate workers at Santa María de Iquique. The workers had gone on strike with relatively moderate demands: they called for an end of payment in scrip, a termination of illegal salary deductions, protections for the right to assemble, and improvements in worker safety. The police gave an order to disperse within five minutes but then immediately fired on the crowd, killing thousands of men, women, and children. As with many of the massacres, it was impossible to determine the exact death toll. The massacre had its intended effect of instilling fear into the survivors, who did not want to admit that their family and friends had been targeted for fear that they would also fall under the taint of having engaged in subversive activities. The aristocracy applauded the suppression of the strike because it reestablished social order in the country.

Journalist Luis Emilio Recabarren (1876–1924) founded and edited numerous working-class newspapers, which contributed to the development of a working-class consciousness in the early-twentieth-century nitrate fields. He was also the founder and chief ideologist of numerous labor unions as well as of the socialist and later the communist party. Recabarren was first elected to congress in 1906, but the conservatives refused to seat him because of his revolutionary views. In 1912, Recabarren formed the Partido Obrero Socialista (POS, Socialist Workers Party) that favored the nationalization of private property and the confiscation of church wealth. Recabarren ran for president in 1920, but the government imprisoned him, thereby preventing him from extending his base of support beyond the northern nitrate regions.

In 1921, Recabarren was again elected to congress as a socialist delegate. In congress, Recabarren countered attacks that blamed working-class agitation on foreign agents. He maintained that the working class was itself capable of fomenting revolutionary action and that such militancy had its roots in Chilean history. He demonstrated that labor activism predated the Bolshevik Revolution in Russia by fifteen or twenty years. Instead, he concluded that the capitalist regime had fostered revolutionary attitudes among the workers. He contended that socialism entailed more than the redistribution of wealth from the rich to the poor; it also included changes in mentality to abolish the imaginary rights of private property.

At Recabarren's urging, the POS joined the Communist International in 1922 and transformed itself into the Partido Comunista de Chile (PCCh, Communist Party of Chile). In 1923, Recabarren traveled to the Soviet Union for the Communist International's fourth congress. The successes of the Russian revolution impressed him. The following year, he committed suicide in the face of a military coup and infighting in the communist party that had undermined its ability to defeat the dictatorship. The communists remained the dominant leftist force in Chile throughout the 1920s, but leaders brought the party increasingly in line with the strict dictates of the Communist International. These restrictions from Moscow incentivized left-wing activists to break off into a separate socialist party in 1932. The socialists subsequently took positions that were sometimes more radical than those of the communists.

ELECTIONS

In 1938, Chile was the first and only Latin American country to elect a popular front government. Pedro Aguirre Cerda served as president of the center-left coalition that included the radical, socialist, and communist parties. The competing political interests, however, limited the influence that leftists had in the government. During the 1950s and 1960s, the Chilean left developed one of the most nondoctrinaire ideological positions in Latin America, which contributed to its growing popular support. The left emerged out of a mass party tradition that predated the 1917

Bolshevik Revolution, and it successfully applied lessons it learned from the Cuban Revolution and other world events in a unique and innovative manner.

In 1952, the socialist party ran Salvador Allende as its candidate for president. The socialists had a poor showing, and Allende finished fourth in a field of four candidates. Allende was not bothered by the loss, because his intent was not to win but to lay the basis for future attempts. Six years later, Allende once again ran as the candidate of the socialist and communist parties. This time he made a much better showing and narrowly lost to Jorge Alessandri, who headed a coalition of the traditional liberal and conservative parties. Allende's support had increased fivefold, and only the candidacy of a left-wing splinter party prevented his victory. In Chile's multiparty races, if no candidate won a majority then congress decided the victor, traditionally the top vote getter. Allende had lost by only 33,500 votes out of the 1.2 million cast. Given the narrow defeat, some leftists pushed for Allende to claim power, by extraconstitutional means if necessary. Allende, however, had faith in Chile's traditions and institutional order. He graciously conceded defeat and encouraged congress to designate his conservative rival as president. He would have to try again in the next election.

Eduardo Frei

Allende's strong showing in 1958, together with socialist gains in a by-election, frightened conservatives. As a result, in the 1964 election they abandoned their party and rallied behind the centrist **Christian Democratic** candidacy of Eduardo Frei to prevent a socialist victory. The Christian Democratic Party had only just formed in 1957, and Frei came in third as the candidate for that party in the 1958 election. Now in 1964, with both conservatives and centrists supporting his candidacy, he achieved the rare feat in Chilean politics of winning an outright victory. Even though Frei won 55 percent of the vote, Allende also boosted his percentage of the vote to almost 40 percent, a significant 10 percent increase from six years earlier.

In office, Frei promised a "revolution in liberty." His reformist government was one of the most progressive administrations in Chilean history. Frei's government featured a series of reforms, including an increase in education spending. Most significant was a 1967 agrarian reform program designed to modernize one of Latin America's most archaic rural structures. A predominance of large, ill-managed agricultural estates that produced little forced Chile to import a quarter of its meat, a third of its milk, and a fifth of its wheat. The land reform program expropriated land from feudal-style estates, legalized peasant unions, and encouraged the formation of cooperatives. For many people, the reforms were moving in the right direction but did not make deep enough changes to satiate their growing demands for profound changes in society.

Frei's second reform entailed a partial nationalization of the copper mines. His goal was to strengthen domestic control over the industry and increase earnings from the exports. After the creation of synthetic alternatives contributed to the collapse of the nitrate industry during the First World War, Chile shifted its dependency to copper. Similar to nitrate exports, wild fluctuations of copper prices on the global

market complicated the creation of coherent economic policies. A common saying
was that as copper went, so went Chile's economy. The copper industry was concentrated in a few hands, and mostly in U.S.-based corporations. The Kennecott
Corporation owned the largest copper mine in world. The mine was very profitable,
but its wealth flowed to the United States rather than remaining in Chile. Copper
mining was more capital than labor intensive, which resulted in fewer economic
gains for miners than during the nitrate boom. The dependence on new technology
required extensive capital investment, and the importation of equipment and parts
undermined the potential industrialization of the country. The departure of most of
the copper profits from the country added to growing resentment toward the industry rather than contributing to a development of the domestic economy.

Frei decided that paying for an outright nationalization of the copper mines was
too expensive. Instead, in a scheme called the "Chileanization" of the copper industry, the government bought part ownership in the mines with an eye toward rein-
vesting the profits and doubling production. The Chilean government bought a 51
percent controlling share in the Kennecott mines and 25 percent of Anaconda. The
plan was not as successful as Frei had hoped. Because of the nature of the contracts,
most of the profits continued to flow to the companies and out of the country.

Many of Frei's reforms were funded with foreign aid, but the loans created a
heavy debt burden for the country. In March 1961, John F. Kennedy announced the
Alliance for Progress as a type of Marshall Plan for the Americas. The goal was to
demonstrate the virtues of capitalism, and champion the United States as a model
for economic development. An intent was to make moderate reforms in order to
prevent another policy disaster such as the Cuban Revolution, and to halt Soviet
influence in the region. Chile became a showcase for the program and received more
per capita funding than any other country. The aid came at the cost of U.S. control
over Chile's domestic policies. In 1964, the CIA contributed three million dollars to
Frei's electoral campaign and spent an additional seventeen million in anti-Marxist
propaganda. The propaganda was aimed particularly at women in an attempt to
convince them that an Allende victory would mean the loss of their children and the
breakup of their families.

Despite Frei's best attempts, he failed to satisfy society's growing demands. His
moderate reforms were too extreme for the conservatives and not radical enough for
the leftists, and as a result he was squeezed between the two extremes. Furthermore,
his programs fell short of their announced goals, and a heavy debt load triggered
an increase in inflation. Frei's progressive reforms also strained his relations with his
conservative allies. In the 1965 midterm congressional elections, the vote for the
traditional liberal and conservative parties fell to 12 percent. Their poor showing
resulted in the dissolution of their parties and the reconstitution in 1967 of the
liberal, conservative, and radical parties as the National Party. With a new face, the
conservative bloc delivered a stronger showing in the 1969 congressional elections,
scoring 20 percent of the vote. Even so, the left was steadily gaining support and
rapidly closing a gap with the center.

BIOGRAPHY: SALVADOR ALLENDE GOSSENS, 1909–1973

Salvador Allende was born in the coastal town of Valparaíso, the son of a well-to-do lawyer. His privileged status allowed him to attend medical school. His training as a medical doctor, similar to Che Guevara, made him aware of the deep class divisions in Chilean society. Recognition that a small number of people could afford proper nutrition while the vast impoverished majority could not contributed to his political consciousness. Unlike other revolutionary leaders, Allende was not a charismatic leader. Instead, what distinguished him was a commitment to making revolutionary changes in society through existing institutional structures.

In 1932, Allende helped found the socialist party. Five years later, and only twenty-nine years old, he was first elected to congress. He spent the rest of his life in government. In 1939, he was named minister of health in the center-left popular front government that included socialists and communists. Allende gained recognition for his humanitarian concerns. In

Salvador Allende at 1973 parliamentary elections

Source: Biblioteca del Congreso Nacional de Chile

that post, he helped thousands of refugees from the Spanish civil war resettle in Chile. In 1945, Allende was elected to the senate and served in that body for the next twenty-five years. He used his political position to fight for healthcare and women's rights. Allende gained a good deal of respect in the senate and in 1968 was elected president of the body. In 1970, after three unsuccessful attempts, Allende won the presidency of the country in a three-way race.

Allende argued that Chile's extreme inequalities required rapid changes. Forty percent of the population suffered from malnutrition, and one-third of those who died were children. Three percent of the population earned 40 percent of the income, while half only had 10 percent. The challenge for Allende was, as he said, that "we must make haste—slowly" in order to address these inequalities but within the constraints of the existing institutional order and in a way that would not destabilize the country and bring the entire political project crashing down on itself.

One way to address Chile's problems of poverty and inequality was to end economic dependency on foreigners. He noted that Chile was rich in natural resources and could be a wealthy country but instead was plagued by poverty. The country was trapped in dependent relations with foreign powers, first with the

Spanish during the colonial period, then the British with the nitrate industry in the nineteenth century, and finally with the United States and copper exports in the twentieth century. Allende wanted to break those colonial and neocolonial ties and redirect those resources to develop Chile's internal economy.

Allende was a close friend and ally of the Cuban revolutionary leader Fidel Castro. Allende was not opposed to armed struggle, but he argued that such a violent path was not necessary, and perhaps even counterproductive, in a country such as Chile with strong and stable democratic structures.

As could be expected after spending most of his adult life in politics, Allende was a strict constitutionalist. He openly proclaimed that he was a Marxist, but he also made a distinction between socialism and communism. He declared that socialists would not imitate the Soviet Union. Instead, Chileans would search for their own path toward absolute independence. He contrasted a socialist emphasis on searching for appropriate policies to address national issues with the communists' internationalism that followed dictates from Moscow.

DOCUMENT: "POPULAR UNITY GOVERNMENT: BASIC PROGRAM," 1970

The Popular Unity drafted a detailed platform for the 1970 presidential elections in which it analyzed the main problems facing Chile and the type of socialist transformation it envisioned for the country. The North American Congress on Latin America (NACLA) translated the entire program into English and published it in the March 1971 issue of its newsletter. Following is an extract from the proposed program.

The revolutionary transformation the country needs can only be carried out if the Chilean people take power into their hands and exercise it effectively. Through a long struggle process the Chilean people have conquered certain liberties and democratic guarantees whose continuity call for the maintenance of an attitude of alertness and combativeness without truce. However, power itself is foreign to the people.

The popular and revolutionary forces have not united to struggle for the simple substitution of one president of the republic for another, nor to replace one party for another in the government, but to carry out the profound changes the national situation demands based on the transfer of power from the old dominant groups to the workers, the peasants and the progressive sectors of the middle classes of the city and the countryside.

The popular triumph will open the way to the most democratic political regime in the country's history.

Concerning political structure the popular governments has a double task:

1. to preserve and make more effective and profound the democratic rights and the conquests of the workers; and
2. to transform the present institutions so as to install a new state where workers and the people will have the real exercise of power.

The popular government will guarantee the exercise of democratic rights and will respect the individual and social guarantees of all the people. Freedom of conscience, speech, press and assembly, the inviolability of the home and the rights of unions and their organization will rule effectively without the limiting conditions presently established by the dominant classes.

For this to be effective the labor and social organizations of workers, employees, peasants, *pobladores* [residents], housewives, students, professionals, intellectuals, craftsmen, small and middle-size businessmen, and other sectors of workers will be called upon to intervene at their respective places in the decisions of the organs of power. For example, in the welfare and social security institutions we will establish the administration by the depositors themselves, thus assuring them democratic elections and the secret vote for their directive councils. Concerning enterprises of the public sector, their directive councils and their production committees will have the direct participation of workers' and employees' representatives.

In organizations concerned with housing, operating within their jurisdiction and at their own level, the Neighbors' Councils and other organizations of slum dwellers will have the use of mechanisms to inspect their operations and intervene in the many aspects of their functioning. These are only a few examples of the new conception of government which we propose—one in which the people truly participate in the state apparatus.

At the same time the popular government guarantees workers the right of employment and strike and to all the people the right of education and culture with complete respect for all religious ideas and beliefs and guarantees of the exercise of worship.

All democratic rights and guarantees will be extended through the delivery to social organizations of the real means to exercise them and the creation of the mechanisms that permit them to act at the different levels of the state apparatus.

The popular government will base its force and authority essentially on the support the organized people give it. This is our idea of a strong government as opposed to that promoted by the oligarchy and imperialism which identify authority with the coercion exercised against the people.

The popular government will be many-partied. It will include all the revolutionary parties, movements and groups. Thus it will be a genuinely democratic, representative and cohesive executive.

The popular government will respect the rights of opposition that is exercised within legal bounds.

The popular government will begin immediately a genuine administrative decentralization as well as democratic, efficient planning which will eliminate bureaucratic centralism and replace it with the coordination of all state organisms.

Municipal structures will be modernized and will be granted the necessary authority in agreement with the coordination plans of the whole state. There will be a tendency to transform these structures into local organisms of the new political organization. They will receive adequate financing and authority for the purpose of caring for, in working with the Neighbors' Councils and in coordination with them, the problems of local interests of the communities and their inhabitants. Provincial Assemblies should also enter into operation with this same idea.

The police force should be reorganized so that it cannot again be employed as a repressive organization against the people and so that on the other hand it fulfills the objective of defending the people from antisocial actions. Police procedures will be humanized so as to guarantee effectively the complete respect of dignity and the physical well-being of the person. The prison system, which constitutes one of the worst defects of the present system, must be completely transformed for the purpose of the regeneration and recuperation of those who have committed crimes.

Source: Popular Unity, "Popular Unity Government: Basic Program," *NACLA Newsletter* 5, no. 1 (March 1971): 9–10.

Popular Unity

In the 1970 presidential election, Chile's entire political spectrum appeared to have shifted significantly leftward. Allende once again ran as a leftist candidate, this time at the head of a Unidad Popular (UP, Popular Unity) coalition. This leftist alliance grouped socialists, communists, the left wing of the Christian Democrats, some dissident radicals, and Christian socialists. Frei was constitutionally barred from running for a second term, so the Christian Democrats ran Radomiro Tomic, who embraced a platform that included some policy proposals that were to the left of Allende. Hard-line conservatives broke from the coalition that they had formed with the centrists in the 1964 election and ran Jorge Alessandri, who had won the 1958 election, as the National Party candidate. Chilean politics had settled into hard thirds, with the population almost equally divided between those who supported conservatives, those who identified with the center, and those on the left.

During the campaign, the Popular Unity coalition published a program that outlined its views on the social and economic situation in Chile and proposed a course of action to improve this situation (see the selection included with this chapter). It noted that due to Chile's dependence on imperialist nations and global capitalism, and the development of an export economy, the Chilean people did not benefit from their great wealth of natural resources. The program pointed to the nature of a class struggle in which workers and peasants suffered from social and economic stagnation and widespread poverty while bourgeois groups refused to address fundamental socioeconomic problems. It concluded that these problems were the result of class privileges that the wealthy would never give up voluntarily.

The Popular Unity advocated replacing the capitalistic and export-oriented economy with a centralized and democratically controlled one. It sought to shift production from luxury items for the wealthy to mass-produced goods for the working class, to free Chile from dominance by foreign capital, to diversify exports, and to combat inflation. The Popular Unity called for measures to end unemployment, legislation to ensure a minimum subsistence wage for workers, elimination of wage discrimination based on sex or age, and an end to high salaries for government employees.

Two main points of the Popular Unity economic policy were the nationalization of foreign capital and national monopolies, and an acceleration of the agrarian reform program begun under the Frei administration. The Popular Unity called for the nationalization of natural resources (the copper, iron, and nitrate mines), banks, foreign trade, strategic industrial monopolies, and the infrastructure (electricity, railroads, air and sea transportation, communications, and petroleum). The Popular Unity also promised to expand an agrarian reform program to benefit small-scale farmers and rural workers. The plan was to transform the economy into one that would serve the entire population.

CHILEAN ROAD TO SOCIALISM

In what became known as the "Chilean Road to Socialism," leftists gained political power in 1970 through the election of Allende to the presidency. On September 4,

1970, Allende eked out a victory in a three-way race with a narrow plurality of 36.6 percent of the vote. The conservative opposition immediately attempted to thwart Allende's ascension to power. In previous elections when one candidate did not win an outright majority, the congress by matter of course confirmed the top vote getter as president. Allende had followed that custom in the 1958 election when he supported Alessandri's confirmation even though he had also only won a narrow plurality of the vote. This time, Alessandri sought to cut a deal with the Christian Democrats. If they would support his candidacy, he would promptly resign and call new elections. Since Frei would no longer be the incumbent, he could thereby dodge the constitutional restriction on reelection. Frei had sufficiently high popularity ratings that he could probably win another election. The Christian Democrats refused to conspire in this scheme, but they did extract guarantees from Allende that he would not restrict political liberties or form a popular militia.

The conservative opposition made one final attempt to stop Allende's assumption of power. The army's commander-in-chief General René Schneider was a strong constitutionalist and opposed a military coup to prevent Allende's inauguration. The CIA supported right-wing military officers in a plan to kidnap the general and thereby open a path to a coup. The plotters botched the kidnap attempt, and Schneider was killed in the process. The incident provoked outrage and led people to rally behind Allende. Two days later, on October 24, the Chilean congress confirmed Allende's victory, and he took office on November 3, 1970. For the first time in history, a Marxist gained the presidency through a democratic process.

Allende, however, had only gained access to one office, which was far short of taking political power. Without a majority vote in the presidential election, he lacked a clear political mandate for his socialist program. He also faced an antagonistic congress in the hands of centrists and conservatives, and hostility from the Chilean ruling class that controlled media outlets and the means of production. Political divisions within the Popular Unity coalition also hindered the viability of Allende's socialist program. Nevertheless, he pushed forward with plans for a fundamental transformation of society.

When Allende took office in November 1970, he immediately focused attention on improving living conditions for the poor. He raised the minimum wage by 35 percent. His policies resulted in a rise in worker income, an increase in consumer buying power, a sharp drop in unemployment, and a fall in inflation rates. Food production increased, industrial manufacturing rose, and the gross national product (GNP) tripled. The government implemented programs of free medical care and supplies, including providing free milk for children, and pregnant and nursing women. The programs had positive outcomes, such as an 11 percent decrease in infant mortality rates. The Popular Unity achieved its short-term goals, and support for the government increased.

Allende pledged to undertake all of these reforms through existing institutional frameworks. He promised to respect democratic structures and individual liberties. In a move away from personalistic forms of governance, Allende ended the practice of placing presidential portraits in government offices. He emphasized that the Popular Unity's political project was much larger than one man. The Chilean

constitution allowed for a single six-year term of office as president with no possibility of reelection. Allende gave no indication that he would attempt to violate that
provision, and by all indications he would step aside at the end of his term and hand
power to whomever won the next election.

Nationalization

By 1970 more than one hundred U.S.-based multinational corporations had investments in Chile. A significant part of the Chilean economy was built on copper
production, and foreign companies (like Kennecott and Anaconda) owned most of
the mines. The Popular Unity government quickly implemented a program that
extended partial government control over key sectors of the economy. On December
21, 1970, only a month after taking office, Allende called for the nationalization of
the foreign-owned copper industry that comprised three-quarters of the country's
exports. The proposal was not that controversial and enjoyed broad popular support.
Not only had Frei started partial ownership through his "Chileanization" of the industry, but also in the 1970 electoral campaign the Christian Democratic candidate
Tomic had called for full nationalization.

On July 17, 1971, the Allende government, with the unanimous support of
congress, nationalized the large copper mines. Based on United Nations principles,
Chile compensated the corporations for the book value of the mines minus excessive
profits. Allende announced that because of excessive profits that the multinational
corporations had taken from Chile over the previous fifteen years they would receive
no compensation. He compared the expropriation to Abraham Lincoln freeing the
slaves in the United States. Lincoln refused to pay the planters both because they
had more than recovered their initial investment in the slaves and because of the
immorality of owning another human. Similarly, the mining companies had earned
far more than a fair profit, and Allende argued that the mines rightfully belonged to
Chile. Despite congressional support, opponents in both the legislature and judiciary
created political roadblocks for the Popular Unity's nationalization efforts. In particular, an oppositional congress refused to provide funding for Allende's socialization programs. As a result, Allende was forced to use laws passed during the Frei and
previous administrations to move ahead with his programs.

Allende's government also nationalized the coal and steel industries, and bought
control of most banks and communications industries. The policies often targeted
foreign firms, in particular International Telephone and Telegraph (ITT) and Ford.
Workers pushed Allende's hand in an attempt to force him to move more quickly on
the expropriations. Workers occupied management offices and refused to leave until
an expropriation took place. By the end of 1971 the Popular Unity had taken over
more than 150 industries, including twelve of the twenty largest companies in the
country. The nationalization programs affected both domestic and foreign corporations. Usually the previous owners were compensated, but sometimes (as in the case
of the copper mines) an agreement was difficult to reach.

The Popular Unity's expropriation campaign concentrated on large corporations. They refrained from attacking small- and medium-sized businesses because they hoped to gain their support for economic changes, although that backing was not always forthcoming. This led to an inherent contradiction as smaller industries employed 80 percent of the workers, precisely those whom the Popular Unity sought to help with their policies. They worked in worse conditions and for less pay than those in the larger corporations that were being expropriated. Because the Popular Unity program did not affect the smaller industries, the vast majority of workers realized little gain from the economic reforms.

Workers put off by the slow pace of the nationalization program began pushing the Popular Unity government to adopt more aggressive policies. On April 25, 1971, workers took over the Yarur textile plant and demanded that it be expropriated. When Allende finally agreed, workers occupied eight other plants with similar demands. This led to workers occupying more small industries that the moderate wing of the Popular Unity did not want nationalized. Slowly, the government began to lose control of the situation as popular demands outpaced what policies the leaders were willing to implement. At the same time, the nationalizations gave the U.S. government an excuse to cut off aid to, and increase economic aggression against, Chile.

Agrarian Reform

The Popular Unity government accelerated the pace of the agrarian reform process begun in 1967 under Frei's administration. In Chile, agriculture was a less important source of employment and export products than in many other Latin American countries. As a result, there was less resistance to agrarian reform and the government could immediately move ahead with plans for a massive, rapid, and drastic agrarian reform program in order to destroy the archaic hacienda system. Allende distributed more land in one year than Frei had in six. By mid-1972 all farms over eighty hectares had been expropriated. The Popular Unity chose to proceed with the existing legislation even though it was not completely consistent with the government's agrarian reform policy out of a concern that the expropriations be legal and that time not be wasted in passing new legislation. Any reforms approved through proper legal channels would be harder to challenge, which improved their potential to achieve permanent structural changes.

In order to increase agricultural production, abandoned and underused state land would be cultivated. Expropriated land would be organized into cooperatives and land titles given to the peasants. A problem that the government faced was that agrarian reform requires more than a redistribution of land. Farmers also needed credit and access to supplies and equipment. The expropriation was to include the assets, capital, credit, and technical assistance necessary for the peasants to farm the land. The land reform happened so fast, however, that often the government could not provide these services, which limited the effectiveness of the entire program.

While the government proceeded in a legal and constitutional manner with its agrarian reforms, leftist elements in the Popular Unity coalition pushed for a more aggressive policy. They argued that adherence to existing laws and institutions only served to retard the transition to socialism and protected capitalists and landowners at a cost to poor farmers. Meanwhile, peasants impatient with the slow pace of reform occupied land, often on small estates not subject to expropriation. Allende condemned these land seizures and the negative influence that they had on rallying the support of the middle class to the cause of the Popular Unity. Some landowners hired armed guards to fight back against the seizures, and others left the country.

Leftist Opposition

The Popular Unity's policies led to significant social and economic gains, which raised expectations for even more fundamental transformations of society. Allende had strained relations with those to his left because he did not move fast enough with his reforms. Workers demanded higher wages, and peasants illegally occupied land in an attempt to push the government's hand. The left-wing faction pushed for accelerated nationalization of the private sector, price controls, and wage increases. Disagreements within the coalition over the pace and direction that the government should take increased after the short-term gains realized in 1971 gave way in 1972 to rising inflation, shortages, and a lack of foreign exchange. The antagonistic congress refused to increase taxes, which forced the government to borrow funds to pay for its massive public works projects that helped stimulate the economy. This economic policy increased inflation, which alienated the middle class. Radicals complained that the economic problems were a result of governmental inaction, and their criticisms weakened the government.

Leftist guerrillas who were skeptical about the viability of a peaceful road to socialism founded the Movimiento de Izquierda Revolucionaria (MIR, Revolutionary Left Movement) in 1965. The MIR challenged Allende's commitment to representative democracy, particularly in the face of an entrenched conservative opposition that from their perspective made a military confrontation inevitable. Instead, they urged the president to suspend the constitution, close congress, arm the people, and move directly to a communist government. They argued that the Popular Unity's commitment to constitutional changes was bound to fail.

The Popular Unity's moderate wing (including the communist party) pressed for slower, more evolutionary change. They opposed the immediate dismantling of the capitalistic economy and the expropriation of small and economically insignificant industries. The moderates accused the "ultra-leftists" of playing into the hands of the conservative opposition. In order to move ahead with their economic programs, the Popular Unity needed the support of the middle class. According to the moderates, leftist actions alienated popular support by provoking clashes with small entrepreneurs and instigating seizures of factories and farms that had no significant economic importance. The moderates believed that compromises and alliances were important to confront reactionary forces that opposed the Popular Unity program.

Even with discontent over the pace of changes, electoral support for the left had continued to grow since Allende's election in 1970. In the April 1971 municipal elections that many viewed as a **referendum** on the Allende administration, the Popular Unity coalition gained almost half of the vote in the country. In the March 1973 midterm congressional elections, the Popular Unity coalition registered an unprecedented 10 percent rise from its vote in the previous presidential contest. Some supporters had hoped that the left would win half the seats in congress, which would allow it to pass legislation over the opposition of its opponents, but it fell short of that goal. Conservatives, meanwhile, also failed to gain a two-thirds majority in order to proceed with plans to impeach Allende. The political polarization of the country intensified.

Conservative Opposition

The Popular Unity faced a formidable conservative opposition to the implementation of its program. The coalition did not control congress. The military, multinational corporations, and most of the media opposed its programs. Opponents organized right-wing paramilitary groups such as Patria y Libertad (Homeland and Liberty) that engaged in terrorist attacks against the government. The Catholic Church moved into the opposition when the Allende government passed an educational reform program to take schools away from church control.

Much has been made of Allende's gender gap, with women traditionally voting more conservatively than men. The left typically organized around class issues, whereas conservatives effectively mobilized women along traditional gender lines. Wealthy women led the opposition to Allende's policies because of how they curtailed privileged access to consumer goods in exchange for popular access to basic commodities. The women effectively played into gender stereotypes and challenged the soldiers' male honor. They organized demonstrations at the houses of army commanders, encouraging them to take action against the socialist government and effeminizing them when they failed to do so. They threw chicken feed at the soldiers, implying they were hens afraid to take action. Upper-class women engaged in marches with empty pots in a display of their discontent. Shortages hit women particularly hard because their gender-defined role was to feed their families. These difficulties led working-class and peasant women to join these protests as well.

Although real wages remained high and unemployment did not increase, in 1972 inflation became rampant. Consumer products became scarce. The middle class moved against the Popular Unity government as the economic situation worsened. In October 1972, truckers went on strike in opposition to the Popular Unity's plans to nationalize their industry. The strike caused shortages, which increased discontent with government policies. Right-wing groups instigated strikes and other activities as part of a broader plan to sabotage the economy. Even some working-class and peasant groups that had become disaffected with the slow pace of change joined in the attempt to shut down the economy.

COUP

On September 11, 1973, army general Augusto Pinochet led a military coup that overthrew Salvador Allende and the Popular Unity government. The coup came on the day that Allende planned to announce a plebiscite to resolve the constitutional crisis facing the country. Instead, Allende attempted to defend the presidential palace with a small group of his closest supporters as the Chilean air force relentlessly bombed the building. In his last radio broadcast Allende stated that history was on the side of the workers and that they would determine the future of the country. He declared that he would repay the loyalty of his supporters with his life. The coup plotters made it apparent that if he surrendered they would not let him go peacefully into exile but instead would torture and humiliate him. The president decided rather to take his own life with a Kalashnikov rifle that Fidel Castro had given to him.

The coup itself did not surprise many. A failed June 1973 attempt had made it obvious that the military and its conservative supporters were moving in that direction. In retrospect, the June attempt appeared to be a test run so that plotters could determine who would join them. What surprised most was the level of physical brutality and the institutional reach of the September coup, and how quickly seemingly entrenched democratic structures crumbled. Many expected that the removal of Allende would lead to new elections and a quick transfer of power, presumably to the Christian Democrats. Instead, the military dismantled the country's sacred democratic institutions and remained in power for seventeen years.

The coup highlighted the extreme polarization in Chilean society. Many conservatives, traditionally allied with the Catholic Church and wealthy landowners, openly embraced a military government in order to save Chile from communism. Many industrialists saw a coup as the only way to maintain a capitalistic system that assured them of their economic power and class privileges. The centrist Christian Democrats initially welcomed the coup as an opportunistic opening that would allow them to return to power but eventually joined a progressive opposition to the military's dismantling of democratic structures. Allende still enjoyed a bedrock of support on the left. On the third anniversary of his September 4, 1970, election, only a week before the coup that removed him from power, Allende's supporters marched in front of the presidential palace in the largest demonstration in Chile's history to publicize their defense of their embattled leader.

As with Arbenz in Guatemala, some militants pressed Allende to arm his supporters in order to remain in power. It was naïve, they argued, to attempt a deep transformation of society without expecting and planning for a conservative reaction such as what happened in the coup. In retrospect, many scholars believe that the overwhelming strength of the Chilean military would easily have crushed the pro-Allende forces. A more likely outcome than a leftist victory would have been a bloodbath. The other alternative would have been to follow the Cuban model and completely dismantle the existing military structures, perhaps including the execution of key leaders who would have been capable of organizing an opposition in exile. Allende, however, was a strong constitutionalist and was unwilling to violate the sacrosanct nature of existing institutions or violate the human rights of his opponents. Those compromises and trade-offs highlight the limitations of attempting to implement a revolution within the confines of the established order.

General Augusto Pinochet

Before joining the coup, Pinochet had been known as a supporter of Chile's constitutional order. Allende had named him as head of the army because of the perception that he was a reliable ally. Only three weeks before the coup, Pinochet had replaced General Carlos Prats as commander-in-chief. Similar to his predecessor Schneider who had been killed in a botched coup attempt just before Allende's inauguration, Prats was also a strong constitutionalist. He had resigned on August 22 when the pressure of the wives of other military leaders calling for a coup had become overpowering. Prats went into exile in Argentina after the coup, where a year later Pinochet's secret police assassinated him.

Pinochet's defection to the side of the conspirators removed the last barrier to the coup moving forward. His betrayal surprised Allende. Scholars have subsequently debated whether Pinochet had always been a closet fascist, or whether the temptation to amass great fame, fortune, and political power provided too great of an opportunity to ignore.

On taking power, Pinochet set out to destroy, not reform, the existing political system. The military regime dissolved congress, suspended the constitution, declared political parties illegal, and outlawed labor unions and strikes. Initially, the plan was to share command among four junta members: Pinochet together with the heads of the air force, navy, and police. Pinochet soon sidelined the other officers and concentrated all power in his own hands. In 1980, Pinochet promulgated a new constitution that ensured his personal and perpetual control over the government. The military named itself the guardian of the state. Former presidents and other top officials were given lifetime seats in the new senate, which guaranteed that conservatives would maintain control over political structures regardless of the outcome of any future electoral contests. The coup represented a staggering blow to the political democracy, liberal freedoms, and social reforms that Allende had championed.

The military government engaged in extensive human rights abuses. They executed over three thousand Chileans and imprisoned and tortured many more, most famously in the national stadium. The regime abolished individual liberties, established curfews, and set strict limits on the media. It took over the universities and in the process violated the tradition of university autonomy. In the weeks after the coup, a "caravan of death" toured the country to arrest leftists and labor activists and execute them. The military used Nazi experts to set up concentration camps and carry out international assassinations. Together with other military governments in South America, they established Operation Condor as a network of secret police forces to eliminate regime opponents who had sought refuge in neighboring countries. A March 1978 amnesty law protected military officials from punishment for their political crimes. The level of brutality perhaps was no worse than other military governments, but what was stunning was that these abuses took place in a country that saw itself as a beacon of democracy and one that enjoyed stable institutions. This type of coup was not supposed to happen in a country such as Chile.

Perhaps as deadly as any of the military government's political policies was the implementation of a neoliberal shock treatment that economist Milton Friedman had designed at the University of Chicago. Chile became a laboratory for the application of free market experiments by economists whom Friedman had trained. These so-called Chicago Boys implemented an unfettered capitalistic economy without having to bother with any of the checks that a functioning democratic system might present. Among their policies were drastic cuts in government spending and a privatization of social security, healthcare, and education. Hundreds of business and industries were privatized and often sold to cronies of the military government or multinational corporations at low prices. Land that Allende had expropriated for rural workers was returned to their previous owners, or sold to a new wealthy upper class that emerged as a direct result of the neoliberal policies.

The result of Friedman's policies was a superficial and short-lived "economic miracle," but it came at the cost of a significant upward redistribution of wealth. For workers, wages declined and social services disappeared. Foreign capitalists gained more control over the country's economy. The rich became richer and the poor poorer, leading to one of most inequitable economies in the world. These economic policies could not have been implemented without the support of a military dictatorship.

In October 1988, Pinochet held a plebiscite to ask the people whether he should remain in power for another eight years. Completely surrounded by supporters, he was convinced that he would easily win the vote. Instead, he lost by a margin of 55 to 43 percent. After vowing to respect the democratic will of the people he could not easily back down from his promise. In this environment, the military allowed a December 1989 electoral contest to move forward. Patricio Aylwin Azocar from the moderate Christian Democratic Party won the election and took office on March 11, 1990. Although Pinochet relinquished the presidency, he remained in power as head of the military and assumed a seat as senator for life and still easily controlled political decisions through those positions. Although a civilian was formally the president, the military set government policy.

On October 16, 1998, police arrested Pinochet in a London hospital, where he was recovering from back surgery. Spain had requested his **extradition** on behalf of two Spanish judges who were investigating crimes that military leaders in Argentina and Chile had committed. They accused Pinochet of engaging in acts of genocide, torture, terrorism, and other crimes against Spanish citizens in Chile. Because of the

1978 amnesty law, he could not be charged for those crimes in Chile. The Spanish judges claimed that the widespread and systematic human rights violations in Chile during the military government amounted to crimes against humanity, and such crimes were subject to universal jurisdiction. Chilean officials fought against the extradition request and launched the extraordinary defense that executions and torture are official functions of government and thereby immune from prosecution. Prosecutors countered with the charge that Pinochet was not exempt for atrocities committed during the unfolding of the coup on September 11, 1973, before formally proclaiming himself as head of state that evening. This charge sent the military generals scrambling to document when exactly they had killed each of their opponents, to prove the deaths had taken place after they had formally taken power. Pinochet's supporters claimed that his actions were justified because he had dispelled a communist threat and brought financial and political stability to Chile. Conservatives championed a cause of national sovereignty and denounced the Spanish judges as a European attempt to recolonize the Americas.

After being held under house arrest for almost two years in London, prosecutors allowed Pinochet to return to Chile on humanitarian grounds. The veil of invincibility, however, had been removed. Half a year later, Chilean courts stripped Pinochet of his immunity and charged him with human rights abuses. The courts declared that kidnapping was an ongoing crime, and in cases where a dead body could not be delivered, the 1978 amnesty did not apply. In July 2001, however, the courts ruled that the former dictator was unable to stand trial because of an onset of dementia. On December 10, 2006, Pinochet died at the age of ninety-one without having had to answer for his crimes.

United States

Unlike the Central American and Caribbean countries of Guatemala and Cuba that lay well within the U.S. geographic sphere of influence, Chile was much more distant and seemingly should have presented less of a challenge to U.S. hegemonic dominance. Allende's socialist policies had sufficiently alienated his domestic conservative opponents that they would have moved against him whether or not the United States existed as an imperial force in the region. Nevertheless, rather than encouraging a continuance of Chile's constitutional system, the United States adopted policies that contributed to an undermining of Chile's democratic institutions.

Throughout the 1960s, the CIA had interfered in Chile's internal affairs to prevent Allende's election. Mailings, leaflets, and media advertisements in the 1970 election warned of the end of religion and family life if Allende were to win. Their propaganda predicted a total economic collapse with a socialist victory and spread rumors of communist firing squads. The CIA also encouraged the international media to write stories critical of Allende.

When Allende won the election, Henry Kissinger, Richard Nixon's presidential assistant for National Security Affairs, declared that he saw no reason "to stand by and watch a country go communist due to the irresponsibility of its own people." He warned that a Marxist government was unacceptable, even though Allende was a strong constitutionalist and had served for decades in the government without violating institutional norms. Kissinger announced that the United States would not be bound by pieces of paper cast into a ballot box in a faraway country. Nixon pledged to smash Allende. His administration pursued a two-track strategy to block Allende from office. The first track was to bribe congress to vote against confirming Allende as president after the close presidential election. That tactic collapsed when the Christian Democrats refused to cooperate with what in essence would have been a constitutional coup. The second track included plans for a military coup, including the removal of generals who supported Chile's constitutional order.

Shortly after Allende's election, Viron Vaky, Kissinger's top aide on Latin America, argued in a secret memo that attempts to prevent the socialist from taking office were a violation of U.S. policy tenets and moral principles. He questioned whether Allende posed a serious threat to U.S. security interests and whether his election would alter a global balance of power. Nevertheless, Washington policy makers viewed the election of an avowed Marxist as a definite psychological setback for U.S. hegemonic control over Latin America and an advance for socialism. As such, it would need to be stopped.

One of the Pinochet administration's most famous attacks against his opponents occurred in the United States. In September 1976, Pinochet's operatives planted a car bomb in Washington, D.C., that killed former Allende ambassador Orlando Letelier and his associate Ronni Moffitt. Letelier was an effective lobbyist against U.S. aid to Pinochet and for that reason needed to be removed. Until September 11, 2001, those murders entailed the most egregious terrorist attack in the country's capital. Secretary of state Henry Kissinger indicated that human rights would not be a priority for the Gerald Ford administration. Instead, he expressed sympathy for Pinochet's political program. President Jimmy Carter tried to press human rights issues when he took office in 1977, but when Ronald Reagan was elected four years later he reversed that policy, to Pinochet's relief. Following in the footsteps of his Republican predecessors, president Bill Clinton cited national security concerns in his refusal to release documents that would have revealed Pinochet's role in the attack on Letelier. Only in 2015 did the U.S. government finally declassify documentation that definitively proved Pinochet's culpability in the attack.

ASSESSMENT

Although Chile and Cuba socialized their economies through different means (electoral versus armed), they followed similar economic programs. Both sought to increase the income of people on the lower rungs of the economic ladder. Both pushed for agrarian reform and nationalization programs. Neither had to deal with an economy destroyed by protracted guerrilla warfare, a situation somewhat unusual for new socialist governments. And both faced enormous opposition, both domestic and from the U.S. government. The Cuban Revolution, however, survived, while the Chilean path to socialism went down in flames. Cuban moderates opposed Castro's rapid pace of change and consolidation of political power, but the physical elimination of his opponents ensured his survival. One potential lesson is that it is impossible to implement a socialist agenda if the revolutionaries do not take the necessary steps to maintain themselves in power.

The Popular Unity's shortcomings together with conservative opposition in Chile and hostility from the United States led to the government's collapse. While Allende's conservative opponents cheered the military for saving Chile from communism, others contended that the coup resulted in a dictatorship much worse than what could have possibly emerged from an Allende government. Rather than confronting a threat to democracy, the decision to launch a coup against Allende was the result of a paranoid fear of communism and a belief in a moral imperative to stop it wherever it emerged. A successful socialist government would present a psychological challenge to U.S. hegemony in the region. It was necessary to make an experiment in socialism appear to be such a failure that no one would ever dare repeat it.

Some scholars have interpreted the Chilean coup as a political, and not a military, defeat for the Popular Unity. From this perspective, the Allende government fell because it employed the rhetoric of a socialist revolution without having the authority to implement such policies. It failed to gain the support of the middle-class and lower-class women who had nothing to lose and much to gain from an attack on economic monopolies and foreign corporations. If Allende had moved faster in transforming society, he may have been more able to fulfill those rising expectations and hence maintain the Popular Unity government in power.

Allende was a strict constitutionalist, and he carefully abided by the legal process to implement the Popular Unity's program. Similar to the removal of Arbenz in Guatemala, his overthrow led some supporters to question whether socialism could only be implemented through armed struggle. Socialism is a threat to the capitalistic mode of production and as such is not an economic policy for the timid. Chile demonstrated the limits of moving in that direction within the constraints of existing institutional orders that would allow conservative opponents to defeat a socialist government and reverse the social gains it achieved. Some contend that a socialization program must be implemented quickly before the opposition has an opportunity to mobilize against it, or it must be given up altogether.

Allende committed suicide in the presidential palace with a machine gun that Fidel Castro had provided him. Several weeks after the coup, Castro justified the gift. He declared, "If every worker and every farmer had a rifle in their hands, there would never have been a fascist coup." The removal of a strong constitutionalist such as Allende raised in the minds of many socialist revolutionaries the question that if those were the parameters, what other choice existed but to follow Cuba's example and close all channels to external subversion and extend democracy only to those who were willing to abide by the rules that the socialist government established. Peaceful paths to revolutionary change no longer seemed as viable as they had only a few years earlier.

SUMMARY

Chile's experiment with a peaceful and constitutional path to socialism raises the question of whether it is possible to make revolutionary changes in society without resorting to violence. The Marxist Salvador Allende won election to the presidency in 1970 after serving in congress for twenty-five years. Although he supported Fidel Castro and the Cuban Revolution, Allende contended that Chile had strong democratic institutions and no need existed to resort to guerrilla warfare. Initially, his Popular Unity government made significant progress in transforming the country's economic structures, but those policies alienated both conservative opponents in Chile and U.S.-based corporations with significant investments in the country. On September 11, 1973, General Augusto Pinochet led a brutal military coup that not only overthrew Allende's government but also dismantled the country's treasured democratic institutions. It took seventeen years for the country to return to civilian rule, but even then the military continued to hold dominance over the country. Chile's path to socialism exemplifies the difficulties that Latin American revolutionaries face in implementing radical changes in their societies.

DISCUSSION QUESTIONS

Did Allende do too much or too little to address Chile's socioeconomic problems?
Was it a mistake for Allende to be such a strict constitutionalist?
Would Allende's government have succeeded had he silenced his opponents?
Why did Allende kill himself?
In retrospect, what could or should Allende have done differently to prevent his government from being overthrown?

FURTHER READING

The Popular Unity government in Chile generated a massive literature, with one joke stating that a thousand books have been published on the topic, one for each day that Allende was in office. The literature is divided into those that examine Allende's government and those that focus on Pinochet's coup and its aftermath.

Burbach, Roger. *The Pinochet Affair: State Terrorism and Global Justice*. London: Zed Books, 2003. A damning critique of the Pinochet dictatorship.
De Vylder, Stefan. *Allende's Chile: The Political Economy of the Rise and Fall of the Unidad Popular*. Cambridge: Cambridge University Press, 1976. A compelling study of the Allende government's economic policies.
Dinges, John. *The Condor Years: How Pinochet and His Allies Brought Terrorism to Three Continents*. New York: The New Press, 2004. A critical examination of terror networks in South America under military dictatorships.

Figueroa Clark, Victor. *Salvador Allende: Revolutionary Democrat.* London: Pluto Press, 2013. A short biography of Chile's Marxist leader.

Hauser, Thomas. *Missing.* New York: Avon Books, 1982. A journalistic account of the execution of the U.S. citizen Charles Horman who was caught in the Pinochet coup.

Kornbluh, Peter. *The Pinochet File: A Declassified Dossier on Atrocity and Accountability.* New York: The New Press, 2003. Declassified documents on the U.S. government's role in undermining the Allende presidency.

Loveman, Brian. *Chile: The Legacy of Hispanic Capitalism.* New York: Oxford University Press, 1979. A historical overview of Chile by a leading historian.

Power, Margaret. *Right-Wing Women in Chile: Feminine Power and the Struggle against Allende, 1964–1973.* University Park: Pennsylvania State University Press, 2002. An impressive examination of women's opposition to Allende.

Stern, Steve J. *Battling for Hearts and Minds: Memory Struggles in Pinochet's Chile, 1973–1988.* Durham, NC: Duke University Press, 2006. The second of a three-volume "memory box of Pinochet's Chile" that starts with the Pinochet coup.

Winn, Peter. *Weavers of Revolution: The Yarur Workers and Chile's Road to Socialism.* New York: Oxford University Press, 1986. A remarkable study of worker mobilizations during the Allende years.

FILMS

The Battle of Chile: The Struggle of an Unarmed People. 1975. A documentary on the fate of Allende's Popular Unity government filmed throughout Chile from February to September 1973.

Death and the Maiden. 1995. Fictional story of a former prisoner who meets her torturer after the fall of the Pinochet dictatorship in Chile.

The House of the Spirits. 1993. Based on Isabel Allende's novel, the film examines political, social, and economic changes in Chile leading to the September 11 coup.

The Last Stand of Salvador Allende: September 11th, 1973; A Documentary. 1998. A remarkable documentary of the final hours of Salvador Allende.

Machuca. 2004. Portrays the 1973 coup from a child's perspective.

Missing. 1982. True story of the execution of Charles Horman after the 1973 military coup in Chile.

National Stadium. 2001. A documentary about the National Stadium that was used as an improvised detention center in the weeks following the 1973 coup.

Salvador Allende. 2004. A documentary on the Chilean president.

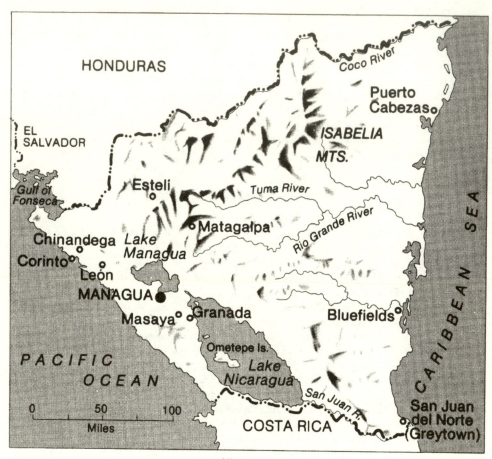

Nicaragua

7

Nicaraguan Sandinistas, 1979–1990

KEY DATES

1856–1860	U.S. **filibusterer** William Walker occupies Nicaragua
1893–1909	Presidency of José Santos Zelaya
1911–1933	U.S. Marine occupation
1927–1933	Augusto César Sandino fights the U.S. Marines to a standstill
1936–1956	Rule of Anastasio Somoza García ("Tacho")
1956–1967	Rule of Luis Somoza Debayle
1961	Founding of the Sandinista National Liberation Front (FSLN)
1967–1979	Rule of Anastasio Somoza Debayle ("Tachito")
December 23, 1972	Managua earthquake
December 27, 1974	Sandinistas crash Somoza's Christmas party
November 8, 1976	Carlos Fonseca killed
January 10, 1978	*La Prensa* publisher Pedro Joaquín Chamorro assassinated
August 22, 1978	Sandinistas seize national palace
June 20, 1979	ABC journalist William Stewart murdered
July 19, 1979	Sandinistas gain power
March 9, 1981	U.S. president Ronald Reagan authorizes paramilitary force (the "contras") to overthrow the Sandinistas
November 4, 1984	Sandinistas win first free elections since 1928
June 27, 1986	International Court of Justice rules against United States for terrorist attacks on Nicaragua
January 9, 1987	Nicaragua ratifies new constitution that provides **autonomy** to Atlantic coast
February 25, 1990	Sandinistas lose elections to Violeta Barrios de Chamorro
January 10, 2007	FSLN leader Daniel Ortega reelected president

On July 19, 1979, a group of guerrillas entered the capital city of Managua, Nicaragua, having overthrown the Somoza family dynasty that had run the country as their personal fiefdom for nearly half a century. The Frente Sandinista de Liberación Nacional (FSLN, Sandinista National Liberation Front) took control twenty years after Fidel Castro led his guerrilla army to power in Cuba. The Sandinistas provide only the second example of a successful armed revolutionary struggle in Latin America. They failed, however, to make changes in societal structures as deep or as permanent as their counterparts had done in Cuba.

With Che Guevara's defeat in Bolivia in 1967 and the 1970 election of Marxist Salvador Allende to the presidency in Chile, leftist sentiments swung away from searching for revolutionary changes through guerrilla struggles and toward using constitutional and institutional means to transform economic and political structures. For a brief period, an armed path to social transformation was largely taken off the table. The collapse of Chile's electoral path to socialism in 1973 ushered in a period of military rule throughout Latin America. With the disappearance of functioning institutional structures, the possibilities for an electoral avenue to revolutionary changes appeared to evaporate. Many leftists now argued that it was naïve to assume that a radical political program could be implemented without the physical elimination of their class enemies. These activists favored returning to armed struggle as the preferred path to power. Only the Sandinistas in Nicaragua realized success with this strategy, while others (discussed in the next chapter) met with failure.

From an orthodox Marxist perspective, Nicaragua was an unlikely candidate for a socialist revolution. Nicaragua was a poor, backward country without a strong working-class base on which to build a proletarian revolution. Other countries seemed to be more likely candidates for a social revolution. Although Cuba was largely a rural society, a long tradition of communist and labor party organization contributed to the success of its revolution. In addition, the nature of labor in the sugarcane fields had the effect of creating a proletarian consciousness among the workers. In Chile, Salvador Allende built on a long history of working-class militancy to win election as president. Nicaragua simply had not developed the basic objective economic conditions deemed necessary for a socialist revolution.

The Sandinistas broke from an orthodox Marxist emphasis on an urban proletariat to provide a vanguard leadership for a revolutionary struggle. They rejected the notion that the peasants were a reactionary force that could not be relied on for the development of a revolutionary movement. The success of the Cuban Revolution strongly influenced the Sandinistas, particularly in terms of the possibilities of a dedicated cadre creating the necessary conditions for an insurrection. They learned from Ernesto Che Guevara that a revolutionary consciousness could be formed in Nicaragua's peasant population. The Sandinistas looked back to the heroic struggle of General Augusto César Sandino (1895–1934) against the U.S. Marine Corps as an example and inspiration for their revolutionary struggle. Facing seemingly insurmountable odds and in the most unlikely of situations, the revolutionaries found success.

CONQUESTS

Nicaragua has few natural resources, which made it a less desirable destination for Spanish conquistadors than Mexico and Peru with their rich gold and silver mines. Agricultural production was dominant, beginning with cacao during the Spanish colonial period, German coffee production during the nineteenth century, bananas in the twentieth century, and cattle and cotton more recently. Even so, Nicaragua's rough terrain meant that only 10 percent of the land was arable, only a third of what could be cultivated in neighboring El Salvador or the United States. By the middle of the twentieth century, a very small political and economic ruling class controlled this limited agricultural production and held the masses in an exploitative and dispossessed state.

The Spanish conquest of Nicaragua began in 1523 from both Panama to the south and Guatemala to the north. Although Nicaragua was not home to the highly stratified Indigenous empires that the Spanish encountered in Mexico and Peru, it did have a sizable native population. Nevertheless, because the conquistadors could not tap into preexisting tribute systems, extracting labor from the natives was difficult. Although the Spaniards quickly established a foothold on the Pacific coast, they never controlled the Caribbean (known locally as the Atlantic) side of the country. Indigenous uprisings repelled Spanish advances into their territory. In 1612 the Spanish embarked on a serious campaign to conquer the interior of Nicaragua, an effort that finally succeeded 150 years later, not through military might but through the religious zeal of Franciscan missionaries. In 1743, over two hundred years after the beginning of the Spanish conquest, a series of fourteen Indigenous revolts challenged Spanish rule. An Indigenous delegation walked from northern Nicaragua to the colonial center of power in Guatemala in 1817 to lodge a complaint with the Spanish officials over the low salaries and bad working conditions under which they suffered. Their action marked one of the first labor protests in Nicaragua.

In the seventeenth century, British buccaneers occupied the eastern Atlantic coast and imported African slaves to grow sugarcane. The British eventually gained control over the Nicaraguan coast as a protectorate. In the nineteenth century, Moravian missionaries brought their Protestant religion to the area. Subsequently, Nicaragua became divided into a western Pacific Spanish and Catholic coast, and an eastern Atlantic seaboard that was of African descent, English speaking, and Protestant.

Nicaragua gained strategic significance during the 1849 California gold rush when Cornelius Vanderbilt developed the country as a transshipment point for prospectors traveling west. Since the sixteenth century, some had dreamed of building a transcontinental canal across Central America. In 1856, the U.S. adventurer and filibusterer William Walker landed in Nicaragua and took over the country as president. Liberals had invited Walker to help them defeat their archrivals the conservatives. As president, he reestablished slavery, implemented a vagrancy law that forced peasants to work, and made English the official language. Walker's abusive policies led Nicaraguans to run him out of the country. He attempted to regain the presidency twice more before a Honduran firing squad executed him in 1860. Although private capital financed his campaign, Nicaraguans subsequently remembered Walker as the first U.S. attempt to dominate their country.

The fiasco of Walker's administration led to a discrediting of the liberals, and as a result the conservatives dominated Nicaraguan politics for the next thirty years. In 1893, the liberals returned to power with José Santos Zelaya, who as president implemented modernizing policies. He favored foreign capital investment but opposed extensive U.S. control. Zelaya was also a nationalist who attempted to extend Nicaraguan sovereignty over the British-controlled Atlantic coast. Conservative leader Emiliano Chamorro launched seventeen revolts against Zelaya before the United States finally intervened in 1909 to help remove the liberal leader from office. Two years later, the conservative president Adolfo Díaz invited the U.S. Marines back to prevent Zelaya from returning to power. From 1911 to 1933, the marines occupied Nicaragua to protect a minority conservative government against liberal insurrection and civil war.

In 1927, the United States sent a special mission to pacify liberal resistance, which resulted in a peace settlement. Rather than having the ruling conservatives run the 1928 elections that inevitably would lead to their victory, the United States supervised the country's first relatively fraud-free vote. The opposition liberals had the support of about two-thirds of the country's electorate and hence won the election. With this agreement, most liberal insurgents laid down their arms. One nationalist general, Augusto César Sandino, refused to give up his fight and continued his guerrilla struggle from his base in the Nicaraguan mountains. In 1932, the U.S. government saw the futility of its ongoing occupation and began to withdraw the marines. They supervised elections, which the liberal Juan Sacasa handily won.

Somozas

The United States trained a nonpartisan national guard to replace the Nicaraguan army and the occupying marines. They placed Anastasio Somoza García (1896–1956, known as "Tacho") in control of the police force. Somoza had trained in business schools in the United States, and the U.S. government liked him because he spoke English and understood their motivation. In 1933, the marines withdrew, and in 1934 Sandino came down from the mountains having achieved his goal of expelling the foreign intruders. Sandino, however, did not understand that Somoza presented a larger threat than the U.S. military. He was the only person with sufficient popular support to challenge Somoza's grasp on power. Somoza invited Sandino to a state dinner and then had him ambushed and killed when he left the national palace.

In 1936, Somoza became president. He subsequently manipulated laws and the constitution to maintain himself in power and sometimes ruled through puppet presidents. At first, Somoza enjoyed some popular support, but then he became more brutal and established his personal empire as a family dynasty. Somoza became the wealthiest man in Nicaragua, and his family owned almost everything of significance in the country. His foreign policy was entirely submissive to U.S. dictates, including declaring war on the Axis powers in the Second World War and implementing an anticommunist agenda during the Cold War. The Somozas allowed the U.S. military to use Nicaragua as a base for attacks on Jacobo Arbenz's government in Guatemala in 1954 and for the 1961 Bay of Pigs invasion in Cuba. Franklin D. Roosevelt allegedly quipped, "Somoza may be a son of a bitch, but he's our son of a bitch." The U.S. government was willing to work with authoritarian leaders if it served its imperial interests.

In 1956, the poet Rigoberto López Pérez assassinated Somoza while the latter was drinking coffee in a sidewalk cafe in León. The death of the dictator did not lead to the expected transformation of society but rather to the ascension of his son Luis Somoza Debayle (1922–1967) to the presidency. The second Somoza was also trained in the United States—in agricultural economics at the University of California, Berkeley. He ruled in a reformist environment, including inviting the Alliance for Progress into the country to help develop and modernize the economy. Most of the resistance to his government came from conservatives who wanted to return to power, rather than from the political left. In 1957, his opponents boycotted what were to be obviously fraudulent elections. In order to create a fiction of democratic pluralism, Somoza created a Conservative Nationalist party to compete in their stead.

In 1967 at the age of forty-four, the second Somoza died of a massive heart attack. Power subsequently passed to his younger brother Anastasio Somoza Debayle (1925–1980, known as "Tachito"). Growing income disparities between the rich and the poor and an unequal distribution of land under his rule contributed to lower-class discontent and unrest. This final Somoza was so militaristic, greedy, and brutal in his quest for more power and wealth that even some of his own upper- and middle-class supporters turned against him and joined in the popular movement that eventually ousted him from power. As political repression and massacres increased, he faced more international pressure due to his blatant human rights violations. Even so, he enjoyed close relations with the U.S. government because of his strongly reliable anticommunist position.

Nicaraguan Socialist Party (PSN)

Except for Sandino's struggle against the U.S. Marines in the 1920s and 1930s, Nicaragua remained largely isolated from the labor and political organizational efforts undertaken in much of the rest of Latin America. Leftists did not organize the first communist party in Nicaragua until 1944, about twenty years later than their counterparts in most of the rest of the hemisphere. As in Cuba, the Nicaraguan communist party called itself socialist, the Partido Socialista Nicaragüense (PSN, Nicaraguan Socialist Party), in order to present itself as less of a threat to the established international capitalist order. Like other Latin American communist parties of this era, the PSN was a pro-Soviet party that followed the rigid ideology and united front strategy of the Communist International. It was formed during the Second

World War under the influence of Earl Browder, the secretary-general of the Communist Party of the United States of America (CPUSA). With Germany threatening the very existence of the Soviet Union, Browder argued that the historic antagonism and contradiction between the bourgeoisie and the working class had disappeared. Members of each country's communist party should unite behind their government and join the war effort to defeat the rise of fascism in Europe. In Nicaragua, the PSN followed the same strategy and for several years worked openly with the Somoza regime, similar to the communist collaboration with Batista in Cuba. This strategy also benefited the Somoza government, which had temporarily adopted a populist stance in order to undercut the strength of leftist labor leaders.

The PSN had the country's small urban proletariat as its base and largely remained removed from rural organizing efforts. The PSN believed that due to the underdeveloped precapitalist economy, the Nicaraguan masses lacked the potential to develop a revolutionary consciousness. From their perspective, Nicaragua did not meet the proper objective conditions for a revolutionary class struggle. Instead, the PSN worked for the development of capitalism as a necessary precondition before attempting to move on to a socialist mode of production. In 1948, with the onset of the Cold War, Somoza García outlawed the PSN and imprisoned or exiled its members, or drove them underground. As in Cuba, this party became ineffective in its opposition to a brutal and oppressive dictatorship.

SANDINISTA NATIONAL LIBERATION FRONT

The success of the Cuban Revolution in 1959 convinced several members of the PSN that they too could organize a guerrilla movement to topple the Somoza dynasty and replace it with a socialist government. Several minor initial attempts in 1959 failed. Nevertheless, young activists believed they could foment a revolutionary consciousness among the Nicaraguan people. Having lost patience with the conservative and passive nature of the PSN, Carlos Fonseca Amador (1936–1976), Tomás Borge Martínez (1930–2012), and others formed the clandestine Sandinista National Liberation Front (FSLN) in 1961. For eighteen years the Sandinistas carried on their efforts at political organization among the Nicaraguan peasant and urban masses before finally claiming victory.

These early Sandinistas condemned the PSN for its policies of class collaboration, support for the bourgeoisie, and acting as an accomplice to U.S. imperialism during the Second World War. The PSN, for its part, denounced the FSLN's efforts as utopian and premature adventurism, much as Cuban communists had previously criticized Fidel Castro's 26th of July Movement. The PSN opted to wait for the proper economic conditions for a social revolution as it continued slowly to organize the proletariat into a working-class movement. Nevertheless, it was out of this situation that a noncommunist guerrilla movement organized a successful armed socialist revolution in Central America.

BIOGRAPHY: CARLOS FONSECA AMADOR, 1936–1976

Carlos Fonseca Amador was largely responsible for shaping Sandinista ideology in the 1960s. Fonseca brought to the FSLN a Marxist-Leninist analysis of Nicaraguan society that he had learned from the PSN. Fonseca, however, used this analysis to challenge the assumptions of the old-line communist party. Similar to José Carlos Mariátegui in Peru, Fonseca emphasized the importance of a creative and flexible approach to revolutionary theory and stressed that a strategy must be specifically adapted to the concrete circumstances of a country rather than dictated by ideologues in distant Moscow.

Mural of Carlos Fonseca (left) together with Che Guevara (in back) and Augusto César Sandino (right) at the Centro Cultural Batahola Norte, Managua
Source: Photo by Marc Becker

Fonseca began his career as a political activist while a high school student in the 1950s in Matagalpa in northern Nicaragua. He was arrested many times during the course of his life for his political activities. Like Che Guevara, the 1954 military coup against Jacobo Arbenz's government in Guatemala woke his revolutionary consciousness. Fonseca believed that the struggle in Nicaragua was not to change a government but to overthrow an entire system. Together with his classmate Tomás Borge, Fonseca formed a student activist group that established contacts with local labor unions. Fonseca earned a reputation as an outstanding student and an avid reader. Through his studies and during a brief tenure as a librarian in Managua, he came in contact with a wide variety of European and Latin American writers who influenced the development of his Marxism. Fonseca graduated at the top of his high school class in 1955 after writing a thesis on Karl Marx's classic work on political economy, *Capital*.

Fonseca and Borge studied law at the National Autonomous University in León where their political activism quickly became more important than their studies. Both joined the PSN in 1955 and together organized a communist party cell and a Marxist study group at the university. In 1957, Fonseca visited the Soviet Union for a youth congress and was imprisoned on his return to Nicaragua. The members of the university study group became increasingly more militant in their belief that they could create a socialist revolution rather than wait for the development of proper economic conditions. The PSN, they contended, was too orthodox, dogmatic, and unrevolutionary in its policies to lead this struggle. Fonseca visited Cuba in July 1959 and returned convinced that a socialist revolution was possible in a backward country. Influenced by the success of the Cuban

Revolution, Fonseca left the communist party in 1959 and joined a guerrilla group that invaded Nicaragua with the intent to overthrow the Somoza dynasty.

The models for guerrilla warfare that Guevara worked out in Cuba strongly influenced Fonseca. He also studied other internationalist philosophies, but ultimately he believed that the FSLN must root its struggle in Nicaragua's own national realities. To this end, Fonseca resurrected the image of General Augusto César Sandino as a national hero and promoted the social and political aspects of Sandino's thought. Somoza had ferociously attacked Sandino, and his image had largely disappeared from the memory of the Nicaraguan public. The PSN criticized Sandino as a petit bourgeois nationalist without a coherent political or economic program and condemned his alleged lack of a proper class analysis of Nicaraguan society. Fonseca, however, looked to him as a symbol of his struggle much as Castro had used José Martí to gain support for the 26th of July Movement in Cuba. Originally the Nicaraguan guerrillas had planned to form a National Liberation Front (FLN), and it was Fonseca who added "Sandinista" to the name. He adopted Sandino's slogan that only the workers and peasants would go all the way to victory.

As the FSLN's leading intellectual, Fonseca stressed the importance of popular education. Borge recounted the story of training a group of peasants in the use of weapons, and when Fonseca arrived he instructed the guerrillas to teach the peasants to read as well. Fonseca's mandate "and also teach them to read" became the slogan of the 1980 literacy crusade that characterized the early years of the revolution. Education was not to remain the sole dominion of the ruling class but a tool to empower the peasant and working-class masses. Fonseca's emphasis on the political education of the peasantry along with his flexible approach to revolutionary theory and his ability to learn from his mistakes contributed to a situation in which the Sandinistas ultimately triumphed in their social revolution.

DOCUMENT: "THE HISTORIC PROGRAM OF THE FSLN," 1969

The Sandinistas presented the following document to the Nicaraguan people in 1969 as a statement of their political, economic, and social demands. It is striking for the broad range of issues that it engages, including the rights of women and Indigenous peoples and a respect for religious beliefs.

The Sandinista National Liberation Front (FSLN) has emerged from the needs of the Nicaraguan people to have a "vanguard organization" capable of taking political power through a direct struggle against its enemies and the establishment of a social system that wipes out the exploitation and poverty that our people have suffered in the past.

The FSLN is a political-military organization whose strategic goal is the seizure of political power through the destruction of the military and bureaucratic apparatus of the dictatorship and the establishment of a revolutionary government based on an alliance of workers and peasants and the cooperation of all patriotic anti-imperialist and antioligarchic forces in the country.

The people of Nicaragua suffer under the subjugation of a reactionary and fascist clique that Yankee imperialism imposed in 1932 when Anastasio Somoza García was named commander in chief of the so-called National Guard (GN).

The Somoza clique has reduced Nicaragua to a neocolonial status exploited by the Yankee monopolies and oligarchic groups in the country.

The current regime is politically unpopular and illegal. Recognition and support from the United States is irrefutable evidence of foreign interference in Nicaraguan affairs.

The FSLN has analyzed the national reality seriously and with great responsibility, and has resolved to confront the dictatorship with weapons in hand. We have concluded that the triumph of the Sandinista Revolution and the overthrow of the regime that is an enemy of the people will emerge as a result of the development of a hard-fought and prolonged popular war.

Whatever maneuvers and resources Yankee imperialism deploys, the Somoza dictatorship is doomed to complete failure in the face of the rapid advance and development of the Sandinista National Liberation Front's popular forces.

Given this historical juncture the FSLN has developed this political program to strengthen and develop our organization, to encourage and stimulate the people of Nicaragua to march forward, determined to fight to overthrow the dictatorship, and to resist the intervention of Yankee imperialism in order to forge a free, prosperous, and revolutionary homeland.

I. A Revolutionary Government

The Sandinista Revolution will establish a revolutionary government to liquidate the reactionary structure that arose from rigged elections and military coups. Popular power will forge a Nicaragua that is free of exploitation, oppression, and backwardness, a free, progressive, and independent homeland.

The revolutionary government shall adopt the following political measures:

A. It will create a revolutionary power structure that will allow the full participation of all people, on both the national and local level.
B. It will guarantee all citizens the full exercise of all individual freedoms and respect for human rights.
C. It will guarantee freedom of thought, leading primarily to the vigorous dissemination of popular and patriotic rights.
D. It will guarantee the freedom to labor organizing in the city and the countryside, and freedom to organize peasant, youth, student, women's, cultural, sporting, and other groups.
E. It will guarantee the right of Nicaraguan immigrants and exiles to return home.
F. It will guarantee the right to asylum for citizens of other countries who are persecuted for participation in the revolutionary struggle.
G. It will severely punish the gangsters who are guilty of persecuting, informing on, abusing, torturing, or murdering revolutionaries and the people.
H. It will strip political rights from individuals who occupy high political posts as a result of rigged elections and military coups.

The revolutionary government will issue the following economic measures:

A. It will expropriate large estates, factories, businesses, buildings, transportation and other property that the Somoza family usurped and accumulated through the misappropriation and waste of the wealth of the nation.
B. It will expropriate large estates, factories, businesses, transportation, and other property that politicians, military officers, and all kinds of accomplices usurped through the current regime's administrative corruption.
C. It will nationalize the assets of all foreign companies engaged in the exploitation of mineral, forestry, maritime, and other resources.

D. It will establish workers' control over the administration of companies and other expropriated and nationalized property.
E. It will centralize the public transit system.
F. It will nationalize the banking system, which will be placed at the exclusive service of the country's economic development.
G. It will establish an independent currency.
H. It will refuse to honor loans that the Yankee monopolies or other powers imposed on the country.
I. It will establish trade relations with all countries, whatever their system of government, to benefit the country's economic development.
J. It will establish an appropriate tax policy, which will be applied with strict justice.
K. It will prohibit usury for both Nicaraguans and foreigners.
L. It will protect small- and medium-sized owners (producers, merchants) while restricting the excesses that lead to the exploitation of the workers.
M. It will establish state control over foreign trade in order to diversify it and make it independent.
N. It will rigorously restrict the importation of luxury goods.
O. It will plan the national economy, putting an end to the anarchy characteristic of the capitalist system of production. An important part of this planning will focus on the industrialization and electrification of the country.

VI. Reincorporation of the Atlantic Coast

The Sandinista Popular Revolution will implement a special plan for the Atlantic coast, which has been abandoned to total neglect, in order to incorporate it into the nation's life.

A. It will end the unjust exploitation the Atlantic coast has suffered throughout history from foreign monopolies, especially Yankee imperialism.
B. It will prepare suitable lands in the area for the development of agriculture and livestock.
C. It will establish favorable conditions for the development of fisheries and forestry.
D. It will encourage the flowering of the region's local cultural values that flow from the specific aspects of its historic tradition.
E. It will wipe out the odious discrimination that the Indigenous Miskito, Sumu, Zambos, and Blacks in that region have faced.

VII. Emancipation of Women

The Sandinista Revolution will abolish the odious discrimination that women have suffered in comparison to men, and establish economic, political, and cultural equality between women and men.

A. It will pay special attention to mothers and children.
B. It will eliminate prostitution and other social vices, which will raise women's dignity.
C. It will end the system of servitude that women suffer that is reflected in the tragedy of the abandoned working mother.
D. Revolutionary institutions will establish equal protection for children born out of wedlock.
E. It will establish daycare centers for the care and attention of the children of working women.
F. It will establish a two-month maternity leave before and after birth for working women.
G. It will raise women's political, cultural, and vocational levels through their participation in the revolutionary process.

VIII. Respect for Religious Beliefs

The Popular Sandinista Revolution will guarantee the freedom to profess any religion.

A. It will respect the right of citizens to profess and practice any religious belief.
B. It will support the work of priests and other religious figures who defend the working people.

XI. Solidarity among Peoples

The Popular Sandinista Revolution will put an end to the use of national territory as a base for Yankee aggression against other sister nations and implement militant solidarity with fraternal peoples fighting for their liberation.

A. It will actively support the struggle of the peoples of Asia, Africa, and Latin America against old and new colonialism and against the common enemy: Yankee imperialism.
B. It will support the struggle of Black people and all the people of the United States for genuine democracy and equal rights.
C. It will support the struggle of all peoples against the installation of Yankee military bases in foreign countries.

XIII. Veneration of Our Martyrs

The Popular Sandinista Revolution will maintain eternal gratitude and veneration of our homeland's martyrs and will continue their shining example of heroism and selflessness.

A. It will educate new generations in eternal gratitude and reverence for those who have fallen in the struggle to make Nicaragua a free homeland.
B. It will establish a secondary school to educate the children of our people's martyrs.
C. It will inculcate in all people the imperishable example of our martyrs, defending the revolutionary ideal: Ever onward to victory!!!

Source: Frente Sandinista de Liberación Nacional, *Programa histórico del FSLN* (Managua, Nicaragua: Departmento de Propaganda y Educación Política del FSLN, 1984; translation by author).

Che Guevara was directly involved with the formation of the FSLN. He helped train and arm the Nicaraguan guerrillas, and at one point he considered personally joining the Sandinistas' struggle in Nicaragua. Guevara's **foco** theory that a small insurrectionary guerrilla army could spark a broad revolution defined the Nicaraguans' military strategy during the first phase of guerrilla operations from 1962 to 1967. In 1967, the Sandinistas organized a rural guerrilla foco at the remote village of Pancasán, where thirty-five guerrillas worked with the local peasants. The Sandinistas accidentally ran into the police who killed all but fifteen of the guerrillas, including key FSLN founders. The national guard responded ferociously to the guerrilla presence, interrogating, threatening, and killing hundreds of suspected Sandinistas. The repression almost wiped out the entire FSLN organization. Rebuilding the guerrilla movement would be a long, slow, hard process.

Historic Program of the FSLN

As part of reconstructing its popular forces, the FSLN outlined its revolutionary aims and ideology in its 1969 "Historic Program of the FSLN" (included as the primary source with this chapter). Fonseca drafted this thirteen-point program that combined nationalist, democratic, and anticapitalist demands. The program called for a revolutionary government that would distribute land to the peasants, enact far-reaching labor legislation, grant equal rights to women, end discrimination against African descendants and Indigenous peoples, respect religious freedom, and carry out a revolution in education and culture. The program called for the nationalization of all of the property that the Somoza family and its cronies owned, all natural resources that foreigners controlled, all large landholdings, and the banking system. Many of these demands were similar to those from the Mexican Revolution and illustrated the persistent influence of that earlier event on the Latin American left.

The FSLN positioned itself as the vanguard of a worker-peasant alliance and called on people to join in a "patriotic anti-imperialist and antioligarchic" struggle. The Sandinista Front professed its commitment to an agrarian reform that would benefit the peasant masses. In addition, the Sandinistas declared their strong support for international solidarity, including encouragement for the peoples of Asia, Africa, and Latin America in their struggles against U.S. imperialism. Much like Mariátegui before them, the FSLN leaders combined anti-imperialist nationalist sentiments with the idea of an international class struggle. The 1969 declaration, nevertheless, stopped short of calling for socialism. The Sandinistas were not fighting for an abstract social or Marxist revolution but one firmly grounded in their own historical reality and experience.

The Sandinistas condemned Somoza's neglect and exploitation of the Atlantic coast and vowed to terminate the racial discrimination that Indigenous and Afro-Nicaraguans faced. The Sandinistas enjoyed a high degree of support from the Indigenous neighborhoods of Monimbó in Masaya and Subtiava in León. The Sandinistas drew on their actions and those of Indigenous peoples in Matagalpa as part of a long history of resistance to colonial domination. During years of political organizing in the Nicaraguan mountains, the Sandinistas came in daily contact with mestizo peasants and members of the Miskito, Sumu, and Rama peoples. While in exile in Chile in the early 1970s, Jaime Wheelock Román, who later served as minister of agriculture in the revolutionary government, wrote a treatise titled "Indigenous Roots of the Anti-colonial Struggle in Nicaragua." He criticized historians for identifying with Spanish colonialists and ignoring the legacy of Indigenous resistance. The Sandinistas gained support because they fought for the rights of marginalized peoples.

The Fall of Somoza

At 12:29 a.m. on Saturday, December 23, 1972, a massive magnitude 6.2 earthquake destroyed central Managua. The earthquake left six thousand people dead, twenty thousand injured, and over a quarter million homeless. As is often the case, the earthquake was as much a political as a natural disaster, and with a better functioning government the damage would not have been so extensive. Only two buildings, the Intercontinental Hotel and the Bank of America, had been built properly to code and survived the quake. In its aftermath, Somoza bought up land on the outskirts of the city and sold it at inflated speculative prices to the homeless who were afraid to return to the city center. He redirected donated aid to his own warehouses and sold it to the displaced. The Red Cross furnished blood for victims, but Nicaragua lacked a sufficiently functioning medical system to use the blood before it expired so Somoza resold it on the international market. When he realized the profits he could make on the sale of blood, he set up centers to collect plasma from Nicaraguans and sold that as well. When the corruption reached the level of vampires, the population began to turn against him. The earthquake and subsequent reconstruction efforts laid bare the unscrupulous nature of Somoza's regime and contributed to a resurgence of the FSLN.

Building on the momentum gained from the 1972 earthquake, the Sandinistas engaged in ever more daring actions. Two years later, they earned widespread notoriety and support when on December 27, 1974, they crashed Somoza's Christmas party and took forty guests hostage. The Sandinistas missed Somoza and the U.S. ambassador who had just left the party—although perhaps that was intentional because their capture might have triggered an undesirable U.S. intervention. The Sandinistas gained freedom for fourteen political prisoners, including future president Daniel Ortega (1945–); a ransom of one million dollars; passage to Cuba; and the promulgation of a communiqué on the radio and in the printed press. The boldness of the action earned the Sandinistas widespread renown. While successful, the action resulted in an increase in repression as Somoza lashed out at the perpetrators.

In 1975 and 1976 the FSLN broke into three factions, or "tendencies." The *proletarios* (proletarians) followed an orthodox Marxist line that favored concentrating political work among the urban poor. They advocated for the formation of an urban, working-class vanguard party to lead a class struggle against the bourgeoisie. Jaime Wheelock Román, the intellectual who had studied economics in Chile during Salvador Allende's government in the early 1970s, led this wing. In contrast, a second tendency, the *guerra popular prolongada* (GPP, Prolonged People's War), emphasized a Maoist strategy of concentrating military forces in the countryside rather than in the city. Those proponents dedicated their efforts to the political and military organization of poor peasants. FSLN founder and future minister of the interior Tomás Borge led this faction. The third tendency, known simply as the *terceristas* (third way) or insurrectionists, favored a flexible ideology and broad alliances, and eventually became the dominant force in the FSLN.

The terceristas combined elements of the proletarians' class consciousness with the GPP's agrarian-based military strategy. They argued that the subjective conditions existed in Nicaragua for a popular insurrection. They brought Social Democrats, the progressive bourgeoisie, and radical Christians into a unified Sandinista-led struggle against the Somoza dictatorship. It was the pragmatic flexibility and ideological

plurality of the terceristas that galvanized Sandinista leadership over a popular insurrection and defined a nationalistic direction for the Nicaraguan Revolution. Daniel
Ortega emerged as the leader of this faction that deviated significantly from orthodox Marxist theory. Partisans of the other tendencies later blamed the Sandinistas'
shortcomings on the lack of a clear ideology that emerged out of this current.

The death of Fonseca in combat on November 8, 1976, was a serious blow to the
Sandinistas. The FSLN founder and chief intellectual was the leader most capable of
bridging the movement's strategic and ideological divides, but he was less effective
as a guerrilla fighter. In 1978, Fidel Castro urged the reunification of these three
tendencies, a task that would have been much easier had Fonseca still been alive.
Castro argued that the best support he could give the Sandinistas was to do nothing
in order to emphasize the local origins of their struggle. He emphasized that Cuba's
assistance would be mostly ideological, moral, and political but not military. From
his own success in Cuba, Castro understood that a guerrilla struggle needed to rely
on the support of the local population. In March 1979, the three FSLN factions
finally managed to reunite their forces. Three members from each tendency formed
a national directorate that set a unified strategy and policy for the movement.

On January 10, 1978, Pedro Joaquín Chamorro, the publisher of Nicaragua's
largest newspaper *La Prensa* and one of Somoza's most outspoken foes, was killed.
Although Somoza was not directly implicated in his assassination, he had the most
to gain from his death. Chamorro came from a leading conservative family, and his
murder galvanized the anti-Somoza business opposition to the dictatorship. Chamorro's death sparked outrage that led to strikes and demonstrations. While most
of the reaction was unorganized, the Sandinistas took advantage of the unrest to
stockpile arms and organize the urban and rural poor.

Building on this growing antagonism, on August 22, 1978, the Sandinistas seized
the national palace in a daring assault. Their raid captured 1,500 people, including
forty-nine deputies, close friends of Somoza, and even Somoza's son. Terceristas Edén
Pastora, known as "Comandante Cero," and Dora María Tellez gained widespread
fame for their flawless design and execution of the attack. As in 1974, Somoza once
again capitulated to the Sandinistas' demands. The guerrillas gained the release
of fifty-nine political prisoners, including FSLN founder Tomás Borge; cash; the
publication of a communiqué; and passage out of the country. The audacity of the
Sandinista action captured the public's imagination. Thousands of cheering supporters lined the streets as the Sandinistas traveled to the airport for their flight to
Panama. The successful operation illustrated the guerrillas' ability to penetrate the
inner reaches of the government and the extent of their widespread support. The
dictator's days were numbered.

In September 1978, the Sandinistas launched a military offensive and a general
strike against the Somoza government. Their actions sparked mass insurrections in
cities across the country. In June and July 1979, the FSLN followed with a final offensive during which they captured and controlled key areas of the country. In the
final months of the Sandinista insurrection, Somoza launched vicious attacks against

the Sandinistas' civilian base, including the aerial bombardment of poor neighborhoods that left them completely destroyed. In the process, the dictatorship killed fifty thousand people and wounded twice as many. The casualty rate in proportion to the total population was higher than that during the 1860s civil war in the United States.

The end of U.S. support for Somoza's regime came with the June 20, 1979, murder of ABC journalist William Stewart. At first Somoza blamed his killing on the Sandinistas and used the death to paint his opponents as cold-blooded assassins. Unbeknownst to Somoza, Stewart's crew had filmed the national guard gunning down Stewart during a traffic stop. ABC broadcast the footage on the evening news, which shifted international sentiments against the regime. After the murders of tens of thousands of Nicaraguans, the death of one U.S. citizen forced president Jimmy Carter to cut off military aid. Without the support of his most loyal ally, Somoza could not hold on to power. Carter called for *Somocismo sin Somoza* (the continuance of a conservative, pro-U.S. government led by wealthy individuals but without the extreme excesses of the Somoza dictatorship), but he could not control the subsequent direction of events.

Somoza left Nicaragua for Miami on July 17, 1979, taking much of the national treasury with him. The Carter administration refused him residency because he had violated an agreement with the U.S. ambassador in Managua not to manipulate his succession in power. Instead, the former strongman settled in Paraguay, where he found a sympathetic environment under the protection of the conservative Alfredo Stroessner administration. Fourteen months later, guerrilla commandos from Argentina and Chile with support from leftists in Uruguay and Paraguay assassinated Somoza in Asunción. The leftists had grown weary of watching dictators destroy their countries and then live out the rest of their lives in comfortable exile, and were determined not to let that happen to the former Nicaraguan tyrant.

LIBERATION THEOLOGY

Nicaragua is a land of poets, and this reality helped emphasize the subjective and emotional aspects of the Sandinistas' revolutionary struggle. Not only did poetry form a large part of Nicaragua's national identity, but also the Sandinistas used it in practical ways, such as to instruct the population in the art of making armaments. During the insurrection, sermons from radical priests proved to be more inspirational than dry economic treatises in mobilizing the masses to action. The Sandinistas became one of the first leftist revolutions to accept openly the role and contribution of religious workers to the process of social change. Rather than seeing religion as a form of alienation and false consciousness as orthodox Marxists tended to do, the Sandinistas believed that religion could be used to heighten people's revolutionary awareness.

Traditionally, the Catholic Church, together with the military and wealthy landowners, had been an ally of the conservative oligarchy. Changes in Catholic theology in the 1960s, including the Second Vatican Council that modernized the church's archaic practices, challenged those alliances. At a 1968 conference at Medellín, Colombia, Latin American bishops declared their "preferential option for the poor." Progressive elements in the church called for religious participation in leftist social movements. Many revolutionaries deemphasized liberal anticlerical views in favor of an acceptance of the positive contributions of religious actors to a revolutionary process. This structural shift in alliances led to the rise of a political and revolutionary popular church and what came to be known as liberation theology. These developments allowed for a greater involvement of religious actors in the political process in Nicaragua than what had occurred with their counterparts in Cuba in the 1950s.

Liberation theology employed Marxist analytical tools of class struggle to reflect critically on societal problems. The Peruvian theologian Gustavo Gutiérrez articulated the central tenets of this approach in his 1971 book *A Theology of Liberation*. The emergence of that theology represented a historic turning point in the attitude of the Catholic Church toward popular movements for social justice. Traditional Christian theology, which emerged from upper-class articulations, endeavored to dictate orders to lower-class workers and peasants. Liberation theologians sought to reverse that relationship, to give hope to the aspirations of the oppressed, and to lead people to realize that they must take a conscious responsibility for their own destiny. Rather than presenting an escapist religion, liberation theology contributed to political empowerment and structural alterations. An important element of liberation theology was the concept of praxis, the combination of theory and practice in a revolutionary situation. For example, catechists would read the biblical story of the Jewish exodus from slavery in Egypt and discuss how it applied to their situation in fighting the Somoza dictatorship. Liberation theology's praxis led far away from the domain of religion and theology into the realm of politics, economics, and history with a goal of addressing societal injustices.

The influence of liberation theology left an unmistakable impression on Nicaragua and Sandinista ideology. Unlike their counterparts in Cuba, the Nicaraguans welcomed religious leaders into their ranks. Several factors account for the different attitudes toward religion in Nicaragua and Cuba. The Catholic Church in Cuba was not the strong institution that it was in Nicaragua. In Cuba, it did not reach much beyond the small urban middle class and was thus divorced from the reality of the majority of the population. With notable exceptions such as Frank País, who was a Baptist Sunday school teacher, few combatants in Castro's 26th of July Movement were religious. Nicaragua, on the other hand, had a strong Catholic tradition, and many devout believers joined the FSLN in the campaign to overthrow the Somoza dictatorship. Liberation theologians had a profound influence on the Sandinistas' open attitude toward religion. Unlike in Cuba, there was no contradiction in Nicaragua between religious involvement and participation in the Sandinista Revolution. Sandinista party militants who had fused religion and politics visited Cuba, and their presence encouraged the Cuban government to reorient official thinking and party policy toward religion. A direct result of that influence in Cuba was the aperture of new spaces for the involvement of religious actors in the construction of a new society. The Nicaraguan experience contributed to a new openness among the left to people of faith across the hemisphere.

Through the initiative and efforts of Catholic priests and local religious organizations committed to social justice known as Christian Base Communities, the struggles of Christians and the Sandinistas were combined into one unified fight against Somoza. During the insurrection, elements of Nicaragua's progressive popular church worked openly with the Sandinista movement, and the Sandinistas willingly accepted their contribution toward the building of a new society. Radical trends in Catholic theology influenced priests who organized social action based on a class analysis of society. Gaspar García Laviana was one such priest who had become frustrated at the failure of peaceful paths to address long-standing problems of poverty and equality. García Laviana joined the Sandinistas and rose to the position of commander in the FSLN's southern front before he was killed in December 1978. Similarly, Father Uriel Molina organized Christian Base Communities to mobilize grassroots support in poor neighborhoods in Managua in favor of the FSLN guerrillas. His church became a sanctuary for activists and a revolutionary armory, with its walls decorated with murals of armed struggle.

Other priests, such as Ernesto Cardenal (1925–), Fernando Cardenal (1934–2016), and Miguel d'Escoto (1933–), also joined forces with the FSLN and took positions in the Sandinista government after the triumph of the 1979 revolution. Trappist father Ernesto Cardenal emerged out of a religious community at Solentiname in Lake Nicaragua in the 1960s to lead the religious opposition to the Somoza dictatorship. His theological reflections contributed to an increased awareness of the economic injustices in Nicaragua and the need for political action to change that reality. A trip to Cuba in 1970 convinced Cardenal that no contradiction existed between Marxism and Christianity. He became an avowed Marxist revolutionary, and he presented the most articulate fusion of Catholic theology and the theory of Marxist class struggle in Nicaragua. Cardenal considered primitive Christian communalism to be a precursor of Marxism, and he believed that Christianity expressed in religious terms the same class struggle that Marx articulated in scientific terms. This struggle extended itself to a battle between the reactionary Christianity of the Somoza dictatorship and the revolutionary Christianity of the proletariat and the popular church. The goal of the Sandinista struggle was the establishment of the biblical kingdom of heaven on earth that would lead to a society without exploitation or domination and a fraternity of love among people.

Miguel d'Escoto was a Maryknoll priest who assumed the position of minister of foreign relations in the Sandinistas' new revolutionary government. Mahatma Gandhi and Martin Luther King Jr.'s nonviolent protests deeply influenced his policies. He echoed their actions by engaging in a hunger strike and leading people on a peace walk in opposition to U.S. attacks on the country. Ernesto Cardenal served as minister of culture in the government. His brother Fernando, a Jesuit priest, was minister of education.

Catholics were not the only Christians who joined forces with the FSLN. A growing radicalism among small protestant sects also contributed to the development of the revolutionary process in Nicaragua. Most significant was the Comité Evangélico Pro-Ayuda a los Damnificados (CEPAD, Evangelical Committee for Aid to the Earthquake Victims) that was formed in the aftermath of the 1972 earthquake. Under the leadership of Gustavo Parajón, CEPAD developed community organizations that established contacts with revolutionary movements. Rather than forming a reactionary force, the Sandinistas believed that a religious faith could aid in the fomenting of a revolutionary consciousness and in the development of a new society. In response, religious actors assumed a larger role in Nicaragua's revolutionary struggle than anywhere else in Latin America.

SANDINISTA POLICIES

On July 19, 1979, the Sandinistas rolled into Managua and ushered in the second successful armed socialist revolution in Latin America. With Somoza gone, a broad range of the dictator's opponents assembled as a Junta of National Reconstruction initially took power. Wealthy conservative business leaders who had been squeezed out of political and economic control over the country sometimes had more reason to despise the Somoza dictatorship than the Sandinistas who attacked the former leader from the left and from below. The pluralistic and ideologically incoherent junta soon gave way to control by a nine-person all-male FSLN national directorate.

The tercerista leader Daniel Ortega was the coordinator of the ruling junta and remained the leader of the Sandinistas during their eleven years in power. Ortega's supporters celebrated the terceristas' pragmatic flexibility and ideological plurality that had galvanized Sandinista leadership over a popular insurrection and defined the unique nationalistic direction of the revolution. The terceristas deviated significantly from orthodox Marxist theory in their analysis of Nicaragua's historical situation as they developed strategies appropriate to their local reality.

Once in power, the Sandinistas implemented the goals of a mixed economy, a plural political system, and a nonaligned foreign policy. They implemented social programs that emphasized a provision of housing, education, and assistance for rural peasants. The government expropriated and nationalized Somoza's property, redistributed land to rural communities, and created new revolutionary institutions. Unlike in Cuba, the Sandinistas did not engage in show trials or the execution of their former torturers in Somoza's national guard. They vowed to lead a humane revolution.

Women

During the insurgency, women made up a third of the Sandinista force. Feminists looked to the FSLN as their best opportunity to gain full equality. In 1977, they organized the Asociación de Mujeres ante la Problemática Nacional (AMPRONAC,

Association of Women Concerned about the National Crisis) with the slogan "No revolution without women's emancipation; no emancipation without revolution." They were committed both to the overthrow of the Somoza regime and achievement of women's equality. In power, the Sandinistas improved the working conditions for women and granted rural women workers the right to control their own income. One of the Sandinistas' first actions was to ban media portrayals of women as sex objects. After the triumph of the revolution, the AMPRONAC renamed itself after a fallen Sandinista leader as the Asociación de Mujeres Nicaragüenses Luisa Amanda Espinoza (AMNLAE, Luisa Amanda Espinoza Association of Nicaraguan Women). Critics charged that AMNLAE was not a feminist organization that aimed for the full emancipation of women but instead was designed to support the Sandinista government. The AMNLAE leadership was accused of paternalistically deciding what was best for Nicaragua rather than representing the class interests of poor and working women. Even with these limitations, many observers recognized AMNLAE as a successful organization.

Even though women had participated actively in the Sandinista insurrection, most notably with the leadership of Dora María Tellez in the August 1978 attack on the national palace, they were largely excluded from positions of power in the new Sandinista government. Tellez served as minister of health, the highest-ranking woman in the new government. Others took similarly significant roles, such as Doris María Tijerino, who served as head of police. But women never reached the proportion of leadership commensurate to their numbers in society, or even to their positions in the insurgent guerrilla force. The feminist poet Gioconda Belli criticized the Sandinista male leadership in her memoir *The Country under My Skin* for expecting women to play the roles of mother and helpmate rather than assuming a role equal to men in building a new country.

One of the most famous images from the revolution was Orlando Valenzuela's *Miliciana de Waswalito* (*Militia Woman of Waswalito*). The photograph showed a smiling young mother breastfeeding her baby with an assault rifle slung over her shoulder. The image was intended to illustrate that a patriotic mother should engage in a civil defense patrol to defend her community from contra attacks. The image, however, could also be read as embracing women's contributions only as long as they also fulfilled a domestic role. Sexist attitudes remained deeply embedded in society.

Elections

In November 1984, strategically scheduled to parallel balloting in the United States, Nicaragua held its first relatively free election since 1928. The FSLN had moved the planned poll up from 1985 in order to gain international recognition and legitimacy for its revolutionary government. One of the reasons for doing so was the October 1983 U.S. invasion of the small Caribbean island of Grenada. A military coup had deposed the popular revolutionary Maurice Bishop, and the invasion took place under the questionable pretext of rescuing U.S. medical students. Many understood that invasion as putting the Sandinistas on notice that the United States would invade Nicaragua next.

The decision to hold elections was not without controversy. Sandinista leader Tomás Borge ridiculed the idea. He proclaimed, "El pueblo ya votó," meaning the people already voted for the type of government they desired through the direct demonstration of a display of arms without the possibility of fraudulent elections corrupting the process. Given Nicaragua's long experience with rigged electoral systems, his concern was not without merit. Nevertheless, the Sandinistas won the multiparty Western-style elections in a landslide with 67 percent of the vote. International observers reported that the vote accurately reflected the popular will of the Nicaraguan people.

Despite broad recognition of the outcome, President Ronald Reagan called the elections a "sham" and a "farce," and refused to acknowledge the outcome. The only elections that the U.S. government would recognize were the ones that they could control and win. They would never allow the Sandinistas to gain legitimacy as the democratic representatives of the Nicaraguan people.

In 1987, Nicaraguans ratified a new constitution that codified the transformations that they sought to make in the country. The most notable provision of the new document was autonomy for the Atlantic coast. Since 1984, the Sandinistas had engaged in conversations with Indigenous peoples to listen to their demands. Together they formed an autonomy commission and devised a plan to preserve Indigenous languages and cultural expressions. Despite initial tensions resulting from the vast cultural divides between the Pacific and the Atlantic sides of the country, the Sandinistas made significant strides in working out agreements that respected the country's cultural and ethnic diversity. The constitution provided people on the Atlantic coast with more control over their economic, social, and political affairs, including jurisdiction over communal lands and natural resources and provisions for political representation.

CONTRA WAR

On March 9, 1981, Reagan signed a secret authorization for the Central Intelligence Agency (CIA) to organize a paramilitary force to overthrow the Sandinista government. Together with the Argentine military, the CIA regrouped Somoza's former national guard and helped arm and train them into a counterrevolutionary force (called the *contras*). Reagan delegated John Negroponte, the U.S. ambassador to Honduras, to run this secret war. The paramilitary force conducted hit-and-run attacks on Nicaragua from Honduras, while the United States positioned warships off the Pacific coast and mined the country's harbors. Rather than direct attacks against military targets, the Reagan administration engaged in a strategy of "low-intensity warfare" that focused on soft targets such as teachers and healthcare providers who were less likely to fight back than men with guns. The contras committed atrocities that included murders, torture, kidnapping, and psychological campaigns against the civilian population. In 1985, the United States implemented a trade embargo against the country. Nicaraguan commerce with the United States fell from a third of its imports and exports to nothing. The goal was to produce an internal economic collapse that would drag the country down and halt agrarian and social reforms.

The anticommunist pope John Paul II visited Nicaragua in April 1983. The very religious population warmly welcomed his visit, but political tensions immediately rose to the surface. A deep divide quickly emerged between a popular church that embraced the tenets of liberation theology and the traditional Catholic hierarchy that retained its conservative alliances. On the tarmac on his arrival at Managua's airport, the pope criticized priests who served in the government. He excommunicated those who refused to resign their posts. The pope denied a mother's request to say a prayer for her sons fallen in combat in the contra war. In a huge outdoor mass, the people chanted that they wanted peace while the pope ordered them to be silent. He attacked the popular church and grassroots movements that supported the leftist Sandinistas and instead joined the church hierarchy in openly allying with the contras.

In response to the ongoing U.S. military and paramilitary attacks, Nicaragua took its adversary to the International Court of Justice. On June 27, 1986, the court ruled that the U.S. intervention in Nicaragua was an "unlawful use of force" and ordered the United States to desist and pay seventeen billion dollars in reparations. Reagan contemptuously dismissed the judgment, declared that the United States would not be bound by the decision, and proceeded to escalate attacks against the country's civilian population. In response, Nicaragua asked the United Nations Security Council to pass a resolution calling on governments to observe international law, but the United States vetoed it. Nicaragua then took a similar resolution to the United Nations General Assembly where it passed almost unanimously, with only U.S. and Israeli opposition. Not only had the International Court of Justice and the United Nations found the United States guilty of engaging in terrorist actions against Nicaragua, but also Reagan was now in violation of international law.

On October 5, 1986, the Nicaraguans shot down a U.S. military supply aircraft. Sandinista soldiers captured a crewmember, Eugene Hasenfus, who acknowledged that the CIA had employed him. This led to the unraveling of the Iran-Contra scandal that implicated Oliver North and other high-ranking officials in the Reagan administration for having secretly sold weapons to Iran and using the profits to supply and train the contras in violation of a series of laws. In 1989, North was convicted of three felonies, although the convictions were later overturned on appeal because he had admitted to the crimes while testifying under immunity in a congressional hearing.

The United States feared the independent example that the Sandinistas had created in Nicaragua and did not want their model of sovereign development to spread to other Central American countries. Overthrowing the Sandinistas became a linchpin of Reagan's foreign policy. This was the case even though Nicaragua was one of the smallest and poorest countries in the Americas. It had few exports and lacked the economic significance of Guatemala, Cuba, or Chile, where the United States had previously intervened against progressive governments. The war, nonetheless, devastated Nicaragua, killing fifty thousand people, making twice as many homeless, destroying entire communities, and leaving the economy in shambles.

Numerous international solidarity groups came to the defense of the Nicaraguan people. More than one hundred thousand U.S. citizens traveled to Nicaragua to support the Sandinistas or to oppose the contra war. Some came as aid workers bringing educational or technical skills, and others traveled to assist with coffee harvests. Many solidarity groups were religiously based. Witness for Peace was built on a concept that the presence of unarmed U.S. citizens would deter contra attacks. This strategy evolved almost by accident when, in 1983, a religious fact-finding delegation to the border town of Jalapa discovered that contra attacks ceased while international observers were present. The influential Pledge of Resistance vowed that if the United States invaded Nicaragua they would engage in massive public resistance. The religious magazine *Sojourners* declared on the front page of its August 1984 issue that Reagan was lying about the political changes in Nicaragua. Those who traveled to Nicaragua returned with a very different image of the country than what he had presented. Instead of a repressive regime, they witnessed a government dedicated to the expansion of healthcare and educational opportunities. These grassroots campaigns were successful in preventing a U.S. military intervention in the country.

1990 Elections

One lasting legacy of the Sandinistas was the implementation for the first time of a functioning electoral system. As the Sandinistas had done in 1984, the revolutionaries once again moved up the date of the 1990 elections to stave off attacks from the United States and gain a larger degree of international legitimacy. The Sandinistas were confident that they would win the vote, as preelection polls had indicated. In a shock to the entire country, the pro–United States candidate Violeta Barrios de Chamorro, the widow of *La Prensa* publisher Pedro Joaquín Chamorro, won instead. Rather than celebrating the electoral defeat of the Sandinistas, the country seemed to go into shock and mourning. Many people apparently had voted against the Sandinistas not because they wanted the conservative Chamorro to win but because they simply wished that the Sandinistas would be more responsive to popular demands. Furthermore, they wanted the contra war to end. Mothers in particular aimed for an end of the military draft of their sons.

In the 1990 election, the United States had offered Nicaraguans two options: vote for the Sandinistas and the economic warfare against the country would continue, or vote for Chamorro and receive extensive aid packages. The United States provided more funding for Chamorro's campaign than Somoza had paid in bribes during his fraudulent elections to justify maintaining himself in power. In the end, the Nicaraguan people cried uncle and hoped a change of government would end the merciless attacks. After Chamorro's election, the U.S. government quickly lost interest in Nicaragua and the promise of aid never materialized.

ASSESSMENT

A decade of U.S.-sponsored contra terror and related economic warfare derailed many of the socialist aspects of the Sandinista Revolution. Economic hardships proved to be more crucial for determining the electoral outcome than did the revolutionary fervor and idealism of the Sandinistas. Rather than subjective factors fomenting a political consciousness, economic factors pulled Nicaraguan society away from its revolutionary idealism, seemingly demonstrating a lack of a revolutionary class consciousness. In retrospect, some intellectuals believe that the fall of Somoza had come too easily and quickly, that through a longer and harder struggle the general public would have gained a higher level of political awareness that would have helped them withstand the imperialist attacks.

The Sandinistas did not institutionalize their revolution to the extent that the Cubans had done. Unlike Castro's declaration in April 1961, the Sandinista leadership never announced the Nicaraguan Revolution to be socialist. Developments in Nicaragua are perhaps a caution against a purely subjective interpretation of a revolutionary process. Economic factors played a large role in the evolution of social and political events. The defeat of the Sandinista government was also a caution that a revolutionary movement could not be a purely (or even chiefly) centralized, statist affair. The lasting revolutionary changes in Nicaragua were those that popular mass-based organizations launched. The revolutionary process is not simply a matter of gaining control of a government but rather a question of transforming the political consciousness of the people.

The 1990 electoral defeat of the Sandinistas raised the question of whether opening the country to liberal reforms led to their defeat. Was it possible to implement socialism through peaceful and democratic means? Was the only viable alternative to follow the Cuban path of closing the country to all opponents of the revolutionary project and only permit the participation of those willing to play by the established rules?

Daniel Ortega ran unsuccessfully again in 1996 and 2001 for the presidency. Finally, in 2007, a much changed and more moderate Ortega regained the presidency. Those to his left complained that he had compromised Sandinista ideals in order to win the election. Ortega came to an accommodation with the conservative Catholic Church hierarchy that had allied with the U.S. government and the contras against his leftist government in the 1980s. His support for reactionary policies that included one of the world's most draconian antiabortion measures led to a falling out with feminists and other social movement activists who otherwise would have provided a bedrock of support for his government. Feminists also reacted negatively to revelations that he had repeatedly raped his stepdaughter, Zoilamérica Narváez. As with the MNR in Bolivia, when the Sandinistas returned to power years later they were not nearly as revolutionary as they had been during their first time in office. Their actions raise the question of whether it is important for the left to gain and hold on to power at all costs.

SUMMARY

The Sandinistas provide only the second example of an armed guerrilla uprising successfully removing a previously entrenched government from power and introducing profound and transformative changes in society. Although the guerrillas fought against the government for eighteen years, their triumph in 1979 came surprisingly quickly as Somoza's former supporters turned against the regime. The Sandinistas soon marginalized their conservative allies from a ruling coalition and took the new government in a leftist direction. Initially Sandinistas achieved significant gains as they expropriated Somoza's property and redistributed resources to marginalized urban workers and rural peasants. They provided land, housing, and education to those who previously did not have access to such social services.

The Ronald Reagan administration quickly moved against the leftist Sandinistas and made their removal from power a linchpin of its foreign policy agenda. Despite international condemnation, Reagan created and trained a counterrevolutionary paramilitary force that terrorized the civilian population. Years of civil war that ravaged the country followed. The Sandinistas turned to elections to gain international legitimacy for their revolution, but instead the ballot became a mechanism for their conservative opponents to turn them out of power. Ironically, one of the most significant achievements of the Sandinista Revolution—the establishment of a functioning and democratic system—led to their undoing. After losing a series of elections, a much-changed Sandinista political party returned Daniel Ortega to the presidency in 2007. This time, they seemed determined to stay.

DISCUSSION QUESTIONS

Was the Sandinista struggle for socialism or for national liberation?

Was Nicaragua prepared for a socialist revolution?

What were the successful policies and actions of the Sandinista government?

Was it a mistake for the Sandinistas to hold elections?

Why did the Ronald Reagan administration see the Sandinistas as such a threat? Were they a threat?

Did religion play a positive or negative role in the Nicaraguan Revolution?

In retrospect, what could the Sandinistas have done differently to maintain themselves in power?

What kind of organization and leadership is necessary to build a revolutionary movement?

FURTHER READING

The Sandinista Revolution led to a cottage industry of publications on Nicaragua, many of the works with red and black covers—the colors of the Sandinista flag. Many of these books from the 1980s are still valuable as historical studies of the revolution.

Alegria, Claribel, and Darwin Flakoll. *Death of Somoza*. Willimantic, CT: Curbstone, 1996. A compelling journalistic account of the execution of Somoza in Paraguay.

Belli, Gioconda. *The Country under My Skin: A Memoir of Love and War*. New York: Knopf, 2002. An autobiography of a Sandinista militant that critiques the revolution's shortcomings.

Booth, John A. *The End and the Beginning: The Nicaraguan Revolution*. 2nd ed. Boulder: Westview, 1985. The standard survey of the Sandinista Revolution.

Cabezas, Omar. *Fire from the Mountain: The Making of a Sandinista*. New York: Crown, 1985. The most famous autobiography of a Sandinista leader.

Hale, Charles R. *Resistance and Contradiction: Miskitu Indians and the Nicaraguan State, 1894–1987*. Stanford, CA: Stanford University Press, 1994. An anthropological examination of Indigenous peoples on the Atlantic coast.

Hodges, Donald C. *Intellectual Foundations of the Nicaraguan Revolution*. Austin: University of Texas Press, 1986. A probing examination of the underlying ideology of the Sandinista Revolution.

Nolan, David. *The Ideology of the Sandinistas and the Nicaraguan Revolution*. Coral Gables, FL: University of Miami, 1984. An important examination of the different ideological currents within Sandinismo.

Peace, Roger C. *A Call to Conscience: The Anti-Contra War Campaign*. Amherst: University of Massachusetts Press, 2012. A survey of opposition to U.S. intervention in Nicaragua.

Walker, Thomas W., ed. *Nicaragua in Revolution*. New York: Praeger, 1982. An impressive collection of essays outlying the initial changes in Nicaragua after the revolution, edited by a preeminent political scientist.

Zimmermann, Matilde. *Sandinista: Carlos Fonseca and the Nicaraguan Revolution*. Durham, NC: Duke University Press, 2001. An outstanding biography of the most important Sandinista ideologue.

FILMS

Latino. 1985. A Chicano Green Beret begins to question the morality of the secret war he is fighting in the Nicaraguan forests.

Pictures from a Revolution. 2007. Photojournalist Susan Meiselas revisits people she photographed during the Sandinistas' insurgency in the 1970s.

Under Fire. 1983. A fictional portrayal of a photojournalist who helps the Sandinistas overthrow Somoza.

8

Guerrilla Warfare

KEY DATES

1959	Hugo Blanco begins to organize peasants in La Convención Valley in Peru
1960	Che Guevara publishes *Guerrilla Warfare*
1963	Police capture and imprison Hugo Blanco
1964	Founding of the ELN in Colombia
1965	Failure of Luis de la Puente Uceda's foco in Peru
1966	Founding of the FARC in Colombia
1967	Founding of the EPL in Colombia
October 8, 1967	Capture of Che Guevara in Bolivia; executed following day
March 24, 1980	Assassination of Salvadoran archbishop Monsignor Oscar Romero
May 17, 1980	Shining Path launches the armed phase of its "People's War" in Peru
January 1981	FMLN general offensive in El Salvador
1984	Founding of the MRTA in Peru
November 1989	FMLN final offensive in El Salvador
1992	El Salvador peace accord; Peruvian police capture Shining Path leader Abimael Guzmán
2009	Election of FMLN presidential candidate Mauricio Funes in El Salvador
2016	FARC signs peace accords with Colombian government

ACRONYMS

CGSB   Coordinadora Guerrillera Simón Bolívar (Simón Bolívar Guerrilla
           Coordinating Board)
ELN   Ejército de Liberación Nacional (National Liberation Army)
EPL   Ejército Popular de Liberación (Popular Liberation Army)
ERP   Ejército Revolucionario del Pueblo (People's Revolutionary Army)
FARC   Fuerzas Armadas Revolucionarias de Colombia (Revolutionary Armed
           Forces of Colombia)
FARN   Fuerzas Armadas de la Resistencia Nacional (National Resistance
           Armed Forces)
FDR   Frente Democrático Revolucionario (Revolutionary Democratic Front)
FMLN   Frente Farabundo Martí para la Liberación Nacional (Farabundo Martí
           National Liberation Front)
FPL   Fuerzas Populares de Liberación (Popular Liberation Forces)
MAQL   Movimiento Armado Quintín Lame (Quintín Lame Armed
           Movement)
MLN–T   Movimiento de Liberación Nacional–Tupamaros (National Liberation
           Movement–Tupamaros)
M-19   Movimiento 19 de Abril (19th of April Movement)
MRTA   Movimiento Revolucionario Tupac Amaru (Tupac Amaru
           Revolutionary Movement)
PCC   Partido Comunista Colombiano (Colombian Communist Party)
PCS   Partido Comunista de El Salvador (Communist Party of El Salvador)
PRTC   Partido Revolucionario de los Trabajadores Centroamericanos
           (Revolutionary Party of the Central American Workers)
UP   Union Patriótica (Patriotic Union)
URNG   Unidad Revolucionaria Nacional Guatemalteca (National
           Revolutionary Guatemalan Unity)

Guerrilla warfare in and of itself is not a revolution; it is simply a form of warfare. Rather than a reliance on large-scale military units as is common in conventional battles, guerrillas depend on small numbers of mobile fighters who live off the land with the support of a local population. The word "guerrilla" comes from the Spanish word for "little war," indicating the irregular nature of the tactics. With only a few combatants, the style of guerrilla warfare can provide a powerful response to a much larger and established military force. Although guerrilla wars are rarely successful, they can cause much larger opponents significant problems and bring their governments to a standstill.

This chapter examines 1980s guerrilla struggles in Latin America that failed to take power. It begins with an examination of the influence that the Cuban Revolution, and in particular the theoretical contributions of the guerrilla leader Che Guevara, had on these movements. This chapter considers the case studies of Colombia, El Salvador, and Peru, the three countries with the largest and most powerful insurgencies. Even though these revolutionaries faced similar conditions to their counterparts in Cuba and Nicaragua, they did not manage to take power through armed struggle. Multiple factors explain that outcome and highlight just how exceptional of an event successful guerrilla uprisings truly are.

CHE GUEVARA

The success of Fidel Castro's 26th of July Movement in Cuba challenged the assumptions of orthodox Marxism and gave hope and inspiration to a new generation of revolutionaries. The triumph of an armed struggle in Cuba led to the flourishing of guerrilla movements throughout the hemisphere. In 1960, Che Guevara published *Guerrilla Warfare* as a manual to guide revolutionaries on how to overthrow a dictatorship and implement a new and more just social order (see the primary source included with this chapter). Guevara analyzed the Cuban Revolution in order to extract general laws and develop a theory of guerrilla warfare. First, he argued that the Cuban Revolution demonstrated that people could organize themselves as a small guerrilla army and overthrow a large, powerful, established regime. Second, popular movements do not have to wait for the proper economic conditions before organizing a revolutionary war; the insurrectionary guerrilla force can create them. Third, Guevara believed that in Latin America revolutionary struggles should be based in a rural, peasant population.

BIOGRAPHY: CHE GUEVARA, 1928–1967

The Guatemalan Spring attracted many leftists and dissidents from across Latin America who were inspired by the ideals and policies of the Jacobo Arbenz administration, particularly in the way it compared to the repressive and exclusionary policies of their own governments. One of those who arrived in Guatemala in 1954 was a young Argentine doctor named Ernesto Guevara de la Serna.

Guevara was born in 1928 to a liberal-left middle-class family that embraced anticlerical ideas and supported the Republicans in the Spanish Civil War. His mother, Celia de la Serna, had a particularly important influence on the formation of his social conscience. Throughout his life, Guevara suffered from severe asthma attacks, but nevertheless he pushed himself and excelled as an athlete. In 1948, he entered the University of Buenos Aires to study medicine. Before finishing his studies, Guevara joined his friend Alberto Granado on a motorcycle trip that took them across Latin America. Although the motorcycle only made it as far as Chile, the two vagabonds continued on foot, hitchhiking, and by boat to Peru, Colombia, and Venezuela. For Guevara, it was a consciousness-raising experience that ultimately changed the direction his life would take. The trip converted Guevara into a pan-Latin Americanist. He believed that the region had a shared destiny

Che Guevara
Source: Photo by Alberto Korda, Wikimedia
Commons

and that national borders only served to divide people in their struggles for a more just social order.

After finishing his medical studies in 1953, Guevara set out on another trip through Latin America that matured his revolutionary political ideology. In Bolivia, he observed the mobilization of workers and the implementation of agrarian reform following a popular 1952 revolution. In Guatemala, he worked with Jacobo Arbenz's revolutionary government. While in Guatemala, he met a Peruvian exile named Hilda Gadea, who introduced him to leftist ideologies. Guevara lived through the military coup that overthrew Arbenz's government, and that experience converted Guevara into a dedicated fighter against U.S. imperialism. It also convinced him that it was necessary to destroy the political and military forces of the old system and to arm the masses to protect a revolution from counterrevolutionary forces. Guevara firmly believed that Arbenz would have survived the coup if he had relied on the peasants and workers to defend the revolutionary government.

After the Guatemalan coup, Guevara hid in the Argentine embassy before escaping to Mexico, where he began a serious study of Marxism. In Mexico, Gadea introduced Guevara to a Cuban exile named Fidel Castro, who was planning to return to his native Cuba to ignite a revolution. In 1956, Guevara joined Castro and eighty other guerrillas to launch an armed struggle against the Fulgencio Batista dictatorship. Castro had invited Guevara, the only non-Cuban in the group, to join as a medic. The Cuban guerrillas gave Guevara the moniker "Che," a Guaraní expression commonly used in Argentina that can be roughly translated as "hey, you." Guevara subsequently became best known by this name.

Shortly after landing in Cuba, the small guerrilla force ran into a military ambush that wiped out about half the group. Forced to choose between a first-aid kit and a box of bullets, Guevara took the ammunition. That decision represented his conversion from a medical doctor to a guerrilla fighter. Guevara fought with the Cubans for two years in the Sierra Maestra mountains, eventually rising to the rank of rebel army commander. He became the third most important leader after Fidel and his brother Raúl Castro.

After the January 1959 triumph of the revolution, Guevara became a Cuban citizen and legally adopted "Che" as part of his name. Drawing on lessons from Guatemala, Guevara advocated the complete destruction of the former regime, including the execution of its members so that they could not launch a counterattack against the revolution. Guevara also engaged in social engineering projects. He advocated the creation of a "new socialist man" who would be motivated to support the revolution through moral rather than material incentives.

Guevara assumed a series of positions in the new revolutionary Cuban government, including working in the agrarian reform institution, as head of the National Bank, and as minister of industry. Guevara, however, was better suited to the life of a vagabond or guerrilla fighter and soon became restless as a bureaucrat. He traveled internationally as an ambassador for Cuba and vocally denounced U.S. imperialism. He advocated the creation of "two, three, or many Vietnams" to strike a deadly blow against imperialism.

In 1965, Guevara renounced his governmental positions and Cuban citizenship and left the island to continue his revolutionary adventures. He first traveled to Africa to join a guerrilla struggle in the Congo, but that proved to be a frustrating experience. In 1966, Guevara arrived in Bolivia to launch a new continental Latin American revolution. Unlike in Cuba, Guevara's guerrillas had difficulties gaining the support of the rural population. The agrarian reform program that had so impressed Guevara on his first trip almost fifteen years earlier had satisfied a peasant hunger for land, and they were not much interested in another revolution. For several months, Guevara engaged in skirmishes with the Bolivian military but was always on the defensive. On October 8, 1967, an antiguerrilla military unit trained by the U.S. Army Special Forces captured Guevara and his few remaining guerrilla fighters. Fearing the potential publicity of a political show trial and possible release or escape, Bolivian dictator René Barrientos ordered his execution. The military publicly displayed his body to prove his death. To many, his corpse looked like a sacrificed Christ, which contributed to an image of Che as a martyr and prophet.

Some critics condemn Guevara for mechanically applying his lessons and theories of guerrilla warfare from Cuba to the Bolivian situation when they were not a good fit and that this ultimately led to his failure and death. Elsewhere in Latin America, revolutionaries attempted to implement his theory that a guerrilla force could create the objective conditions necessary for a guerrilla war and similarly met with disaster. Others have criticized Guevara for overemphasizing the role of armed struggle in a revolutionary movement and have pointed out that although a relatively small guerrilla force overthrew Batista in Cuba, this came only after years of leftist political agitations and rising worker expectations.

Although a dedicated communist revolutionary, Guevara was highly critical of bureaucratic Soviet communism for having lost its revolutionary fervor. Following in the footsteps of earlier Latin American Marxist thinkers such as José Carlos Mariátegui, Guevara argued that subjective conditions, including the role of human consciousness, were more important for creating a revolutionary situation than an objective economic situation. Rather than waiting for a highly developed capitalist economy to collapse due to its internal contradictions, he believed that a dedicated cadre must engage in the political education of the masses.

Guevara's efforts to launch a continent-wide revolution to overthrow capitalism and usher in a socialist utopia ultimately failed. Nevertheless, many young idealists admired Guevara for his selfless dedication to a struggle against oppression and for social justice. Decades after his death, Che Guevara continues to be championed as a revolutionary hero in the struggle for social justice and against oppression, exploitation, and marginalization. Although often reduced to a chic icon on T-shirts, his life represents a selfless dedication to the concerns of the underclass, a struggle to encourage people to place the needs of the broader society above their own personal wishes and desires, and a willingness to make extensive personal sacrifices to achieve a more just and equitable social order.

DOCUMENT: CHE GUEVARA, *GUERRILLA WARFARE,* 1960

Che Guevara published Guerrilla Warfare *in 1960 as a manual to guide revolutionaries in other countries on how to launch their own revolutions. In the first several pages, Guevara outlines the general principles he extracted from the Cuban Revolution that he thought applicable to other situations.*

The armed victory of the Cuban people over the Batista dictatorship was not only the triumph of heroism as reported by the newspapers of the world; it also forced a change in the old dogmas concerning the conduct of the popular masses of Latin America. It showed plainly the capacity of the people to free themselves by means of guerrilla warfare from a government that oppresses them.

We consider that the Cuban Revolution contributed three fundamental lessons to the conduct of revolutionary movements in America. They are:

(1) Popular forces can win a war against the army.
(2) It is not necessary to wait until all conditions for making revolution exist; the insurrection can create them.
(3) In underdeveloped America the countryside is the basic area for armed fighting.

Of these three propositions the first two contradict the defeatist attitude of revolutionaries or pseudo-revolutionaries who remain inactive and take refuge in the pretext that against a professional army nothing can be done, who sit down to wait until in some mechanical way all necessary objective and subjective conditions are given without working to accelerate them. As these problems were formerly a subject of discussion in Cuba, until facts settled the question, they are probably still much discussed in America.

Naturally, it is not to be thought that all conditions for revolution are going to be created through the impulse given to them by guerrilla activity. It must always be kept in mind that there is a necessary minimum without which the establishment and consolidation of the first center is not practicable. People must see clearly the futility of maintaining the fight for social goals within the framework of civil debate. When the forces of oppression come to maintain themselves in power against established law, peace is considered already broken.

In these conditions popular discontent expresses itself in more active forms. An attitude of resistance finally crystallizes in an outbreak of fighting, provoked initially by the conduct of the authorities.

Where a government has come into power through some form of popular vote, fraudulent or not, and maintains at least an appearance of constitutional legality, the guerrilla outbreak cannot be promoted, since the possibilities of peaceful struggle have not yet been exhausted.

The third proposition is a fundamental of strategy. It ought to be noted by those who maintain dogmatically that the struggle of the masses is centered in city movements, entirely forgetting the immense participation of the country people in the life of all the underdeveloped parts of America. Of course the struggles of the city masses of organized workers should not be underrated; but their real possibilities of engaging in armed struggle must be carefully analyzed where the guarantees which customarily adorn our constitutions are suspended or ignored. In these conditions the illegal workers' movements face enormous dangers. They must function secretly without arms. The situation in the open country is not so difficult. There, in places beyond the reach of the repressive forces, the armed guerrillas can support the inhabitants.

We will later make a careful analysis of these three conclusions that stand out in the Cuban revolutionary experience. We emphasize them now at the beginning of this work as our fundamental contribution.

Guerrilla warfare, the basis of the struggle of a people to redeem itself, has diverse characteristics, different facets, even though the essential will for liberation remains the same. It is obvious—and writers on the theme have said it many times—that war responds to a certain series of scientific laws; whoever ignores them will go down to defeat. Guerrilla warfare as a phase of war must be ruled by all of these; but besides, because of its special aspects, a series of corollary laws must also be recognized in order to carry it forward. Though geographical and social conditions in each country determine the mode and particular forms that guerrilla warfare will take, there are general laws that hold for all fighting of this type.

Our task at the moment is to find the basic principles of this kind of fighting and the rules to be followed by peoples seeking liberation; to develop theory from facts; to generalize and give structure to our experience for the profit of others.

Source: Che Guevara, *Guerrilla Warfare* (Lincoln: University of Nebraska Press, 1998), 7–9.

The most controversial aspect of *Guerrilla Warfare* was Guevara's belief that a guerrilla force could create the objective conditions necessary for a guerrilla war. Previous revolutionary theorists had argued that certain political and economic conditions were necessary for a successful struggle. In what became known as his *foco* theory of guerrilla warfare, Guevara argued that the Cuban Revolution demonstrated that a small insurrectionary guerrilla army (the foco) operating in the countryside could spark a revolution that would then spread to the cities. Only a handful of guerrillas in each country were necessary to begin a process that would transform Latin America. This caused him to emphasize the importance of a proper geographic setting for an armed struggle. A jungle environment that provided good cover for the guerrillas was more important than the ideological preparation of a large civilian base of support.

Almost every Latin American country had a guerrilla insurgency in the 1960s. Attempts to lead foco-style insurrections against Batista-style dictatorships in Panama, Nicaragua, the Dominican Republic, and Haiti quickly met with defeat. A series of guerrilla attempts in Peru initially realized more success but also showed the shortcomings of the foco theory. Hugo Blanco was a Trotskyist and a charismatic peasant organizer in La Convención Valley north of Cuzco. He significantly expanded peasant activism under the slogan "land or death" that combined Zapata's "land and liberty" with Castro's "homeland or death." An attempt to lead an armed insurrection failed because Blanco was more of a peasant organizer than guerrilla fighter. A second attempt, by Luis de la Puente Uceda, also failed because of divisions on the left, poor site selection, and a misreading of the political situation. Blanco's movement had organized peasants in desperate need of guerrilla support. They had seized land but had no guns to defend it. In contrast, de la Puente's guerrillas failed because of a lack of support from an organized peasantry. They had guns but no peasants to defend. A third attempt, by Héctor Béjar, similarly failed due to ideological, organizational, and personalist fragmentation, and a lack of organic connections with rural communities. The failure of these three guerrilla attempts ended guerrilla activity in Peru for fifteen years until the Shining Path emerged in 1980.

The failure of the Peruvian focos foreshadowed the defeat and execution of Guevara in neighboring Bolivia. Guevara had left Cuba to continue revolutionary struggles elsewhere, first in the Congo in 1965, where he faced defeat, and then in Bolivia, where he was executed in 1967. Guevara hoped his Bolivian foco would trigger a hemispheric revolution, but he seemed to ignore key aspects of his own theory. Some critics condemned Guevara for mechanically applying his lessons from Cuba and theories of guerrilla warfare to the Bolivian situation where they did not fit well. He appeared unable to learn lessons, including from his failure in Congo. Furthermore, many have criticized Guevara for overemphasizing the role of armed struggle in a revolutionary movement. He ignored the fact that a relatively small guerrilla force overthrew Batista in Cuba only after years of leftist political agitations and rising worker expectations. In fact, some argued that he fundamentally misinterpreted why the Cuban Revolution succeeded and as a result misunderstood the lessons of that victory. Nevertheless, Guevara became a renowned martyr for his selfless dedication to a revolutionary struggle. In death, he became a more powerful symbol than he had been in life.

Guevara's death led to a shift from rural- to urban-based guerrilla movements. Abraham Guillén, an exiled veteran of the Spanish Civil War who lived in Uruguay and Argentina, published *Strategy of Urban Guerrilla* in 1966. Guillén argued that with demographic shifts to urban areas, it was no longer viable to launch guerrilla warfare from the countryside. He believed that Guevara's foco theory was a recipe for disaster and would only lead to a mounting death toll. These urban movements were largely rooted in student and intellectual populations. One of the most significant was the Movimiento de Liberación Nacional–Tupamaros (MLN–T, National Liberation Movement–Tupamaros) in Uruguay that took its name from the colonial rebel Tupac Amaru. They engaged in spectacular robberies and kidnappings, and distributed food in poor neighborhoods, which gained them an image as Robin Hood–style fighters. Critics blamed the Tupamaros' practice of kidnappings and assassinations for inciting police repression that resulted in a military dictatorship in 1973. After the return to constitutional rule in 1985, the Tupamaros resumed life as a peaceful political party. The former Tupamaro political prisoner José "Pepe" Mujica won election as president of Uruguay with the leftist coalition Frente Amplio (Broad Front) in 2010. Mujica gained renown for his austere lifestyle rather than leveraging his political success for personal material gain.

WOMEN

Women have always played a significant role in warfare, but with this new wave of guerrilla movements they transitioned from support networks that sustained male fighters to armed combatants themselves. The gendered division of labor in guerrilla groups always reflected a certain amount of sexism, but women participants also understood that they aroused less suspicion than men in carrying out clandestine operations. Women could more easily and safely ferry weapons and messages than men and exploit their femininity to infiltrate the opposition. Haydée Tamara Bunke Bider (1937–1967) was an Argentine-born East German communist who joined Guevara's guerrilla army in Bolivia. Under the **nom de guerre** Tania, she effectively penetrated the upper echelons of the Bolivian government, becoming very close to president René Barrientos. When her cover was blown, she joined Guevara as a guerrilla fighter until she was killed in a military ambush. Tania was the only woman in Guevara's insurgent force and as such became the most famous female guerrilla.

By the 1980s, women regularly comprised about a third of many guerrilla armies and played roles equal to men. Several factors contributed to their increased involvement. In part their participation was a reflection of economic and social changes, including migration from rural to urban areas and an increase in the number of women in the labor force. These factors broke traditional gender roles that previously limited women to the domestic sphere. A change in guerrilla tactics from small foco groups to mass political mobilizations also necessitated broader popular participation. Inevitably women were swept up in these movements along with others in their communities.

Women had to fight hard to become accepted in guerrilla movements. One Colombian guerrilla declared that women "had to shoot to be heard," and women came to be respected only after they proved themselves in combat. Comandanta Ramona was one of the most important leaders of the neo-Zapatista guerrillas in Mexico in the 1990s and led their delegation in peace talks. It was a long struggle, however, and women were never represented in positions of leadership proportional to their numbers in the guerrilla ranks, much less to their portion of society. Feminists commonly complained that guerrilla movements failed to develop a serious women's agenda and that gender issues were always subordinate to a class struggle. Sexism was something that would be addressed in the new society after the war was won, but even then issues of survival always seemed to take precedence over gender equality.

COLOMBIA

The Fuerzas Armadas Revolucionarias de Colombia (FARC, Revolutionary Armed Forces of Colombia) was Latin America's oldest, largest, and longest-running guerrilla movement. For half a century the FARC fought a long and bloody war against the Colombian government. Some combatants spent their entire adult lives within

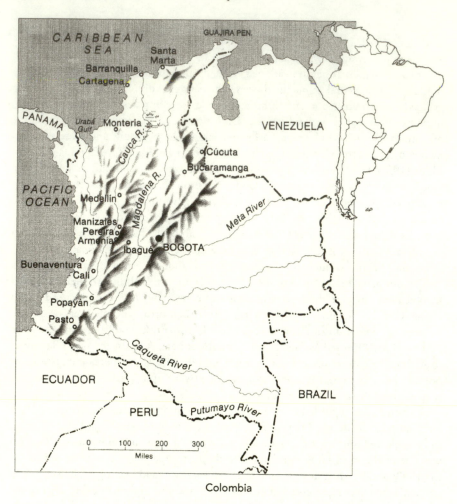

Colombia

the guerrilla force. As the war dragged on, it increasingly relied on the drug trade to fund its struggle. In the face of high levels of U.S. support for the Colombian government, the guerrillas stood little chance of a military victory. Although at different times the FARC managed to control significant swaths of territory, its popularity declined. The FARC provides a cautionary tale of the negative consequences of engaging in a guerrilla struggle without end.

The FARC's origins lie in the 1950s when a monopoly on power between the conservatives and liberals resulted in the social, economic, and political exclusion of other organized political movements. On April 9, 1948, an assassin killed Colombian liberal leader and presidential candidate Jorge Eliécer Gaitán. His death triggered a massive riot known as the *bogotazo* that left thousands dead and injured, and much of downtown Bogotá destroyed. That social explosion introduced a decade of violence (called "La Violencia") between liberals and conservatives for control of the countryside that left at least two hundred thousand people dead. That period of bloodletting ended with a power-sharing agreement between the two parties that shut out other political parties. The exclusionary nature of Colombian society created the objective conditions for a civil conflict.

With the end of the civil war, one of the guerrilla fighters, Pedro Antonio Marín, under the nom de guerre Manuel Tirofijo ("Sureshot") Marulanda, retreated to the community of Marquetalia, Tolima, with his supporters. Their goal was to create a society that would meet the needs and concerns of Colombia's rural population. Marulanda formed a self-defense group to protect agrarian interests, which prompted the government to fear a Cuban-style guerrilla movement in what it dubbed the independent Republic of Marquetalia. In 1964, the Colombian army attacked the community. Marulanda escaped to the mountains along with forty-seven other guerrilla fighters. Survivors of that battle met with members of other communities and formed the Southern Bloc guerrilla group that called for land reform. Two years later, the Southern Bloc reestablished itself as the FARC. It became the military wing of the Partido Comunista Colombiano (PCC, Colombian Communist Party) and shifted to more offensive tactics. In 1982, the FARC changed its name to the FARC-EP or Ejército del Pueblo ("People's Army"), although in common parlance it was always known simply as the FARC.

The FARC kidnapped politicians and wealthy individuals for ransom to pay for the costs of its guerrilla camps and the social services it provided to communities under its control. In the 1970s, the FARC began to tax drug traffickers. The new revenue stream allowed the guerrilla group to grow rapidly, even as the association with the drug trade began to erode the FARC's reputation as politically motivated. Some recruits joined the insurgents for financial rather than ideological reasons, particularly when the FARC paid soldiers higher wages than the Colombian military. Wealthy landowners formed paramilitary groups with names such as Muerte a Secuestradores (MAS, Death to Kidnappers) and the Autodefensas Unidas de Colombia (AUC, United Self-Defense Forces of Colombia) in alliance with the Colombian military to fight back against the guerrillas. The conflict gained the characteristics of a civil war, although one in which combatants targeted the civilian supporters of their opponents rather than armed groups that had weapons with which to fight back.

In the 1980s, the FARC entered into peace talks with the Colombian government under president Belisario Betancur. In 1984, the two parties reached an agreement for a bilateral ceasefire that lasted for three years. As part of the agreement, the FARC together with the PCC founded a political party called the Union Patriótica (UP, Patriotic Union). The UP initially experienced much success and realized a strong showing in the 1986 elections. Right-wing paramilitary groups, drug cartels, and the Colombian military, however, killed thousands of its members and leaders, causing the party to disappear as an important political force.

The FARC grew in size to eighteen thousand soldiers. Almost half of its members were women, and they trained and fought alongside men and rose to positions of leadership in the guerrilla army. The FARC also gained high-profile foreign recruits, including the Dutch woman Tanja Nijmeijer (Alexandra Nariño), who rose through the ranks to become an assistant to a senior commander. Having children within a mobile guerrilla force is very complicated, and in fact was forbidden in the FARC. Some have condemned the FARC for forcing pregnant women to undergo abortions and to work as sex slaves for guerrilla commanders. Human rights groups have also criticized the FARC for recruiting child soldiers.

In 1997, the U.S. State Department added the FARC to its list of Foreign Terrorist Organizations. In 2000, U.S. president Bill Clinton initiated a nine-billion-dollar military aid program called Plan Colombia to combat the guerrillas and the drug trade. In 2002, the conservative politician Álvaro Uribe won the presidency and launched an aggressive campaign against the guerrillas. The military successes of his defense minister Juan Manuel Santos slowly led to its decline as a significant threat. The Colombian military gained access to U.S. technology that allowed it to engage in targeted assassinations of FARC commanders, which further undermined the group's coherence.

In 2012, Uribe's defense minister Santos won the presidency and restarted the peace process with the FARC. Government and guerrilla negotiators gathered in Havana, Cuba, for discussions that stretched out for years. In 2016, the belligerents finally signed a five-point peace accord and agreed to a ceasefire. The agreement committed the Colombian government to investment in rural development and would allow the FARC to transform itself into a legal political party. In order to give the accord a higher degree of legitimacy, Santos brought it to a public referendum. Santos's predecessor Uribe campaigned fiercely against the referendum, which contributed to its defeat at the polls. Santos, meanwhile, won the Nobel Peace Prize for his efforts to bring the long conflict to an end. The government and guerrillas returned to the negotiating table and quickly hammered out a revised agreement that they hoped would be more acceptable to the broader public. It remained to be seen whether the peace initiative would be more successful than previous attempts. An unknown was whether a peace accord would solve the exclusionary nature of Colombian society, or whether new guerrilla forces would emerge in its aftermath.

Other Guerrilla Movements

Several other guerrilla groups emerged alongside the FARC in Colombia. In 1964, students, Catholic radicals, and left-wing intellectuals formed the Ejército de Liberación Nacional (ELN, National Liberation Army), modeled after Guevara's guerrilla struggles. Its most famous member was the priest Camilo Torres Restrepo (1929–1966), a well-known and liked university professor who was attracted to liberation theology's radical ideas. Although Torres came from the upper class, he was openly critical of the social and economic inequality in Colombia. He joined the ELN as a simple soldier rather than a commander, including participating in kitchen and guard duty. In Torres's first combat action, he participated in an ambush of a military patrol that killed four soldiers. The army mounted a counterattack and killed Torres. The military buried the former priest in an unmarked grave. He subsequently became a highly regarded ELN symbol.

The ELN never grew as large as the FARC and mobilized about seven thousand fighters at the height of its operations. To fund itself, the ELN kidnapped wealthy Colombians and extorted funds from oil corporations and other businesses in what it called "war taxes." Along with the FARC, the United States listed the ELN as a Foreign Terrorist Organization. Occasionally the FARC and ELN attempted to collaborate, but just as often they competed for the allegiance of populations under their control. The ELN also entered into preliminary peace talks with the Santos administration, although they did not advance as quickly as those conducted with the FARC.

The Movimiento 19 de Abril (M-19, 19th of April Movement) was a more moderate Colombian guerrilla movement than either the FARC or ELN. It formed in the aftermath of the allegedly fraudulent April 19, 1970, presidential elections from which it took its name. The M-19 drew much of its support from radical students and urban movements. The M-19 employed a leftist populist and anti-imperialist discourse but, unlike many other guerrilla groups, not one that was explicitly Marxist.

The M-19 gained renown for its spectacular and highly symbolic urban guerrilla actions. In 1974, members stole one of independence leader Simón Bolívar's swords from a museum, and in 1980 they took fourteen ambassadors hostage in a raid on a Dominican Republic embassy cocktail party. In 1985, they held hundreds of lawyers and judges captive in a siege of the Palace of Justice. This plan, however, backfired when the Colombian army attacked the building, setting it ablaze, and killing the M-19 commandos and many of their hostages, including eleven supreme court justices. That failure led to the decline of the group, and it entered into peace negotiations. The demobilized guerrillas formed a political party but faced the same problem as the UP of having drug cartels and right-wing death squads killing many of its members.

A Maoist offshoot of the PCC formed the Ejército Popular de Liberación (EPL, Popular Liberation Army) in 1967. It never gained the size or presence of the other guerrilla groups. The EPL demobilized in 1991 and formed the political party Esperanza, Paz y Libertad (Hope, Peace, and Freedom). As with the other groups, the EPL did not gain a significant presence in the electoral realm.

In 1984, Indigenous activists formed the Movimiento Armado Quintín Lame (MAQL, Quintín Lame Armed Movement) in Cauca, a part of Colombia with a large native population that suffers from unequal land distribution. The group was named after Manuel Quintín Lame Chantre (1880–1967), a leader from the early twentieth century who defended Indigenous rights. The MAQL fought to protect Indigenous communities from landowner and military attacks. They negotiated a demobilization agreement with the Colombian government in 1990, which included their participation in a constituent assembly the following year. As a political force, the MAQL achieved major concessions and the incorporation of Indigenous rights into the 1991 constitution.

In 1987, the five guerrilla groups (FARC, ELN, M-19, EPL, and MAQL) formed an umbrella organization known as the Coordinadora Guerrillera Simón Bolívar (CGSB, Simón Bolívar Guerrilla Coordinating Board). Similar to the M-19's theft of Bolívar's sword, the CGSB's use of the independence hero's name appealed to nationalist sentiments in an attempt to legitimize the guerrilla movement. Competing political ideologies and interests, however, meant that the diverse guerrilla groups failed to merge their organizations. A lack of unity in the face of a common enemy contributed to the failure of their revolutionary agenda.

EL SALVADOR

In 1980, El Salvador seemed to be following Nicaragua on a path toward the victory of an armed guerrilla uprising. A small oligarchy known as "the fourteen families" controlled most of the land, the entire banking system, and most of the country's industry. In contrast to their wealth, the majority of the country's inhabitants lived in deep poverty. This ruling class engaged in extreme political repression in order to retain their class privileges. The violence and injustice resulted in a civil war that stretched for twelve long years, from 1980 to 1992. After a bloody fight, however, the guerrillas were unable to take power through armed means. Instead, the process of struggle contributed to the creation of a very strong and highly politicized civil society.

Similar to Nicaragua, revolutionary movements in El Salvador had a strong base in liberation theology and grassroots Christian-based communities. These religious communities engaged poor people in rural areas and urban barrios with a combined

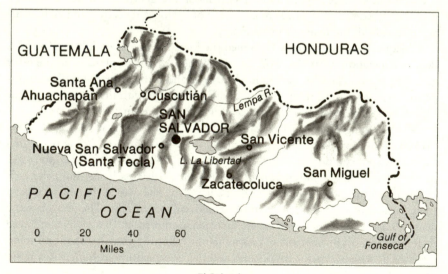

El Salvador

study of the Bible and an analysis of economic and social problems. Catholic priests emphasized social justice and the rights of the poor and oppressed. With rising social unrest, the government organized death squads that terrorized the civilian population in order to maintain their class privileges. Repression of these communities led to further politicization and radicalization. Rutilio Grande, a Jesuit who worked in the community of Aguilares, was one of the first killed as the repressive violence began to increase dramatically in the late 1970s. In March 1977, a death squad murdered him along with a teenager and a seventy-two-year-old peasant while on his way to say mass.

The death of Rutilio Grande deeply influenced Archbishop Monsignor Oscar Romero. Romero became increasingly vocal in denouncing human rights violations and calling for social justice. He appealed to U.S. president Jimmy Carter to suspend his support of the government because U.S. aid was only being used to repress the civilian population. Instead, the United States continued to prop up the government with more than a million dollars of military funding a day. Romero slowly moved toward support of armed struggle as the only option, given the increased repression. When asked if he feared for his life, Romero declared, "If I am killed, I shall rise again in the struggle of the Salvadorian people." On March 24, 1980, under instructions from army major Roberto D'Aubuisson, a death squad assassinated Romero while he was celebrating mass. His death provided a powerful catalyst for popular struggles.

After Romero's death and with government-sanctioned violence on the rise and all peaceful paths to political changes seemingly exhausted, many members of civil society joined guerrilla armies. In 1970, communist party leader Salvador Cayetano Carpio, together with the leader of the educational union Mélida Anaya Montes and university professors Clara Elizabeth Ramírez and Felipe Peña Mendoza, founded the Fuerzas Populares de Liberación (FPL, Popular Liberation Forces) as a military and political organization. A second group, the Ejército Revolucionario del Pueblo (ERP, People's Revolutionary Army), emerged several years later out of disaffected youths. Under the leadership of Joaquín Villalobos, the ERP emphasized military action over political work. When internal disputes within the ERP resulted in the assassination of leading ideologue Roque Dalton in 1975, a breakaway faction formed the Fuerzas Armadas de la Resistencia Nacional (FARN, National Resistance Armed Forces). The FARN assumed a more moderate social democratic position than the previous two groups and was willing to collaborate with reformist elements in their opposition to the Salvadoran oligarchy.

Previously the Partido Comunista de El Salvador (PCS, Communist Party of El Salvador) had assumed an orthodox communist position of favoring peaceful political organizing over armed struggle, but in 1980 they agreed to join the FPL, ERP, FARN, and the Partido Revolucionario de los Trabajadores Centroamericanos (PRTC, Revolutionary Party of the Central American Workers) in coordinated military activities. The five leftist groups representing different ideologies and constituencies formed the Frente Farabundo Martí para la Liberación Nacional (FMLN, Farabundo Martí

National Liberation Front), named after the communist leader who directed the failed 1932 uprising. The FMLN coordinated its activities with a broad opposition coalition called the Frente Democrático Revolucionario (FDR, Revolutionary Democratic Front). Under the leadership of Guillermo Ungo and Rubén Zamora, the FDR developed a political platform together with the FMLN that called for social and economic reforms to benefit the poor, a mixed economy, and a nonaligned foreign policy. They stopped short, however, of calling for socialism.

In January 1981, the FMLN launched a general offensive that tried but failed to overthrow the government. In response, the military increased its ferocious attacks on civilian communities. It pursued a policy of draining the ocean of civilians in order to exterminate the guerrilla "fish." In one attack, the elite U.S.-trained counterinsurgency Atlacatl Battalion killed almost one thousand civilians in the village of El Mozote. As a result, many people in rural communities were forced into exile in refugee camps in neighboring Honduras.

Years more of bloody warfare followed that caused the deaths of thousands of civilians. Government repression of those suspected of leftist sympathies destroyed existing organizational structures. Many, including women, who felt they had no alternative, joined the FMLN in large numbers. About 40 percent of the FMLN members were women, including 30 percent of the combatants and 20 percent of the military leaders. During this entire time, the Salvadoran government continued to hold legislative and presidential elections that provided the regime with a veneer of legitimacy. Despite the mass popular support for the FMLN, the guerrillas were never able to make the label of dictatorship stick to their opponents.

In November 1989, the FMLN launched a massive "final offensive" in another attempt to take power. This uprising also failed, and the military again took advantage of the battles to engage in a new wave of repression. Most notably, soldiers shot six Jesuit priests at the Central American University whom they considered the FMLN's intellectual leaders, together with their housekeeper and her daughter. At first the military blamed the guerrillas for the murders, but evidence later emerged that once again the Atlacatl Battalion was the culprit.

By 1992, after twelve years of war and with seventy-five thousand dead and right-wing death squads having "disappeared" an unknown number more, it became apparent that the FMLN could not win militarily. Even with endless U.S. aid, neither could the Salvadoran government defeat the insurgents. Out of this stalemate emerged a peace accord that brought the fighting to an end. The FMLN transitioned from a guerrilla army to a political party and continued its struggle for social justice in the electoral realm. In 2009, the FMLN finally realized success with the election of Mauricio Funes as president. In 2014, the vice president and previous guerrilla leader Salvador Sánchez Cerén won the election. Even with the FMLN in office, gang warfare ravaged the country that resulted in homicide rates higher than those during the height of the civil war in the 1980s. Perhaps the FMLN's most significant legacy, however, was creating a highly politicized and aware civil society that continued to struggle against neoliberal economic policies and social exclusion through peaceful means.

A common revolutionary slogan in the 1980s was "Nicaragua won, El Salvador is winning, and Guatemala will win." Popular movements in Guatemala, however, faced a much more genocidal war than those in the other Central American republics. As in Nicaragua and El Salvador, rural mobilizations strengthened in Guatemala in response to exclusionary political and economic conditions and with the encouragement of religious workers, progressive political parties, and labor unions. In 1982, a coalition of four guerrilla forces joined together as the Unidad Revolucionaria Nacional Guatemalteca (URNG, National Revolutionary Guatemalan Unity). Similar to the FMLN, the URNG did not call for socialism but an end to government repression, equality for the Maya, agrarian reform, and social and economic policies that would meet basic human needs. The Guatemalan guerrillas attempted to replicate the success of the Sandinistas in Nicaragua and the war the FMLN appeared to be winning in El Salvador. The URNG, however, never gained the strength of those other two groups. The military launched a counterinsurgency campaign that killed as many as a quarter million civilians. With their backs against a wall, in 1996 the guerrillas were forced to accept a peace agreement. The accords brought an end to Central America's deadliest and longest-running civil war, although it left exclusionary structures more entrenched than anywhere else in the region.

PERU

The Sendero Luminoso (Shining Path) in Peru was the largest and most violent of the 1980s guerrilla movements. It emerged in the context of a military government that brought a series of failed guerrilla experiments in the 1960s to an end. In 1968, General Juan Velasco Alvarado (1910–1977) overthrew Fernando Belaunde's elected civilian government. At first, the military coup appeared to be just another change in the occupant of the presidential palace that would leave existing social structures intact. Velasco quickly clarified that this was not his intent. He announced a plan to pursue a third path of national development that would be neither capitalist nor socialist in nature. Velasco's Revolutionary Government of the Armed Forces pursued a top-down approach that emphasized a radical program of nationalization of the means of production, promotion of worker participation in the ownership and management of industries, and an agrarian reform plan named after Tupac Amaru. After twelve years in power, the pace of Velasco's reforms slowed and even reversed. A 1978 constituent assembly for the first time extended citizenship rights to Indigenous peoples, and a 1980 election returned Belaunde to office. Shining Path militants, however, were not interested in peaceful paths to power.

In 1970, Abimael Guzmán, a philosophy professor at the University of Huamanga in the highland city of Ayacucho, broke from the mainline communist

Peru

party. He announced his intent to push forward "por el sendero luminoso de José Carlos Mariátegui," by the shining path of José Carlos Mariátegui, the founder of Latin American Marxist theory. Guzmán's party came to be known as the Partido Comunista del Perú—Sendero Luminoso (Communist Party of Peru—Shining Path), and finally shortened in common parlance to simply "Sendero Luminoso," or the Shining Path, although militants never self-identified as such. Under the nom de guerre of Presidente Gonzalo, Guzmán began to develop his own "Gonzalo thought" that positioned the Shining Path as the "fourth sword" of Marxism after Marx, Lenin, and Mao.

Rather than joining leftist coalitions that participated in massive national strikes that pushed Peru toward a civilian government, the Shining Path decided in a 1979 Central Committee meeting to prepare for armed struggle. In 1980, as the rest of the country went to the polls to elect a new president, the Shining Path launched its "People's War" with symbolic actions such as hanging dogs from lampposts and blowing up electrical towers. The dogs represented the notion of "running dogs of capitalism," meaning people who served the interests of exploitative capitalists. They gained popular support through their emphasis on popular justice and moral behavior, including holding "people's trials" that often ended in the execution of abusive property owners, police officers, and other unpopular figures. Much of their support came from rural students and schoolteachers who found their social mobility blocked by racial prejudice and economic stagnation. At the height of its activities, the Shining Path had ten to twelve thousand people under arms and could draw on the collaboration of a civilian base perhaps ten times that size.

Initially the Shining Path gained sympathy both within Peru and internationally because of its idealism and stance on behalf of the marginalized and impoverished rural masses. The Shining Path had a special appeal to women, and many of its members were women. The party provided women with a protected space in which they knew they would not face humiliation or discrimination for being poor, Indigenous, and female. The Shining Path pursued a Maoist strategy of prolonged popular war that included laying siege to the cities from the countryside, eventually bringing its war to poor shantytowns on Lima's periphery.

The Shining Path imposed a top-down leadership style. An authoritarian approach eliminated the divisive ideological and personal tendencies that had torn earlier guerrilla movements apart. A vertical hierarchy and carefully designed autonomous cell structure provided for efficient actions and tight security that proved very difficult for the government to penetrate. The capture of one militant could only provide officials with very limited information rather than intelligence that would lead to the apprehension of more leaders. These strengths, however, were also weaknesses. The Shining Path's authoritarian nature and failure to empower people at a grassroots level alienated potential supporters and ultimately limited its effectiveness.

As the guerrilla army grew larger, its brutal tactics and dogmatic philosophy became more apparent. It made what others would see as serious tactical mistakes, including imposing control over agricultural harvests and commerce, placing young people in control of communities where elders traditionally had assumed leadership roles, and executing violators of social norms rather than using lesser and more appropriate punishments. It accepted no opposition to its policies and often treated other leftists more harshly than members of the oligarchy. It accused those engaged in social reforms of sustaining a fundamentally unjust system rather than discarding it in favor of something new and better.

One of the Shining Path's most noted victims was the community leader María Elena Moyano in Villa El Salvador in 1992. She had organized community soup kitchens and was head of the neighborhood Vaso de Leche ("glass of milk") program that offered breakfast to impoverished children. Moyano provided strong and independent leadership, and called for an end to both Shining Path's violence and government repression. The guerrillas blew up her body with dynamite in front of her family, not so much to eliminate a competitor as to intimidate and instill fear in those who might challenge the Shining Path's dominance.

The war killed an estimated seventy thousand people, most of them civilians, with a disproportionate number of rural and Indigenous victims. What was unusual in Peru was that the Shining Path was responsible for a large share of the deaths, while in most guerrilla wars the military and right-wing paramilitary death squads committed the lion's share of the murders. The war also displaced a quarter million peasants and resulted in $24 billion in property damage. It appeared that militarily the Shining Path could not take power and that the government was incapable of destroying the movement. Nevertheless, given the Shining Path's ruthless dedication to the pursuit of its ultimate goal, eventual victory—whether it took one generation or one hundred years—seemed inevitable.

On September 12, 1992, the government captured Abimael Guzmán. The tightly centralized control over the party that had made the Shining Path so powerful now proved to be its undoing. Anonymous military tribunals with 97 percent conviction rates and other judicial abuses not only helped collapse the Shining Path's support structures but also resulted in the imprisonment of many innocent people. From jail, Guzmán called for an end to the armed struggle and negotiated a peace agreement with the government. The deadly violence had accomplished little, and Peru seemed no closer to a socialist revolution than before the war started. Latin America's most deadly guerrilla war had come to an end, but the underlying conditions of poverty and exclusion that had originally led to the insurgency remained unresolved.

A smaller Peruvian guerrilla group was the Movimiento Revolucionario Tupac Amaru (MRTA, Tupac Amaru Revolutionary Movement). It fought to establish a socialist government in Peru. In 1995, the police arrested U.S. citizen Lori Berenson and accused her of collaborating with the MRTA. She was sentenced to twenty years in prison. In the MRTA's most famous action, in December 1996 fourteen guerrillas stormed the Japanese ambassador's residence in Lima. They held seventy-two people hostage for more than four months. In April 1997, the military attacked the residence, killing one of the hostages and all of the guerrillas. It was later revealed that the soldiers had summarily executed several of the guerrillas after they had surrendered.

The government captured many of its other leaders, and the MRTA lost its strength. Although the MRTA followed a very different ideological and strategic path than the Shining Path, it was no more successful in achieving its ultimate objectives.

SUMMARY

The Cuban Revolution was a watershed event in twentieth-century Latin America, and for leftists it came to be seen as a normative manner by which to transform society. Examining the efforts of other revolutionaries who attempted but failed to emulate the Cuban example provides instructive counterexamples. Although revolutionaries found Che Guevara's foco theory of guerrilla warfare very compelling in the early 1960s, by the 1970s it had become largely discredited. Activists looked elsewhere for models on which to base their transformation of society.

Achieving change through a guerrilla struggle is a very difficult undertaking, as revolutionaries in Colombia, El Salvador, and Peru discovered. In each case, activists launched powerful insurgencies, but in each case their efforts devolved into lengthy and bloody civil wars. Deep ideological and strategic divisions separated revolutionaries in Colombia and Peru, while their counterparts in El Salvador were more successful in unifying their efforts. Peace agreements had a limited effect on solving underlying problems of exclusionary social structures. Most successful was El Salvador, where the guerrilla struggle resulted in a civilian population with a high level of political consciousness. Even that country, however, was plagued with gang warfare that killed more people than had died in combat during the 1980s. Achieving permanent and sustainable revolutionary transformations remained an elusive goal.

DISCUSSION QUESTIONS

What leads people to turn to violence to solve political problems?

To what extent is guerrilla warfare an inherently male undertaking?

Is the FARC's pursuit of state power through violent means for half a century an example of admirable determination or an abject failure?

Could the FMLN have won the presidency in El Salvador without engaging in a twelve-year-long civil war?

Why did the Shining Path become more violent than other guerrilla groups?

FURTHER READING

The literature on guerrilla movements is extensive. Included here is a highly selective list largely focusing on ethnographic treatments of the 1980s guerrilla movements discussed in this chapter. Not included are theoretical works on guerrilla warfare and those that discuss an earlier wave of movements in the 1960s.

Anderson, Jon Lee. *Che Guevara: A Revolutionary Life*. New York: Grove Press, 1997. A comprehensive biography of the famous guerrilla leader.

Brittain, James J. *Revolutionary Social Change in Colombia: The Origin and Direction of the FARC-EP*. London: Pluto Press, 2010. A sympathetic overview of the Colombian guerrilla insurgency.

Danner, Mark. *The Massacre at El Mozote: A Parable of the Cold War*. New York: Vintage Books, 1994. Examination of a brutal 1981 massacre of a village by an elite Salvadoran military force.

Degregori, Carlos Iván. *How Difficult It Is to Be God: Shining Path's Politics of War in Peru, 1980–1999*. Madison: University of Wisconsin Press, 2012. Collection of essays from a leading Peruvian critic of the Shining Path.

Gavilán Sánchez, Lurgio. *When Rains Became Floods: A Child Soldier's Story*. Durham, NC: Duke University Press, 2015. A rare autobiography from a Shining Path soldier.

Gorriti Ellenbogen, Gustavo. *The Shining Path: A History of the Millenarian War in Peru*. Chapel Hill: University of North Carolina Press, 1999. Journalistic account of the founding and early years of the Shining Path guerrilla insurgency.

Henríquez Consalvi, Carlos. *Broadcasting the Civil War in El Salvador: A Memoir of Guerrilla Radio*. Austin: University of Texas Press, 2010. Description from a journalist as to how he maintained a radio station for the guerrillas in El Salvador during the war.

Kampwirth, Karen. *Women and Guerrilla Movements: Nicaragua, El Salvador, Chiapas, Cuba*. University Park: Pennsylvania State University Press, 2002. Interviews with women in guerrilla movements.

Leech, Garry M. *The FARC: The Longest Insurgency*. Halifax, NS: Fernwood, 2011. Journalistic overview of guerrilla insurgency in Colombia.

Stern, Steve J., ed. *Shining and Other Paths: War and Society in Peru, 1980–1995*. Durham, NC: Duke University Press, 1998. Edited collection of critical scholarship on the Shining Path.

Todd, Molly. *Beyond Displacement: Campesinos, Refugees, and Collective Action in the Salvadoran Civil War*. Madison: University of Wisconsin Press, 2010. Sympathetic study of human impact of the civil war in El Salvador.

Vásquez Perdomo, María Eugenia. *My Life as a Colombian Revolutionary: Reflections of a Former Guerrillera*. Philadelphia: Temple University Press, 2005. Autobiography of an M-19 guerrilla.

FILMS

Courage. 1998. Based on the life of community leader María Elena Moyano whom the Shining Path executed in February 1992.

The Dancer Upstairs. 2002. Fictional portrayal of the capture of Shining Path leader Abimael Guzmán from the police perspective.

"Fire in the Mind." 1993. Part nine of a ten-part PBS documentary, *Americas*, examining revolutions in El Salvador and Peru.

La Boca del Lobo. 1988. A study of a bloody encounter between the Peruvian Army and the Maoist Shining Path in Chuspi, a small isolated village in the Andes.

Maria's Story: A Portrait of Love and Survival in El Salvador's Civil War. 1990. Documentary based on the life of Salvadorian guerrilla leader María Serrano.

1932 Scars of Memory. 2002. Documentary on 1932 peasant uprising in El Salvador that the military brutally repressed.

Plan Colombia: Cashing In on the Drug-War Failure. 2003. Documentary of U.S. involvement in the Colombian conflict.

Proof of Life. 2000. Fictional portrayal of a U.S. aid worker kidnapped by the FARC guerrillas in Colombia.

Romero. 1990. Moving depiction of assassination of Archbishop Oscar Romero in El Salvador.

Salvador. 1985. An Oliver Stone movie about the civil war in El Salvador through the eyes of a U.S. journalist.

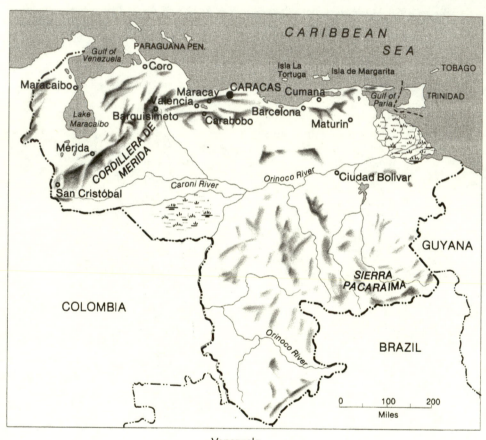

Venezuela

9

Venezuela's Bolivarian Revolution, 1999–

KEY DATES

1958	Pact of Punto Fijo establishes power-sharing agreement between the two main political parties
1976	President Carlos Andrés Pérez nationalizes the petroleum industry
1982	Hugo Chávez forms the Bolivarian Revolutionary Movement 200 (MBR-200)
February 27, 1989	Massive street riots known as the *caracazo* against structural adjustment measures
February 4, 1992	Chávez leads a military-civilian coup d'état against Pérez
1997	Chávez founds the Fifth Republic Movement (MVR)
December 6, 1998	Chávez elected president
December 15, 1999	Voters approve new constitution
July 30, 2000	Chávez reelected under new constitution
April 11, 2002	Failed coup against Chávez
August 15, 2004	Chávez handily wins recall referendum
January 30, 2005	Chávez declares the socialist nature of the Bolivarian Revolution
December 3, 2006	Chávez wins third term and forms the United Socialist Party of Venezuela (PSUV)
October 7, 2012	Chávez wins fourth term as president
March 5, 2013	Chávez dies and power passes to Nicolás Maduro
April 14, 2013	Maduro wins a special election to replace Chávez

By the end of the twentieth century, extreme socioeconomic polarization character-ized Venezuelan society. Eighty percent of the population, overwhelmingly those of African and Indigenous descent, lived in poverty despite the fact that the country had one of the largest petroleum reserves in the world. Wealth and power were con-centrated in the hands of the other 20 percent of the population who were primar-ily of European heritage and worked in professional jobs related to the petroleum industry. It was in this context that Hugo Chávez won election as president in 1998 on the promise of implementing policies that would shift resources toward the most disadvantaged sectors of society. In the process, Chávez introduced a new wave of revolutionary fervor that swept across Latin America.

More than any other contemporary experiment in socialism, Chávez embodied many of the debates regarding revolutionary rule that flowed throughout the twen-tieth century. After a failed 1992 coup, Chávez rejected armed struggle and turned toward electoral politics to gain power. Rather than contradictory or ironic, these competing strategies simply indicate the presence of different and not necessarily op-posing paths in a common revolutionary struggle. As with previous revolutionaries, Chávez was a charismatic leader who provided the inspiration that drove his move-ment. Similar to how Fidel Castro appealed to José Martí and Carlos Fonseca to Au-gusto César Sandino, Chávez embraced Latin American independence leader Simón Bolívar (1783–1830) as his symbolic nationalist hero. Even though Venezuela is pri-marily an urban country, Chávez emphasized the importance of, and drew support from, rural peasant and Indigenous peoples. His fervent anti-imperialist rhetoric led to strong opposition from the United States, but unlike Salvador Allende in Chile, he weathered an April 11, 2002, right-wing coup attempt and consolidated his hold on power. Meanwhile, Chávez's social programs brought education and healthcare to the working class and significantly raised their standard of living. Chávez not only learned the lessons of a century of revolutionary movements but also embodied a synthesis of their struggles and gains.

PETROLEUM ECONOMY

Christopher Columbus made his first landfall in South America in 1498 in what today is the country of Venezuela. Located in the northeastern part of the continent, its rich resources allowed disparate local populations to thrive based on hunting, gathering, and agricultural production. Venezuela's Indigenous peoples lived in an environment of plenty and never needed to create the large centralized empires of the high Andes or Mexico's central valley to provide for a population that placed pressure on the land's carrying capacity. Unable to tap into preexisting tribute systems, the Spanish made slow progress in colonizing the region and turned instead to Catholic missions to "civilize" the native population. Indigenous leaders such as Guaicaipuro (1530–1568) led resistance to European encroachments onto their lands. Because they faced difficulties in extracting labor from the local population, the Spanish colonizers imported slaves from Africa to work their plantations.

In 1821, Bolívar led Venezuela to independence from Spain with the vision of unifying all of Latin America against foreign domination. Bolívar's dream failed, and Latin America fragmented into separate republics. Meanwhile, the descendants of the colonizers continued to hold Indigenous and African peoples in a subjugated position. The nineteenth-century peasant leader Ezequiel Zamora advocated a far-reaching land reform program to address their oppression but failed to dislodge the land-owning aristocracy.

At the beginning of the twentieth century, the government of Juan Vicente Gómez (1908–1935) discovered oil in Venezuela and subsequently emphasized the development of the petroleum industry. Peasants flooded to urban areas to join in the oil boom, but most of the wealth flowed to trained professionals who worked in the oil industry or for foreign companies. Over time, the abandonment of agriculture led to a highly distorted economy. Land ownership became extremely unbalanced, with 5 percent of the population owning three-quarters of the agricultural land. Much of that land was poorly used, forcing the country to import most of its food.

Rómulo Betancourt (1908–1981) came to power in 1945 in a military coup. He founded the Acción Democrática (AD, Democratic Action) party to lead the country on a path of nationalist, bourgeois development. Conservative military officers under the leadership of Colonel Marcos Pérez Jiménez (1914–2001) overthrew Betancourt in a 1948 coup. On January 23, 1958, a popular uprising removed Pérez Jiménez from power. The AD and a Social Christian party known as the Comité de Organización Política Electoral Independiente (COPEI, Independent Political Electoral Organization Committee) entered into a power-sharing agreement called the Pact of Punto Fijo. These two parties governed in favor of privileged groups and excluded the vast majority from participation in politics. Because of this pact, and unlike in most of Latin America, after Pérez Jiménez's removal in 1958 Venezuela did not return to military rule.

In 1960, about two-thirds of Venezuela's six million people lived in the countryside and worked in the agriculture sector. About 60 percent of those agricultural laborers toiled on large plantations, leaving them poor, landless, and unable to support themselves. U.S. development programs such as the Alliance for Progress favored capital-intensive industrialized agricultural production that did little to provide peasants with education, training, or access to land. Rather than increasing Venezuela's ability to feed itself, these schemes only deepened the country's economic dependence on foreign powers.

A second oil boom, in the 1970s, turned Venezuela, a cofounder of the Organization of the Petroleum Exporting Countries (OPEC), into one of the world's largest petroleum producers. The wealth, however, was not equally shared across society and instead increased economic and social inequity. The government ignored rural areas and focused its attention primarily on urban and industrial sectors. In response, peasants flooded into urban areas in search of jobs and economic prosperity. With few other options, these internal migrants settled into "misery belts" that surrounded Venezuela's cities. Unemployment, a lack of utilities including water and electricity, and high crime rates plagued these slums. At the end of the twentieth century, 87 percent of the country's twenty-five million people lived in cities. Not only did this policy leave the countryside underdeveloped, but also it increased problems in urban areas.

A legacy of this history of unequal development was that most of the country's resources, population, and wealth were concentrated in large cities. The cities were overpopulated and the countryside was underpopulated, thus limiting Venezuela's potential for economic development and ability to feed itself. While Venezuela was one of the world's largest oil exporters, it imported about 70 percent of its food even though it had plenty of rich agricultural land. It had the smallest agricultural sector in all of Latin America (6 percent of its gross domestic product [GDP]) and remained the only country in the region that was a net importer of agricultural products. In this distorted economy, the wealthy gained the most value from oil production while displaced peasants lacked work and went hungry because they no longer had land on which to practice subsistence agriculture.

1992 COUP

Hugo Chávez first burst onto the political scene in Venezuela after a failed February 4, 1992, military-civilian coup d'état against the elected government of Carlos Andrés Pérez (1922–2010). In 1976 during a previous term as president, Pérez had nationalized the oil industry. When he returned to office in 1989, Pérez implemented draconian International Monetary Fund (IMF) structural adjustment measures that curtailed social spending and removed price controls on consumer goods. These neoliberal policies were designed to halt inflation, and they disproportionately hurt poor people. An increase in bus fares and bread prices triggered massive street protests in the capital city of Caracas on February 27, 1989, that became known as the *caracazo*. In response, security forces killed hundreds of protesters.

Although Chávez did not play a role in these protests, they set the stage for his eventual rise to power. The caracazo convinced him, along with a growing number of fellow military officials, that Venezuela's political system was fundamentally corrupt. He blamed the Pact of Punto Fijo for excluding the vast majority of Venezuelans from participating in the political system. He believed that the military could force an end to the pact, which led to the failed 1992 coup attempt. After the power grab fell apart, Chávez made a brief appearance on national television to call for other rebels to lay down their arms to prevent further bloodshed. His statement that they had failed "por ahora," or "for the moment," indicated that he would continue the struggle through other means. Taking a stand against corruption and the exclusionary rule of privileged groups made him a hero for Venezuela's impoverished masses who had not benefited from the country's petroleum-fueled economic growth.

Due to popular pressure, Chávez received a presidential pardon after spending only two years in prison. He continued his political struggle and in 1997 organized the Movimiento Quinta República (MVR, Fifth Republic Movement) to call for a refounding of the country based on progressive principles designed to benefit the country's excluded majority. Now, rather than engaging in military coups, the former military official entered the electoral realm.

BIOGRAPHY: HUGO RAFAEL CHÁVEZ FRÍAS, 1954–2013

Venezuelan president Hugo Chávez was a contentious and polarizing figure. He was a charismatic and personalistic leader who appealed to those who felt as if they never before had anyone in power who understood them, but his political ideology and working-class status alienated him from the traditional power brokers. To his opponents, Chávez's nationalist and populist rhetoric was seen as authoritarian demagoguery that harmed Venezuela's economic growth and threatened its political stability. For the poor, Indigenous, and Afro-Venezuelan underclass who formed his base of support, Chávez represented their best hope for remaking the world so that it responded to their needs.

Hugo Chávez with Latin American Indigenous and peasant leaders in October 2003
Source: Photo by Marc Becker

Chávez was born on July 28, 1954, the child of provincial schoolteachers. He was a career military officer, one of the few avenues for social advancement available to common people in Latin America. In the military, Chávez had access to positions of power that otherwise would not have been available to him. Eventually he rose to the rank of lieutenant colonel. Chávez gained a political consciousness in the military barracks as he witnessed economic exploitation and racial discrimination. He was part of a tradition of military socialists in Latin America that dated to the 1930s and permeated lower-class sectors of the military. Rather than operating in its traditional role as an upper-class tool of oppression of marginalized communities, these low-ranking officers used the military as a mechanism to bring economic development to marginalized areas, even as they did so in a centralized and hierarchical fashion. In 1982, with both military and civilian co-conspirers, Chávez formed the Movimiento Bolivariano Revolucionaro 200 (MBR-200, Bolivarian Revolutionary Movement 200), so named for the birth of Venezuelan independence hero Simón Bolívar, to challenge the existing political system and open the way for social change.

Chávez always remained an outsider to the wealthy and powerful European-oriented world of the capital city of Caracas. Unlike previous leaders in Venezuela and throughout Latin America who gravitated toward Europe and the United States, Chávez was proud of his Indigenous and African heritage. He claimed that one of his grandmothers was a Pumé Indian and that a great-grandfather was an agrarian revolutionary. During his 1998 presidential campaign, he signed a "historic commitment" to rule on behalf of the country's half-million Indigenous peoples. He kept that promise, and doing so earned him the undying support of that sector of the population. At the same time, those policies gained him the animosity of the traditional power brokers who bristled at the thought of an Indigenous or African Venezuela. Chávez spoke directly to the country's population in a weekly live call-in program, *Aló Presidente* (Hello president). He broke from a centralized vision of the country and proclaimed his desire to rule on behalf of all Venezuelans. He traveled to rural communities and invited people to join him on TV. He proposed programs to bring government benefits to previously overlooked regions and sectors of the country.

DOCUMENT: HUGO CHÁVEZ, WORLD SOCIAL FORUM, 2005

In a speech to the 2005 World Social Forum in Porto Alegre, Brazil, Hugo Chávez declared for the first time the socialist nature of the Bolivarian Revolution.

Ignacio Ramonet, in his introduction, mentioned that I am a new kind of leader. I accept this, especially coming from a bright mind such as Ignacio's, but many old leaders inspire me.

Some very old like for example Jesus Christ, one of the greatest revolutionaries, anti-imperialist fighters in the history of the world, the true Christ, the Redemptor of the Poor.

Simón Bolívar, a guy who crisscrossed these lands, filling people with hope, and helping them become liberated.

Or that Argentine doctor, who crisscrossed our continent on a motorcycle, arriving in Central America to witness the gringo invasion of Guatemala in 1954, one of so many abuses that North American imperialism perpetrated on this continent.

Or that old guy with a beard, Fidel Castro, Abreu Lima, Artigas, San Martín, O'Higgins, Emiliano Zapata, Pancho Villa, Sandino, Morazán, Tupac Amaru, from all those old guys one draws inspiration.

Old guys that took up a commitment and now, from my heart, I understand them, because we have taken up a strong commitment. They have all returned.

One of these old guys, he was being ripped into pieces, pulled by horses from each arm and leg. Empires have always been brutal, there are no good or bad empires, they are all aberrant, brutal, perverse, no matter what they wear or how they speak. When he felt he was about to die, he shouted, "I die today but some day I'll return and I'll be millions." Atahualpa has returned and he is millions, Tupac Amaru has returned and he is millions, Bolívar has returned and he is millions, Sucre, Zapata, and here we are, they have returned with us. In this filled up Gigantinho Stadium.

I'm here because the World Social Forum is the most important political event in the world. I'm here because, with my comrades from the Venezuelan delegation, we have come to learn. In Venezuela what we are honestly doing is a test run and as every test run it needs to be monitored and improved; it is an experiment open to all the wonderful experiences happening in the world.

The World Social Forum, in these five years, has become a solid platform for debate, discussions, a solid, wide, varied, rich platform where the greater part of the excluded, those without a voice in the corridors of power, come here to express themselves and to raise their protests, here they come to sing, to say who they are, what they want, they come to recite their poems, their songs, their hope of finding consensus.

I don't feel like a president, being president is a mere circumstance. I'm fulfilling a role as many fulfill a role in any team. I'm only fulfilling a role, but I'm a peasant, I'm a soldier, I'm a man committed to this project of an alternative world that is better and possible, necessary to save the Earth. I am one more militant of the revolutionary cause.

I have been a Maoist since I entered military school, I read Che Guevara, I read Bolívar and his speeches and letters, becoming a Bolivarian Maoist, a mixture of all that. Mao says that it is imperative, for every revolutionary, to determine very clearly who are your friends and who are your enemies. In Latin America this is particularly important. I'm convinced that only through the path of revolution we will be able to come out of this historical conundrum in which we have been stuck for many centuries.

Today we also have the Missions, for example Barrio Adentro. It is a national crusade involving everybody, civilians, soldiers, old, young, communities, the national and local governments, grassroots community organizations, helped by Revolutionary Cuba. Today there are almost 25 thousand Cuban doctors and dentists living among the poorest, plus Venezuelan male and female nurses. The budget to pay the medicine, for which the people pay not one cent, to pay the doctors and the transportation systems, the communication systems, ambulatory center building, the equipment, all that, the majority of all these is paid for with income from the oil industry, money that before left the country. In 2004 the mission Barrio Adentro took care of 50 million patients, completely with free medicine.

Another example of the Venezuelan revolution, those kids are in the Bolivarian University, which is a year old. The majority of these kids were waiting for years to enter universities, but couldn't because they were privatized. That's the neoliberal, imperialist plan. The health system was privatized; that cannot be privatized because it's a fundamental human right. Health, education, water, energy, public services—they cannot be given to private capital that denies those rights to the people. That's the road to savagery. Capitalism is savagery.

Every day I'm more convinced, less capitalism and more socialism. I have no doubt that it is necessary to transcend capitalism, but I add, capitalism cannot be transcended from within. Capitalism needs to be transcended via socialism, with equality and justice, that's the path to transcend the capitalist power—true socialism, equality, and justice. I'm also convinced that it's possible to do it in democracy but watch it, what type of democracy not the one Mr. Superman wants to impose.

Although I admire Che Guevara very much, his thesis was not viable. His guerrilla unit, perhaps 100 men in a mountain, that may have been valid in Cuba, but the conditions elsewhere were different, and that's why Che died in Bolivia, a Quixotic figure. History showed that his thesis of one, two, three Vietnams did not work.

Today, the situation does not involve guerrilla cells, that can be surrounded by the Rangers or the Marines in a mountain, as they did to Che Guevara, they were only maybe 50 men against 500, now we are millions, how are they going to surround us. Careful, we might be the ones doing the surrounding . . . not yet, little by little.

Empires sometimes do not get surrounded, they rot from inside, and then they tumble down and get destroyed as the Roman Empire and every empire from Europe in the past centuries. Some day the rottenness that it carries inside will end up destroying the US Empire.

Goliath is not invincible. The empire is not invincible. Three years ago only Fidel and I, in those president's summits, other than us, it was like a neoliberal choir and one felt almost like an infiltrated agent, conspiring. Today almost nobody dares to defend the neoliberal model. So that is one of the weaknesses that undresses the empire. The ideological weaknesses are evident. Even the economic weaknesses are evident. And everything indicates that these weaknesses will increase. It's enough to see the internal repression in the U.S. The so-called PATRIOT Act is nothing more than a repressive law against North American citizens. They speak about freedom of expression, but they violate it every day.

So here we are in Latin America, it is not the same Latin America of even five years ago. I cannot, out of respect for you, comment on the internal situation of any other country. In Venezuela, particularly the first two years, many of my partisans criticized me, asking me to go faster, that we had to be more radical. I did not consider it to be the right moment because processes have stages. Compañeros, there are stages in the processes, there are rhythms that have to do with more than just the internal situation in every country, they have to do with the international situation. And even if some of you make noise, I will say it: I like Lula, I appreciate him, he is a good man, with a big heart, a brother, a compañero, and I'm sure that Lula and the people of Brazil, with Néstor Kirchner and the Argentine people, with Tabaré Vázquez and the Uruguayan people, we will open the path towards the dream of a United Latin America, different, possible.

A big hug, I love you all very much, a big hug to everybody, Many, many thanks.

Source: Hugo Chávez Frías, "Capitalism Is Savagery," *Z Magazine* (November 2006): 44–46, https://zcomm.org.

ELECTIONS

In December 1998, Chávez won Venezuela's presidential election with nearly 60 percent of the vote. The previously dominant political parties AD and COPEI had followed neoliberal economic policies that eliminated social spending as well as foodstuff, petroleum, and agricultural subsidies. These discredited policies harmed the country's poor and marginal populations. Chávez won largely based on the support of lower-class people who had previously been excluded from the country's economic development.

Chávez took office on February 2, 1999, and immediately began to remake Venezuela's political landscape. He implemented policies that expanded social spending and halted privatization plans, although he never took steps away from the country's extreme dependency on petroleum exports. The president's failure to break from a monoculture export economy led some early observers to comment that Chávez's bark was worse than his bite—that his strident anti-neoliberal rhetoric was not reflected in his economic policies. Nevertheless, building on his support among the poor, Chávez proceeded to redraw the country's political structures. He drafted a new constitution to replace the one in force since 1961. The new constitution increased presidential power while at the same time implementing socioeconomic changes—including expanding access to education and healthcare. It increased civil rights for women, Indigenous peoples, and others marginalized under the old system. Symbolically, the constitution included gender-inclusive language. It also changed the name of the country from the "Republic of Venezuela" to the "Bolivarian Republic of Venezuela," pointing to an internationalist vision that built on Bolívar's pan-Latin Americanism.

The new constitution so fundamentally rewrote Venezuela's political structures that it required new congressional and presidential elections. Chávez handily won reelection in 2000 with about 60 percent of the vote, a margin of support that he consistently enjoyed. Despite earlier involvement in a military coup, Chávez was content to remake the face of Venezuela through the political process and relished the challenges of electoral campaigns.

International observer missions, including the Carter Center, declared Venezuela's electoral system to be one of the most clean, transparent, and accurate in the world. Duplicate systems to prevent fraud included electronic thumbprint identification machines and paper printouts of each vote. Former U.S. president Jimmy Carter acknowledged that the Venezuelan process was cleaner and more legitimate than the 2000 vote in the United States that awarded the presidency to George W. Bush, even though he had lost the popular vote to Al Gore.

Missions

Following the consolidation of his power, Chávez proceeded to implement a series of social programs called "missions" designed to attack the endemic poverty that plagued about a third of Venezuela's population. Often these were named after national heroes. One of the most successful was Plan Robinson, a literacy program named after Simón Rodríguez, Bolívar's mentor who was nicknamed Robinson because of his fascination with the novel *Robinson Crusoe*. The program employed the Cuban literacy campaign that eradicated illiteracy from that island in 1961. Venezuela was the eighteenth country to use that program and successfully taught 1.2 million people who did not previously know how to read and write. Plan Ribas, named after independence hero José Félix Ribas, provided diplomas to five million high school dropouts. Other missions provided subsidized food to poor people, supported women's reproductive and family planning rights, recognized women's work as mothers and caretakers, and provided mothers with social security payments.

In the first years of Chávez's administration, public spending on healthcare quadrupled. Venezuela led the world in the number of plastic surgeons and beauty queens but lacked doctors who were willing to engage in general practice, particularly in poor urban and rural areas. In order to address this shortage, Barrio Adentro (Into the Neighborhood) brought Cuban doctors to poor neighborhoods that never before had received sufficient medical attention. The government also provided scholarships so that more Venezuelans could train to be doctors. The expansion of rural clinics and free emergency care led to a dramatic drop in the infant mortality rate. The Misión Milagro or miracle plan extended this funding to eye care, providing the "miracle" of vision to people who could not previously see.

In order to address the failures of previous agrarian reform programs, in November 2001 Venezuela enacted a law to foster land and agricultural development. The legislation instituted a cap on the size of landholdings, imposed taxes on properties that were not in production, and provided for the distribution of land to landless peasants. The main goals of this legislation were to address issues of social injustice and to increase agricultural production. In order to speed up the process of agrarian reform, on February 4, 2003, Chávez signed a presidential decree that formally launched Plan Zamora. Named after the radical nineteenth-century peasant leader, this plan supported sustainable agricultural development based on a philosophy of a just distribution of land in accordance with values of equality and social justice. Plan Zamora was key to achieving the government's goals of food security, economic self-sufficiency, and ending dependence on imported goods.

Together with these social reforms were ideas of creating a new form of "participatory protagonist democracy" in which people could have a tangible voice in the political process. Mechanisms such as communal planning councils fostered citizen engagement. A goal was to replace a representative democracy that entrenched wealth and power in the hands of the ruling class with grassroots organizations that empowered local communities.

Populism and Socialism

Chávez was often called a populist, which, in Latin America, has the negative connotations of the authoritarian and corporatist legacy of Getúlio Vargas in Brazil and Juan Perón in Argentina. Populists often opportunistically appeal to the impoverished masses for support but implement policies designed to secure their hold on power rather than remake state structures with the goal of realizing social justice for the dispossessed. Detractors complained that Chávez used skyrocketing petroleum prices to fund social programs to shore up his base, while supporters noted that these were precisely the policies on which he had campaigned. Chávez was sometimes called a "left populist" to indicate that he used rhetoric to appeal to the poor but also implemented concrete policies to shift wealth and power away from the upper class. His potential for success provided much hope to his supporters, while at the same time feeding apprehension among his opponents.

Initially Chávez denied that he intended to implement a socialist agenda in Venezuela. Instead he emphasized a nationalistic "Bolivarian Revolution" that followed in Bolívar's footsteps. As Chávez consolidated power, however, he embraced a socialist discourse. At the World Social Forum in Porto Alegre, Brazil, in January 2005, Chávez declared, "Every day I'm more revolutionary. It's the only path we can take to break down hierarchy and imperialism." He pointed to the failures of savage capitalism and argued that capitalism can only be transcended with socialism through democracy. It was his first public statement in favor of socialism. The following year the World Social Forum moved to Caracas, where Chávez presented an even stronger statement in favor of socialism. He proclaimed that the world faces two choices: socialism or death, "because capitalism is destroying life on earth." He consistently utilized religious language, calling Jesus Christ "one of the biggest anti-imperialist and revolutionary leaders in history" who contributed "to the socialist project of the twenty-first century in Latin America." In December 2006, after winning a third term in office, Chávez announced that all of the disparate political parties that had supported his candidacy would now join forces in one Partido Socialista Unido de Venezuela (PSUV, United Socialist Party of Venezuela). The PSUV subsequently became Venezuela's dominant political force.

Opposition

Everything from Chávez's lower-class mannerisms and colloquial speech patterns to his social policies and economic priorities alienated him from Venezuela's small minority that had long held political power. During his first term in office under the new constitution (2000–2006), Chávez faced three significant challenges and overcame each one. The first and most dramatic was an April 11, 2002, coup that removed Chávez from office for two days, but a wellspring of popular support from poor neighborhoods brought him back to power. A December 2002 employer strike in the state oil company Petróleos de Venezuela (PDVSA, Venezuela Petroleum) and other industries significantly damaged the economy but failed to undermine Chávez's popular support. Finally, after failing in these extraconstitutional efforts to remove Chávez, the upper class turned to a provision in Chávez's own constitution that allowed for the recall of elected officials midway through their terms. Chávez handily won the August 15, 2004, vote, further strengthening his hold on power. These defeats discredited the entire opposition, including both traditional political parties AD and COPEI and newer ones such as Primero Justicia. Facing the prospects of a complete rout in the 2005 congressional elections, conservatives withdrew from the campaign and handed Chávez and his leftist allies complete control over the national assembly.

The actions of a mobilized rural population threatened the privileged position of wealthy landholders who, in alliance with traditional political parties, exercised significant control in rural areas. Paramilitary groups operated with impunity and killed hundreds of peasant leaders. At the same time, low prices for agricultural commodities frustrated peasants' attempts to earn a living. These peasants wanted Chávez to do more and move faster to transform societal inequalities.

Internationally, the Bush administration denounced and undermined Chávez through a variety of avenues. The National Endowment for Democracy (NED) supported and funded opposition groups. Chávez accused the United States of plotting his assassination and stridently condemned U.S. imperialism and neoliberal economic policies. He signed commercial agreements with China, India, and other new markets in an attempt to break Venezuela's dependency on oil exports to the United States. Chávez presented the Alternativa Bolivariana para América Latina (ALBA, Bolivarian Alternative for Latin America) as a substitute to the U.S.-sponsored Free Trade Area of the Americas (FTAA). His demands to put people before profits gained him a good deal of international support as he challenged U.S. hegemonic control over the region.

Death and Legacy

After struggling with cancer for two years, Chávez died on March 5, 2013. Power passed to his vice president and anointed heir, Nicolás Maduro. Even in his death, observers disagreed whether Chávez was a democrat dedicated to transforming Venezuela to benefit the poor or an archetypical autocrat bent on amassing personal power.

During fourteen years in office, Chávez's policies cut poverty in half and reduced extreme poverty by more than 70 percent. Income inequality fell from one of the highest to the lowest in the region. Unemployment was slashed in half, and the number of people eligible for public pensions tripled. Reversing a twenty-year decline before Chávez's presidency, per capita income grew by more than 2 percent annually from 2004 to 2014. Investment in social missions improved the quality of life of the country's poor majority, vastly expanding access to healthcare, education, and housing. Chávez's policies also significantly increased citizen participation in politics.

Despite these economic gains, Venezuela faced significant problems at the end of Chávez's life. Homicides quintupled during his time in office, reaching one of the highest murder rates in the world. Corruption, waste, and incompetence among government officials continued to be major problems. The country also faced high inflation rates that undermined the significant increases in wages and social services. Further complicating the economic situation, a slump in oil prices in 2014 dried up a revenue stream that funded government subsidies and social programs. Critics blamed the problems on the economic mismanagement of Chávez's successor Maduro, including his maintenance of multiple foreign currency exchange rates that encouraged the smuggling of subsidized goods at a cost to the country's poor and marginalized populations. Supporters instead accused opponents of sabotaging the economy and pointed to the inherent difficulties of building a socialist economy in a country still dominated by a capitalist mode of production.

SUMMARY

The election of Hugo Chávez as president in 1998 rocked Venezuela's political establishment and set the continent on a leftist political trajectory. His triumph seemingly reinforced the idea that dramatic political changes in Latin America could be made through institutional structures rather than resorting to armed struggle to alter the existing order. While conservative opponents ceaselessly opposed Chávez's government, previously marginalized populations rallied to his cause. Despite the significant problems and reversals that it faced, the Bolivarian Revolution appeared to be a truly transformative event.

DISCUSSION QUESTIONS

Is representative or participatory democracy better at governing in the interests of the popular will of the people?

What was it about the Bolivarian Revolution that imperial powers found so threatening? Were these fears justified?

How important was charismatic leadership for the success of the Bolivarian Revolution?

How much did the Bolivarian Revolution change Venezuela? Was this a true revolution?

FURTHER READING

Hugo Chávez's election as president of Venezuela triggered a burst of interest among political scientists and journalists in the Bolivarian Revolution, leading to the publication of a large number of outstanding works on the leftist government.

Angosto-Ferrández, Luis Fernando. *Venezuela Reframed: Bolivarianism, Indigenous Peoples and Socialisms of the Twenty-First Century.* London: Zed Books, 2015. An examination of Indigenous support for the Bolivarian Revolution.

Ciccariello-Maher, George. *Building the Commune: Radical Democracy in Venezuela.* London: Verso, 2016. An exploration of Venezuela's efforts to build a participatory democracy.

———. *We Created Chávez: A People's History of the Venezuelan Revolution.* Durham, NC: Duke University Press, 2013. An influential book that convincingly argues that grassroots movements, not vanguard leadership, defined the direction of the Bolivarian Revolution.

Ellner, Steve. *Rethinking Venezuelan Politics: Class, Conflict, and the Chávez Phenomenon.* Boulder, CO: Lynne Rienner, 2008. A careful analysis of the Chávez government from a leading Venezuela scholar.

Gonzalez, Mike. *Hugo Chávez: Socialist for the Twenty-First Century.* London: Pluto Press, 2014. A short and sympathetic biography of the Venezuelan president.

Gott, Richard. *Hugo Chávez and the Bolivarian Revolution.* London: Verso, 2005. A solid journalistic summary of Chávez's rise to power.

Martinez, Carlos, Michael Fox, and JoJo Farrell. *Venezuela Speaks! Voices from the Grassroots.* Oakland, CA: PM Press, 2010. A collection of interviews with social movement activists who were supportive of the Chávez government.

Ponniah, Thomas, and Jonathan Eastwood, eds. *The Revolution in Venezuela: Social and Political Change under Chávez.* Cambridge, MA: Harvard University David Rockefeller Center for Latin American Studies, 2011. Distinguished authors analyze social change in Venezuela from a broad range of ideological perspectives.

Tinker Salas, Miguel. *Venezuela: What Everyone Needs to Know.* Oxford: Oxford University Press, 2013. An introduction to Venezuela by a preeminent historian.

Wilpert, Greg. *Changing Venezuela by Taking Power: The History and Policies of the Chávez Government.* London: Verso, 2007. A critical appreciation of the strengths and shortcomings of the Chávez administration.

FILMS

Hugo Chavez at the 2005 World Social Forum, Porto Alegre, Brazil. 2005. Venezuelan president Hugo Chávez discusses the goals and achievements of his administration.

The Revolution Will Not Be Televised. 2002. A powerfully moving film that describes Venezuelan president Hugo Chávez's removal from power on April 11, 2002, and his return to power three days later.

Venezuela Bolivariana: People and Struggle of the Fourth World War. 2004. A documentary about the Bolivarian Revolution of Venezuela and its links to the worldwide movement against capitalist globalization.

10

Socialisms of the Twentieth and Twenty-First Centuries

KEY DATES ("PINK TIDE" GOVERNMENTS)

Hugo Chávez (Venezuela, 1999–2013)
  April 11–13, 2001: Failed military coup
Ricardo Lagos (Chile, 2000–2006)
Jean-Bertrand Aristide (Haiti, 2001–2004)
Luiz Inácio Lula da Silva (Brazil, 2003–2010)
Néstor Kirchner (Argentina, 2003–2007)
Evo Morales (Bolivia, 2005–)
Tabaré Vázquez (Uruguay, 2005–2010)
Manuel Zelaya (Honduras, 2006–2009)
  June 28, 2009: Military coup
Michelle Bachelet (Chile, 2006–2010)
Daniel Ortega (Nicaragua, 2007–)
Rafael Correa (Ecuador, 2007–2017)
  September 30, 2010: Failed police mutiny
Cristina Fernández de Kirchner (Argentina, 2007–2015)
Fernando Lugo (Paraguay, 2008–2012)
  June 22, 2012: Express impeachment
Mauricio Funes (El Salvador, 2009–2014)
José "Pepe" Mujica (Uruguay, 2010–2015)
Dilma Rousseff (Brazil, 2011–2016)
  August 31, 2016: Impeached on politically motivated charges

Nicolás Maduro (Venezuela, 2013–)
Michelle Bachelet (Chile, 2014–)
Salvador Sánchez Cerén (El Salvador, 2014–)
Tabaré Vázquez (Uruguay, 2015–)

Hugo Chávez's election as president of Venezuela in 1998 was followed at the dawn of the twenty-first century with the election of Evo Morales in Bolivia and Rafael Correa in Ecuador. Those two leaders pursued a similar road of implementing progressive policies that Chávez had paved before them. Voters elected less radical leftist governments in most other South American countries (particularly Argentina, Brazil, and Chile) as well as in Nicaragua and El Salvador in Central America. Latin America had moved significantly from the 1970s when the military governed in most of the region. With the return to civilian rule in the 1980s, armed struggle was largely off the table as a path for the left to assume political power. Civilian rule, however, did not mean democracy in the sense of a popular government that implemented policies that benefited the majority of the population. Before Chávez's election, conservative governments held power in all of Latin America with the sole exception of Cuba. They implemented neoliberal economic policies that privatized public resources to the benefit of the upper class, with a resulting increase in inequality and poverty for the lower class. In what some have termed the "**pink tide**," by the end of the first decade of the twenty-first century almost the entire region was under leftist rule.

NEW SOCIAL MOVEMENTS

A resurgence of mass mobilizations against neoliberal economic policies in the decade before Chávez's election opened political space for the election of progressive governments across the hemisphere. With the electoral defeat of the Sandinistas in 1990 and the failure of other guerrilla movements in Latin America, academic and political attention had shifted away from armed paths to power. Instead, activists formed social movements, sometimes called popular movements because of their roots in marginalized populations, which fought for the realization of civil or social rights. Rather than engaging in electoral campaigns or guerrilla struggles with the goal of gaining direct control over governmental structures to transform society, these social movements typically had more limited goals of influencing specific policies. They functioned as part of civil society and were known as nonstate actors.

Sociologists distinguished new social movements (NSMs) from older movements that were rooted in traditional political parties, labor unions, or guerrilla insurgencies that advocated for political and social changes. Researchers interpreted NSMs as responding to immediate and specific crises with focused and definitive demands. Examples of NSMs included gender and women's rights organizations, neighborhood associations, human rights promotion, ecological activism, support for political prisoners and the disappeared, and champions for Indigenous peoples' rights. While the old movements were commonly rooted in a Marxist understanding of class struggle, NSMs embraced identity politics. Leftist scholars challenged this as an artificial divide and noted that the "old" movements had not entirely ignored identity politics and the "new" ones had not discarded economic demands. More important was to understand how various forms of identity (including class, ethnicity, and gender) interact with each other in specific historical contexts.

A key demand of many social movements in the 1990s was to roll back the neoliberal economic policies that many of Latin America's conservative governments had implemented in the 1980s. International lending agencies such as the International Monetary Fund (IMF) had encouraged countries to privatize state enterprises and reduce subsidies for public programs such as transportation and education. A goal was to halt high rates of inflation and fuel economic growth, but these policies increased socioeconomic inequality and undermined the livelihoods of the most marginalized members of society. Movements initially formed as apolitical groups to address specific matters soon found themselves engaging with much larger structural concerns. These new movements opened up political spaces, articulated popular demands, and politicized issues (such as gender rights) that had been formerly confined to the private realm. To achieve their objectives, they engaged in similar strategies and tactics of earlier movements such as demonstrations, strikes, and marches in order to wrestle concessions from the government.

Brazil's Movimento dos Trabalhadores Rurais Sem Terra (MST, Landless Workers Movement) was one of Latin America's largest social movements and bridged the artificial divide between the demands and strategies of old and new movements. Rural activists formed the MST in the late 1970s to defend the rights and lives of peasants who had been expelled from their lands. The MST engaged in land occupations as a strategy to pressure the government for positive policy changes, including an agrarian reform that included access to land, healthcare, education, dignity, infrastructure, water, housing, and support for the young to stay on the land. The MST helped found the Via Campesina (Spanish for "Peasants' Way") in 1993 as an international movement to raise family farmers' voices in international debates. The Via Campesina opposed corporate-driven agriculture that destroyed the environment and instead defended small-scale sustainable agriculture as a way to promote social justice and dignity. They proposed the concept of food sovereignty as the right of communities to produce healthy food on their own land rather than relying on neoliberal export economies that contributed to poverty and climate crises.

The 1992 quincentennial of Columbus's arrival in the Americas raised the profile of Indigenous struggles. One of the best-organized Indigenous movements was the Confederación de Nacionalidades Indígenas del Ecuador (CONAIE, Confederation of Indigenous Nationalities of Ecuador). Leading up to the quincentennial, CONAIE organized a powerful uprising that paralyzed Ecuador for a week. Activists blocked roads with boulders, rocks, and trees that halted the transportation system, effectively cutting off the food supply to the cities and shutting down the country to force the government to negotiate agrarian reform demands. The movement's most controversial proposal was to revise the constitution to recognize the "plurinational" character of Ecuador. Activists called for the incorporation of the unique contributions of diverse populations into state structures, a proposition that the dominant culture repeatedly rejected as undermining the unity and integrity of the country.

The World Social Forum (WSF) was the largest gathering of civil society and presented the most significant challenge to neoliberal economic policies. The WSF first met in Porto Alegre, Brazil, in 2001, but had its roots in earlier organizing efforts such as the 1992 Earth Summit at Rio de Janeiro, Brazil, and the First International Encounter for Humanity and against Neoliberalism that the Zapatistas organized in Chiapas, Mexico, in 1996. It quickly grew from an assembly of ten thousand people (mostly from Latin America, France, and Italy) who gathered to talk about creating a "globalization from below," to more than one hundred thousand within three years. Under the slogan "Another World Is Possible," the WSF presented a direct challenge to the conservative British prime minister Margaret Thatcher's claim "There is no alternative" to the ravages of neoliberal capitalism. The forum created an open platform for activists to discuss strategies of resistance to neoliberal globalization and to present constructive alternatives.

The WSF provided an arena for perennial discussions concerning the relationship between social movements and political parties in achieving social change. With an emphasis on civil society, the WSF excluded political parties and armed groups from its discussions. With the rise of new left governments in Latin America during the first decade of the twenty-first century, many activists began to rethink the relationship between social movements and political parties. Although parties could not mobilize massive demonstrations the way social movements did, those movements lacked the governmental authority necessary to implement positive policy proposals. Organized as part of civil society, the WSF was better situated than any other force to open up the political spaces necessary for the election of a new wave of left-wing governments in Latin America.

LATIN AMERICA'S LEFT TURN

Chávez's Bolivarian Revolution blazed a pathway forward and provided a model for subsequent leftist governments in Latin America. Unlike Cuba half a century earlier, all of them came to power through what were widely recognized as open and free elections. Critics spoke of two lefts: a more moderate trend represented by Néstor Kirchner in Argentina, Luiz Inácio Lula da Silva in Brazil, first Ricardo Lagos and then Michelle Bachelet in Chile, and Tabaré Vázquez and José "Pepe" Mujica in Uruguay; and a "populist" left of Chávez in Venezuela, Evo Morales in Bolivia, and Rafael Correa in Ecuador. The "good" left was willing to work within the confines of existing market economies, while opponents condemned a more radical left for returning to allegedly discredited nationalist, **clientelist**, and statist models of governance. None of the governments, however, approached the radical policies of the twentieth-century revolutions that led to the expropriation of Standard Oil in Mexico, United Fruit Company land in Guatemala, tin mines in Bolivia, sugar mills in Cuba, or copper mines in Chile.

In reality, all of these governments took very different directions. Instead of two, Latin America had many different lefts. A year after Chávez's victory in 1998, the socialist lawyer Ricardo Lagos won election in Chile, seemingly returning the country to a path that had been interrupted with Augusto Pinochet's military coup in 1973. Lagos played a significant role in a 1988 plebiscite that brought Pinochet's dictatorship to an end. In what appeared to be a repeat of history, the socialist Lagos succeeded the son of the Christian Democrat Eduardo Frei (also named Eduardo Frei) who preceded Salvador Allende in power in the 1960s. Six years later, the socialist, medical doctor, and single mother Michelle Bachelet succeeded Lagos in office and returned for a second term four years later. Chilean radicals criticized Lagos and Bachelet for their relatively moderate policies and failures to break from Pinochet's neoliberal economic policies. Institutional policies implemented during Pinochet's regime, including constitutional provisions that ensured conservative control over the legislature, restricted the pace of changes that socialists could make. This legislative control limited possibilities to reform Pinochet's 1980 constitution that would have allowed reforms to end neoliberal economic policies that contributed to Chile's continuing high rates of socioeconomic inequality.

After three unsuccessful campaigns for office, labor leader Luiz Inácio Lula da Silva won the presidency in Brazil in 2003 as the candidate for the Partido dos Trabalhadores (PT, Workers' Party). After two terms in office, he passed the mantle to his chief of staff, Dilma Rousseff, a student activist and guerrilla member in the 1960s whom the military government had imprisoned and tortured. As leaders of the world's eighth-largest economy, both presidents followed fairly moderate reform policies that made only modest gains in addressing Brazil's severe socioeconomic inequalities. The MST in particular expressed disappointment that they did not dismantle the country's agroindustrial export economy.

Néstor Kirchner of the left-populist Peronist party also won election in Argentina in 2003. After serving a term in office, his spouse Cristina Fernández de Kirchner succeeded him in 2007. Under their neo-Keynesian state-led development policies, poverty rates dropped by 70 percent and extreme poverty by 80 percent. Unemployment fell from more than 17 percent to less than 7 percent. Their approach alternated between inflammatory populist positions designed to motivate their base and quite orthodox policies that alienated that same base. Their leftist rhetoric also earned them the animosity of the U.S. government. Kirchner's plan to alternate terms in office with his wife was undermined when he died in 2010. His widow Fernández won reelection in 2011 and successfully served two terms in office.

The physician Tabaré Vázquez led the left to its first presidential victory in 2005 in neighboring Uruguay. As the candidate of the Frente Amplio (Broad Front) leftist coalition, Vázquez introduced middle-class social democratic policies that led to considerable improvements in education and working conditions, a significant expansion of the welfare system, and a dramatic reduction in poverty. In 2010, José "Pepe" Mujica, a former guerrilla fighter with the Tupamaros, succeeded Vázquez in office. Mujica gained renown for his austere lifestyle, including giving up many of the perks of the presidential office. He preferred instead to live in his own simple house and drive his old Volkswagen Beetle. In 2015, Vázquez returned for a second term in office.

In contrast to these relatively moderate governments from South America's southern cone, Hugo Chávez in Venezuela gained two strong allies on the radical left in the Andes with the election of Evo Morales in Bolivia in 2005 and Rafael Correa in Ecuador the following year. Both followed Chávez's lead in revising their countries' constitutions in a way that fundamentally remapped political structures. The new constitutions increased presidential power, including allowance for presidential reelection. Opponents charged that the leaders sought to maintain themselves permanently in power while advocates feared that their positive gains would be turned back without strong leadership. All three presidents used the earnings from the export of commodities to fund economic development. They implemented social programs that significantly reduced poverty and inequality. The new constitutions protected the rights of Indigenous and African-descent peoples, and pledged to follow a path of local, sustainable economic development. The three presidents also had complicated relations with the social movements that helped place them in power. Sometimes they tangled more with radicals who tried to push their revolutions in a leftist direction in favor of more thoroughgoing redistributive policies than they did with the members of the discredited traditional oligarchy who wished to return to neoliberal economic structures that privileged a wealthy minority.

Many of the new left governments faced significant threats to their hold on power. In 2006, Manuel Zelaya won election with the liberal party in Honduras. Once in office, he moved significantly to the left and implemented policies to benefit the country's impoverished majority. His proposals threatened the traditional oligarchy that had initially supported his presidency. Three years into his term, the military removed him from office under the questionable charge that he attempted to revise the constitution to allow for presidential reelection. The military coup triggered massive grassroots protests as marginalized communities pressed for the realization of the policy objectives that Zelaya had proposed.

In 2008, the bishop Fernando Lugo, who had been influenced by liberation theology, won the election in Paraguay. A lack of support in congress continually frustrated his goal of implementing policies to benefit the poor Paraguayan farmers to whom he had ministered as a priest. In 2012, the legislature engaged in an express impeachment without giving the president time to prepare a defense. His removal took the form of a constitutional coup. In countries with an entrenched and conservative oligarchy, winning the presidency only meant a tenuous hold on one office. Electoral victories remained distant from the goal of actually gaining power and altering political and economic structures. These defeats highlighted the limitations of institutional paths to power that proscribed a complete dismantling of the structures of the old regime.

In 2007, after two failed campaigns, the Sandinista Daniel Ortega returned to office in Nicaragua. He made extensive compromises with the conservative Catholic Church hierarchy and the U.S. government in order to engineer his election. These concessions provided him with a high level of approval and ensured his continuance as president but came at the cost of significantly limiting the ability to implement socialist policies. Once he was back in the presidency, opponents complained that he dismantled democratic institutions to guarantee his hold on power.

In El Salvador, the leftist Farabundo Martí National Liberation Front (FMLN), which had fought a bloody guerrilla war in the 1980s, finally won the presidency through electoral means in 2009 with the journalist Mauricio Funes at the head of the ticket. Five years later, the former guerrilla fighter Salvador Sánchez Cerén succeeded him in office. The aftermath of the civil war left violent criminal gangs in place, resulting in higher homicide rates than those at the height of the fighting in the 1980s. Gaining power through existing institutional structures meant that the FMLN had limited means to address the significant problems facing the country.

Many of the key issues that faced revolutionaries at the dawn of the twentieth century were still very much present a century later, although they would often be focused through the specific lens of a current historical context.

Charismatic Leadership

Charismatic and strong leaders dominated Latin America's new left governments. If the leaders left office, the projects they headed threatened to fall apart. The presence of such commanding presidents led to doubts as to whether they ruled in the interests of the broader public, or whether they followed a nineteenth-century *caudillo* tradition of an all-powerful leader. An open question was whether their political projects were designed to maintain one person, typically a male, in power, or to transform societal structures. Some supporters willingly traded the limitations of egotistical leadership for the very real social gains they were able to implement. Others feared that reliance on one leader might mean a political project could fall apart were that person to disappear, and they advocated instead for taking advantage of the new political openings to train new leaders.

Opponents charged that leftist presidents maintained themselves in office through clientelistic programs of strategic handouts designed primarily to solidify their electoral support. Government defenders contended that shifting resources to disadvantaged populations was not an opportunistic move but a fundamental part of the governments' redistributive goals. Conservatives charged that these governments irresponsibly spent resources on social programs rather than saving for a rainy day. Leftist militants cautioned that clientelism and handouts replaced the more difficult task of raising people's political consciousness. Instead, they advocated prioritizing fundamental structural alterations to address underlying issues of oppression and exploitation and to transform society.

Social Movements and Electoral Politics

Elected leftist governments in the twenty-first century emerged on the back of social movements that had created new political spaces in which they could operate, but they often clashed with those movements that should have been their firmest and most loyal allies. In a sense, these conflicts were part of a long-running feud between anarchists and Marxists over the role of the state in making transformational changes. This friction also provided a contemporary counterpart to the tensions that Allende felt in Chile in the 1970s when he wanted to make permanent societal changes through institutional structures, while those to his left hoped to move much more quickly to a socialist society. Brazil's Landless Workers Movement (MST) initially had high expectations when Lula da Silva was elected in 2003 but vocally complained about the president's compromises once he was in office. Political parties cautioned these "ultra-leftists" against making unrealistic demands of their new governments. With conservatives out of power and their neoliberal economic policies largely discredited for having contributed to poverty and inequality, twenty-first-century socialist presidents often worried that those to their left presented more of a threat to the stability of their governments than their traditional enemies in the oligarchy. For grassroots social movements, winning a presidential election was simply one more step in a centuries-long struggle against oligarchical domination of their country.

Leftist political parties learned that winning an election is not the same as taking power. The presidency is only one of many political offices, and an antagonistic legislature and judiciary can significantly curtail their actions. In Venezuela, for example, it took Hugo Chávez a decade to consolidate control over government structures and move forward with socialist reforms. These are the limitations of working within the confines of a constitutional framework rather than gaining power through an armed struggle that destroyed the ancien régime, as happened in Cuba and Nicaragua.

Although twenty-first-century leftist governments used revolutionary rhetoric, their policies were more moderate than any of those from the twentieth century. They rarely spoke of nationalizing industries, or changing the mode of production. A common debate in the twentieth century was whether to reform existing systems or replace them with much more radical solutions. In the twenty-first century, the socialist governments opted for social evolution rather than violent revolution that might disrupt the smooth functioning of society. Their relative moderation and failure to deliver on more radical promises led some social movements to conclude that the current governments represented a continuation rather than a radical break from previous capitalist policies.

Neoextractivism

Latin America's new left governments flourished in the midst of a commodity boom. They were able to fund an expansion of social programs with windfall profits from petroleum and mineral extraction. As a result, their economies grew dramatically and poverty rates plummeted. Chávez and other left-populist governments that followed him claimed that their socioeconomic gains were a direct result of their return to state-centered development projects that previous neoliberal governments had disassembled.

Leftist critics complained that pursuing such policies failed to make a fundamental break with previous export-dependent economies. Environmental and social movement activists criticized the unsustainable nature of these policies, as well as the fact that local communities that bore the brunt of these endeavors rarely shared in their benefits. Protests against mineral extraction spread across the Americas, with both left and right governments arguing that large-scale mining was preferable and less ecologically damaging than the alternative of small-scale artisanal mining.

In one of many examples of the tensions between leftist governments and social movements, Indigenous organizations in Bolivia in 2011 marched to protest government plans to build a highway through the Isiboro-Sécure Indigenous Territory and National Park (TIPNIS) ecological reserve. Evo Morales was an Aymara who leveraged his credentials as a leader of Bolivia's powerful social movements to win election as president. In office, he pressed for construction of the road because it was key to Bolivia's economic development. At first Morales refused to listen to protests that the road would destroy one of the world's most biodiverse regions, but social movements pressured him to change his position. He learned to negotiate policies with rural communities in order to maintain both high approval ratings and impressive economic growth rates.

In 2013, Ecuadorian president Rafael Correa announced his decision to drill for oil in the ecologically sensitive Yasuní National Park in the eastern Amazonian forest. A proposal not to exploit the Ishpingo Tiputini Tambococha, or ITT, oil fields in exchange for international development aid was a signature policy objective of his administration and one of the president's most popular proposals. Although Indigenous and environmental organizations opposed the policy reversal, the plan was consistent with the president's actions since he first took office in 2007. Correa favored resource extraction in an attempt to fund programs to end poverty and fuel economic development, even though it threatened to sacrifice marginalized communities. It was a trade-off he was willing to make, even as it also earned him the animosity of those his policies were designed to benefit the most.

The developmental policies of new left governments highlight how difficult it is to break from the capitalist logic of an export-driven economy. Bolivian vice president Álvaro García Linera in particular championed what he termed Andean-Amazonian capitalism as a method of developing the country. He advocated exporting natural resources and investing that income to lift marginalized people out of poverty. Such policies echoed the arguments of orthodox Marxists in the 1950s that Latin America lacked the proper objective conditions to implement socialist policies. Instead, the intermediate goal should be to build capitalism to develop the economy before moving on to the more advanced stage of communism. This was, of course, an argument that Fidel Castro in Cuba and Carlos Fonseca in Nicaragua rejected. Nevertheless, a perennial question was how quickly a leftist government could change society and whether administrations should focus on moderate reforms rather than striving for a much more radical socialist revolution that might destabilize society.

These resource-extraction strategies challenged the claims of 1960s dependency theorists that export-oriented economies would underdevelop the Latin American periphery. Most of the value from the export of natural resources accrues to the industrial core that converts the imports into finished products. A failure to end dependent relations on industrialized countries in Europe and North America ran Latin American governments afoul of those who should have been their strongest supporters on the Indigenous and environmental left. Leftist governments and social movements continued a complicated dance to realize mutual objectives of sustainable development that would benefit all peoples.

After a decade of record-high commodity prices and significant social gains, petroleum and mineral prices dropped and an economic boom came to a halt. During the boom years, some critics questioned how much specific governmental policies had contributed to economic growth and whether such gains would have been realized under any government. As economies stalled and inflation rates rose, voters turned back to the previously discredited conservative politicians who still held to their neoliberal doctrines of privatization and austerity. It appeared as if in good economic times, the general public was willing to turn toward leftist socialists with their promises of redistribution, but during tougher periods they preferred conservative capitalists with their emphasis on economic growth.

Capturing the Narrative

A common complaint leveled against many of Latin America's new left governments is that in their drive to advance social programs they had sacrificed individual liberties, particularly freedom of the press. Theoretically, one might ask why social and individual rights often convey the impression of being in tension with each other, but in examining historical realities it does not appear to be much of a mystery. In Guatemala in the 1950s, for example, the CIA broadcast anti-Arbenz propaganda into the country, and those media campaigns undermined the government. In Nicaragua in the 1980s, the opposition press played havoc with the economy simply by falsely reporting an upcoming shortage of a commodity and thereby causing a run on that item and as a result artificially creating a supply problem. Other progressive administrations faced similar problems. The conservative aristocracy retained a firm hold on media outlets and exploited them to advance their economic and political interests even when out of office. If a leftist government attempted to forward an alternative narrative, the oligarchy inevitably cried foul and claimed censorship. Fighting disinformation was always a significant problem.

In the twenty-first century, despite impressive social and economic gains, one would be hard pressed to find positive stories in the international mainstream media about Latin America's new socialist governments. News outlets openly cheered the reversal of political gains for the working class. This antagonism was even true of nominally leftist media outlets such as London's *Guardian* that one would typically expect to be sympathetic to these socialist programs. Most reporters, and many academics as well, enter a country in the company of the middle or upper classes and hence report from that perspective, often remaining largely unaware of the advances that social programs have brought to the working class. Deep racial divides mean that they have little contact with marginalized sectors of the society that provide a bedrock of support for leftist governments, and have little understanding of, or sympathy for, their perspectives when they do. For many of these governments caught up in a fight to advance a social revolution, the nicety of freedom of the press was a luxury they could hardly afford if the opposition refused to play fair.

Despite a common narrative that leftist governments control the local press, in most countries the owners of the mainstream media outlets are members of a conservative oligarchy who are committed to neoliberal economic policies and are deeply antagonistic to the redistributive policies of socialist governments. Given their class position, one could hardly expect them to act otherwise. It is for this reason that left governments create their own media outlets in an attempt to craft their own narrative. In the process, they discount or ignore any legitimate critique of their policies and turn to propaganda to reinforce public support for their administrations. Resorting to these tactics often comes at the cost of the leaders' own detriment, as they create an echo chamber in which officials become numb to growing popular discontent. In part, this is what led to the Sandinistas' electoral defeat in Nicaragua in 1990. Outside observers are left confused by competing narratives that talk past each other. An easy solution to this conundrum is not readily apparent in an environment where class opponents of a socialist experiment are dedicated to its overthrow by any means necessary.

Imperialism

At the dawn of the twenty-first century, the heavy imperial hand of the U.S. government continued to be as present in Latin America as it had been throughout the twentieth century. U.S. opposition to leftist governments was rarely expressed through overt military intervention. Rather than attempting to colonize Latin America directly as William Walker had done in Nicaragua in the 1850s, the United States favored neocolonial economic policies in which the value of raw commodities in Latin America accrued to corporations in the United States rather than supporting local development. Instead of focusing policy on a geopolitical conflict with the Soviet Union as during the Cold War, the largest threat to U.S. hegemony was China, which sought the region's resources to fuel its own economic development.

More common than direct U.S. military intervention in Latin America's internal affairs was to work through covert means, as had happened in Guatemala and Cuba, with the domestic opposition as in Chile, or with proxy paramilitary forces as was the case with the contras in Nicaragua. International lending agencies such as the IMF also made it difficult for governments to fund social programs. On occasion, the U.S. government also followed the policy that it had implemented with the MNR in Bolivia of attempting to draw what could otherwise be an antagonistic government into its sphere of influence. While not common, such a policy could be the most effective way to moderate what otherwise would have been radical policy objectives of a leftist government.

Conservative Restoration?

After a decade of almost hegemonic control of leftist governments in Latin America, previously discredited conservative politicians who favored a return to the capitalist neoliberal policies of privatization and austerity measures appeared to be making a comeback in 2015 with electoral victories in Argentina and Venezuela. Pontificating pundits proclaimed, seemingly with little basis in factual data, that during a period of economic downturn, leftist presidents preferred to sit out a term of office rather than see their popularity compromised, with plans to return once the economy returned to its previous growth patterns. The pundits also declared, with a certain amount of glee, that the populace had "tired" of the socialist policies of redistribution and voted for a return to "democracy."

Others argued that a resurgent right was part of typical political swings. After two terms of socialist rule in Chile under Lagos and Bachelet (2000–2010), the conservative billionaire Sebastián Piñera won, only to have Bachelet return to office four years later. After twelve years of Kirchner rule in Argentina (2003–2015), the conservative Mauricio Macri won the presidency on an openly neoliberal economic platform that denounced Venezuela, pledged loyalty to the United States, and pursued anti-immigrant policies. Several weeks later, voters flipped control of Venezuela's national assembly to a stridently anti-Chávez but politically incoherent opposition. In Brazil, the conservative congressional leader Eduardo Cunha led a politically motivated impeachment campaign against president Dilma Rousseff. Her vice president, Michel Temer, assumed office and moved quickly to undo thirteen years of progressive policies. After a successful first term in office, Chilean president Michelle Bachelet faced very low poll numbers during her second term, and the conservative Sebastián Piñera appeared positioned to win the 2017 election. Ecuador's Rafael Correa faced a constitutional ban on his reelection in 2017, and in Bolivia, Morales lost a referendum that would have allowed him to run for reelection in 2019, although he searched for ways to continue in office. The international media cheered these developments as the end of Latin America's left turn. In reality, various elements determined these political outcomes, and similar issues had influenced the rise and fall of social revolutionary projects during the twentieth century. No single factor explains the emergence of a revolutionary situation or its defeat, but often these historical developments are the result of a complex interplay of many different considerations including leadership, ideology, and access to resources.

The conservative victory in Argentina in November 2015 can be similarly understood as a result of the weakness of the nominally leftist candidacy of Daniel Scioli, the failures of his previous administration as governor of the province of Buenos Aires, divisions on the left with many supporting instead the insurgent candidacy of the more radical Sergio Massa, the personalist nature and campaign style of Macri, and an antagonistic media campaign against the Kirchner governments, not to mention objective conditions of rising inflation that undermined economic growth. In an electoral system, an effective campaign and the personal appeal of a candidate can play a larger role in determining an outcome than a political ideology or specific economic programs.

Similarly in Venezuela, high crime rates, low oil prices, bad government economic policies, corruption, and the fact that Nicolás Maduro was significantly less charismatic than Hugo Chávez all contributed to the left's legislative defeat in December 2015. Leading up to the election, the conservative opposition charged that the voting would be rigged, or that the government would refuse to recognize the results. Similar to the Sandinistas' electoral beating in Nicaragua in 1990, many Venezuelans voted against the government not because they favored a return to capitalism but because they wanted officials to pay more attention to a rapidly declining economic situation. After an almost unbroken seventeen-year stretch of leftist electoral victories (the only loss was a 2007 referendum to reform the constitution), Maduro accepted the defeat with grace. Despite a conservative opposition determined to remove the socialist government by any means necessary, as with the 1980s Sandinista Revolution, one of the most significant triumphs of the Bolivarian Revolution was the entrenchment of a transparent and legitimate electoral system.

SUMMARY

Contemporary leftist governments confront many of the same issues that revolutionaries faced throughout the twentieth century. This book has explored competing paths that revolutions have taken in Latin America. All of them followed diverse paths and realized varying degrees of success. The 1910 Mexican Revolution introduced a century of profound changes in the hemisphere and highlighted that the movements responded to local concerns and forwarded solutions that emerged out of domestic interests. A pair of midcentury reform movements in Guatemala and Bolivia opened a path to deep societal transformations before they were eventually slowed and stopped with military coups. The 1959 Cuban Revolution was the most successful revolution in Latin America and provides a standard by which others are measured. Unfortunately, none of the other twentieth-century movements achieved their transformative potential. Salvador Allende's elected socialist government ended in a military coup, whereas the Sandinistas came to power in Nicaragua through an armed uprising only to be evicted in an election. In contrast, Chávez used these same institutions to collapse the old order in Venezuela and introduce a period of profound and revolutionary changes. He left existing power structures largely intact, however, and those forces continued to challenge the Bolivarian Revolution.

Historians have not reached consensus on which events should be labeled as revolutionary. As this book demonstrates, revolutions need not be violent, and some of the most significant transformations can be achieved through peaceful and institutional means. A barrier to permanent change, however, was the persistence of preexisting power structures that remained intact and threatened the left's hold on power. For a revolution to be successful, wealth and power must be transferred from the upper class to a previously impoverished and dispossessed group of people. Those revolutions were informed by a socialist ideology that envisioned a more equal and just society without profound class divisions.

In addition to a clear ideology, revolutions relied on a variety of other factors to realize success. Charismatic vanguard leadership that could provide guidance for movements was a key theme that ran throughout twentieth-century revolutions in Latin America. Despite an assumption that revolutions emerged out of repression and deprivation, in reality they required the mobilization of significant material and human resources. Revolutions also succeeded in the midst of the collapse of a previous discredited political system. They surfaced in a political vacuum as much as a result of a successful armed struggle. Furthermore, armed struggles were only victorious when available legal avenues for change appeared to be closed off.

A variety of issues underlie all of these movements. Participants debated how quickly they should and could make changes, and whether a gradual reform of existing structures was preferable to rapid and potentially destabilizing change. They questioned whether successful and permanent changes were better achieved through peaceful and legal means, or via violent and extraconstitutional avenues. Revolutionaries disagreed on how broad to build a movement and whether tightly controlled governing structures best ensure success. Ideologues and tacticians also disagreed on which sectors of society are the most revolutionary. They deliberated whether struggles need to be rooted in a working-class consciousness as Marx envisioned, or whether in Latin America revolutions would emerge in the countryside among agrarian farmers. Warfare has traditionally been gendered male, and revolutionaries struggled with the relegation of women to marginal and domestic roles. Over the course of the twentieth century the function of the Catholic Church evolved. Whereas religious leaders traditionally allied with wealthy landholding interests, after the Second Vatican Council in the 1960s a new and popular church associated with the aspirations of poor and marginalized people materialized. Finally, revolutionaries disagreed whether to mobilize primarily around local issues, or whether to embrace transnational aspects of a movement.

Revolutions are inherently messy and complicated business, and raise intrinsically complicated issues. Transforming unequal and unjust societal structures is a difficult undertaking that does not lend itself to simple solutions. Understanding present-day political events helps in analyzing earlier developments, and studying Latin America's revolutionary history contributes to a fuller appreciation of the current challenges the hemisphere faces.

DISCUSSION QUESTIONS

Did social movements in the 1990s emerge out of the successes or the failures of the 1980s guerrilla wars?
What role do social movements play in defining the policies of leftist governments?
How important are elections to leftist strategies?
Are new left governments a threat to democratic governance?

FURTHER READING

The Bolivarian Revolution in Venezuela introduced a left turn in South America as well as an explosion in literature on new progressive governments. Given the current nature of these events, political scientists have published the bulk of the scholarly work on the subject, and much of it has appeared as essays in edited volumes.

Burbach, Roger, Michael Fox, and Federico Fuentes. *Latin America's Turbulent Transitions: The Future of Twenty-First-Century Socialism*. London: Zed Books, 2013. A broad exploration of Latin America's left turn.

Castañeda, Jorge G., and Marco A. Morales, eds. *Leftovers: Tales of the Latin American Left*. New York: Routledge, 2008. A conservative, quantitative critique that condemns the policies of leftist governments.

Dangl, Benjamin. *Dancing with Dynamite: States and Social Movements in Latin America*. Oakland, CA: AK Press, 2010. A journalistic account of the complicated dynamics between social movements and leftist governments.

Ellner, Steve, ed. *Latin America's Radical Left: Challenges and Complexities of Political Power in the Twenty-First Century*. Lanham, MD: Rowman & Littlefield, 2014. A collection of essays that explores Latin America's leftward turn.

Levitsky, Steven, and Kenneth M. Roberts, eds. *The Resurgence of the Latin American Left*. Baltimore: Johns Hopkins University Press, 2011. A critique of leftist governments by mainstream political scientists.

Prevost, Gary, Carlos Oliva Campos, and Harry E. Vanden, eds. *Social Movements and Leftist Governments in Latin America: Confrontation or Co-option?* London: Zed Books, 2012. A collection of essays that analyzes the complicated dynamics between social movements and leftist governments.

Ross, Clifton, and Marcy Rein, eds. *Until the Rulers Obey: Voices from Latin American Social Movements*. Oakland, CA: PM Press, 2014. Interviews with social movement activists behind Latin America's leftist turn.

Sader, Emir. *The New Mole: Paths of the Latin American Left*. London: Verso Books, 2011. A thoughtful analysis from a preeminent Brazilian sociologist of the need to support leftist governments.

Stahler-Sholk, Richard, Harry E. Vanden, and Marc Becker, eds. *Rethinking Latin American Social Movements: Radical Action from Below*. Lanham, MD: Rowman & Littlefield, 2014. Provides a social movement perspective on leftist governments.

Webber, Jeffery R., and Barry Carr, eds. *The New Latin American Left: Cracks in the Empire*. Lanham, MD: Rowman & Littlefield, 2013. A collection of essays that explores Latin America's leftward turn.

FILMS

South of the Border. 2010. Director Oliver Stone visits seven presidents in five countries in South America to gain an understanding of the political and social ideas underlying Latin America's new left-wing governments.

Strong Roots (*Raiz forte*). 2000. Documentary on the Brazilian Landless Workers Movement (MST).

Glossary

agrarian reform. Government program of redistributing land from wealthy owners with extensive holdings to those who work the land, as well as provision of the resources such as credit, technical training, and distribution networks necessary to work it.

anticlericalism. Opposition to the institutional power of the Catholic Church because of its outsize influence on political and social affairs, with a desire that a secular government replace religious control over education, marriage, and other institutions.

autonomy. Control over local decisions affecting a self-governing territory while remaining part of a larger political unit or country.

bourgeoisie. Capitalist class that owns the means of production and typically embodies materialistic values or conventional attitudes to ensure the preservation of their privileged position in society.

capitalism. An economic theory that favors private ownership of the means of producing economic goods, with an emphasis on profit rather than use.

Christian Democracy. A political philosophy that combines traditional Catholic social teachings with modern democratic ideals, typically conservative on social issues and liberal on economic ones.

científicos. Porfirio Díaz's technocratic advisers trained in positivist "scientific politics" with a goal to modernize Mexico.

class consciousness. Awareness of one's place in a system of social classes, especially as it relates to a class struggle.

clientelism. Gaining political support in exchange for providing goods or services.

communism. An economic and political system that stresses that decisions related to the production of economic goods should reside in the hands of the workers.

Communist International. An international political party with local branches in different countries founded in Moscow in 1919 to lead a global revolution.

conservative. A reliance on the Catholic Church, the military, and wealthy landholders to maintain a highly stratified society.

coup. from the French term "coup d'état," or blow against the state, the illegal seizure of government through a sudden, violent military action.

death squad. Armed vigilante group that conducts extrajudicial killings or forced disappearances of people for the purposes of political repression.

democracy. Rule of the people, including the idea that people should have equal access to, and a say in, the distribution of the wealth and resources of a country. A representative democracy is where a small group of people are selected to rule on behalf of an entire society, and a participatory democracy is one in which everyone has an equal voice in making decisions.

dependency. Control of one country over another, often through economic means.

dictatorship. Absolute rule by an authoritarian leader; commonly used in a derogatory sense to delegitimize a political opponent.

ejido. A communally owned and operated farm, with community members individually working specific plots that rotate from year to year to maintain a balance of equal access to better and lesser quality land.

embargo. A ban on trade with another country. The Cuban government calls the U.S. embargo on Cuba a "blockade," which means sealing off a place to prevent goods or people from entering or leaving.

expropriation. The act of a government confiscating private property to use it in the public interest.

extradition. Transfer of a suspected or convicted criminal between countries to stand trial or serve a prison sentence.

fascism. An extremely authoritarian, militarist, and nationalist ideology. Relies on a strong leader, is based on a corporate organization of society, and subjugates individual liberties to the interests of the government and business interests.

feminism. Advocacy for equal rights for all. First-wave feminism in the nineteenth century fought for suffrage rights for women, a second wave beginning in the 1960s campaigned for legal and social equality, and a third wave emerged in the 1990s as a reaction against second-wave feminism that treated the interests of women from privileged classes as normative.

filibusterer. A military adventurer who engages in an unauthorized military expedition to foment a change of government in another country.

foco. A theory that emerged out of the Cuban Revolution that a small insurrectionary guerrilla army could spark a broad revolution.

gross national product (GNP). A broad measure of a country's total economic activity.

guerrilla. From the Spanish word for "small war," refers to an irregular form of fighting against a larger, established military force.

hacienda. Large, landed estate similar to a plantation that exploits rural labor, commonly owned either by a wealthy individual or the Catholic Church.

imperialism. The domination of a larger and more powerful country over a smaller and weaker one, typically through economic, diplomatic, or military means.

indigenista. Representation of Indigenous peoples by non-Indians, typically motivated by paternalistic notions of improving their lives.

Indigenous. The original inhabitants of an area, often retaining a unique culture that distinguishes them from the rest of society.

junta. A military or political group that rules a country after taking power by force.

latifundia. A system of large, landed estates (known as latifundios—fundos—or haciendas) on which impoverished peons work to the benefit of an absentee landowner.

left. A broad term for those who support communal concerns over individual liberties. The term comes from the 1789 French Revolution when those favoring the monarchy sat to the president's right in the national assembly, and supporters of the revolution, to his left.

Leninism. Political theory that the organization of a vanguard party is necessary for a socialist revolution, as developed by Vladimir Lenin in the context of the 1917 Bolshevik Revolution.

liberalism. An ideology that champions individual rights, civil liberties, and private property.

liberation theology. A Catholic approach to social problems that utilizes Marxist tools of class struggle.

Maoism. Political theory derived from Mao Zedong's peasant-based communist revolution in China.

massacre. Indiscriminate killing of a large number of people.

national guard. A militia with police powers that often acquires the characteristics of a formal military force.

nationalization. Placing private industries under public ownership so that the profits benefit an entire society rather than select individuals.

neoliberalism. Economic policies of privatization, austerity, deregulation, free trade, and reduction in government spending.

nom de guerre. A pseudonym under which a person fights.

oligarchy. A power structure in which a small group of wealthy people command authority over the rest of society.

Pan-Americanism. Advocacy of political or economic cooperation among people or governments on the American continents.

paramilitary. An unofficial military force, often organized in parallel with a professional military or recognized government but technically separate to avoid legal sanction.

peasant. Poor rural farmer, often with negative connotations of being uneducated and ignorant.

pink tide. Wave of left-wing electoral victories in the first decade of the twenty-first century.

plebiscite. A poll of public opinion on an important, frequently constitutional, issue.

popular front. A policy that the Communist International adopted in 1935 to ally with liberal and other leftist political parties in a broad coalition against conservative or fascist forces.

populism. Personalistic rule by a nationalist and charismatic leader.

proletariat. The working class, often wage earners in an industrial society.

referendum. An up or down vote on a political question.

Sandinistas. Members of the Frente Sandinista de Liberación Nacional (FSLN, Sandinista National Liberation Front) that took power in 1979 after an eighteen-year guerrilla struggle.

social movement. A group of people organized around a specific issue on a civic rather than political or military basis.

socialism. An economic, social, and political doctrine that advocates for the equal distribution of wealth through the elimination of private property and the exploitative ruling class.

syndicate. A group of people organized to promote a common interest, typically related to working conditions and wages.

suffrage. The right to vote (also called the franchise) as a condition of citizenship.

terrorism. Use of violence and intimidation of a civilian population to achieve a political purpose.

Trotskyism. A radical form of socialism named after the Russian revolutionary Leon Trotsky, who argued in favor of a permanent revolution or an ongoing global revolutionary process.

Index

Italicized page numbers refer to illustrations.

About the Author

Marc Becker is professor of Latin American history at Truman State University. His research focuses on constructions of race, class, and gender within popular movements in the Andes. He is the author of *Pachakutik: Indigenous Movements and Electoral Politics in Ecuador* (2011), as well as *The FBI in Latin America: The Ecuador Files* (2017), *Indians and Leftists in the Making of Ecuador's Modern Indigenous Movements* (2008), and *Mariátegui and Latin American Marxist Theory* (1993); coeditor (with Richard Stahler-Sholk and Harry E. Vanden) of *Rethinking Latin American Social Movements: Radical Action from Below* (2015) and (with Kim Clark) of *Highland Indians and the State in Modern Ecuador* (2007); and editor and translator (with Harry Vanden) of *José Carlos Mariátegui: An Anthology* (2011). Becker has received Fulbright, SSRC-MacArthur, and other fellowships to support his research. He is a participating editor for *Latin American Perspectives*. Becker has served on the executive committees and has been web editor of the Ecuadorian Studies and Ethnicity, Race, and Indigenous Peoples (ERIP) sections of the Latin American Studies Association (LASA); the Andean and Teaching Materials committees of the Conference on Latin American History (CLAH); the Peace History Society (PHS); and Historians against the War (HAW). See http://www.yachana.org.